T0339798

WORLD GOVERNMENT: UTOPIAN DREAM OR CURRENT REALITY

VOL. 2

World Government: Utopian Dream or Current Reality?

Vol. 2

Lessons of History: The United States and the European Union

Raymond Converse

Algora Publishing
New York

Library of Congress Cataloging-in-Publication Data —

Converse, Raymond W.
    World government, utopian dream or current reality volume 2 : lessons of history
from the United States and the European Union / Raymond W. Converse.
        p. cm.
    Includes bibliographical references and index.
    ISBN 978-0-87586-828-8 (soft: alk. paper) — ISBN 978-0-87586-829-5 (hard: alk.
paper) — ISBN 978-0-87586-830-1 (ebook) 1. International organization. 2. International
cooperation. I. Title.
    JZ1318.C65776 2011
    341.2'1—dc22
                            2010051030

Front cover: ImageZoo

Printed in the United States

Table of Contents

PREFACE TO VOLUME 2

The world is in trouble, at the national and international level; of that there can be no doubt. A true federal system based on liberal representative democracy is still the most viable solution to the challenges facing the world currently, even though problems exist within such systems. Here, using the history of the United States and later the history of the European Union, an attempt will be made to identify the problems with such systems and their potential solutions, and to outline a way that such a federal system based on liberal representative democracy can be implemented worldwide for the benefit of the greatest part of the populace.

This volume begins with the adoption of the assumptions that were set forth in Volume 1:

First, the assumption that a world union will be established on the basis of the tenets of representative democracy, using the US Constitution as a guide;

Second, that all member nations will either be representative democracies or convert to the use of representative democracy within a reasonable time after joining the world union;

Third, any nation choosing not to join the world union will find its isolation from the union unsustainable and seek to join the union within a short period of time;

Lastly, that a meaningful liberal education is necessary to prepare individuals for their role as politically, economically, and socially informed citizens.

All of these assumptions are based on the last four or five centuries of evolution politically, economically and socially within the current system of nationalism. The system of nationalism is in turn based upon the real or Utopian, as the case may be, tenets of the Age of Enlightenment, the Age of Reason, and the age of scientific and technological development. These assumptions notwithstanding, notice can and should be taken that the various nations' positions within that evolution can be very divergent, that is, one nation may be well developed within this general scheme while another may not have even begun the path along this development. Large scale adjustments will have to be made in each of the assumptions as they are actually applied to the various nations included within the general world union.

One place to test the general readiness of the various nations to cooperate in bringing the assumptions made into reality is to see whether or not agreement can be reached in the one area that could release the funds to produce a level playing field for all: that is to say, a general and total disarmament.

In addition to testing the nations' readiness to move toward these goals, it will be necessary to challenge each of the assumptions made and to adjust functions of the world union as necessary to resolve the problems that will arise. We will attempt to anticipate some of those problems and solutions in this work.

Volume 1 of this work set forth a proposed constitution for a world government (on the model of the US Constitution) and arguments that support its ratification based upon 19th-century liberalism. Volume 2 assumes that such a constitution has in fact been drafted and has been ratified by the necessary number of countries, and that the government it established is now operating.

The main lines of evolution that have led to the current political environment in the US, the European Union, and the United Nations can inform us as to what issues a world government may face and at the same time illustrate the factors which have both promoted and prohibited the full development of representative democracy in these institutions. These issues and approaches to their solution are explored in this book.

THE FIRST ISSUE

Disarmament will be the very first issue to face the World Union established under the conditions set forth in the original volume. There, it was suggested that it would be best if disarmament could be agreed upon or even accomplished before the institution of the world government. For the sake of presentation it will be assumed here that only an agreement between the participating nations has been obtained before initiation of the World Union. This being the case, one of the first orders of business will be to institute the procedures under which disarmament will take place; to initiate reliable procedures for the verification of disarmament; and to install procedures for the safe destruction and disposal of all weapons included in disarmament. One of the most difficult problems will be the destruction and disposal of weapons of mass destruction.

The establishment of the total disarmament package will, of course, take a considerable period of time and effort. The initial legislation session might need to limit its activities to the drafting and passage of general legislation to implement disarmament procedures. All of the research needed to set up the procedures would have to be conducted and completed during the lead-up to this session: the period of time needed to draft the constitution, ratify the constitution, and to initiate the first session of Congress.

THE FIRST LEGISLATIVE SESSION

The legislation needed would include laws requiring all member nations to immediately institute procedures to provide manpower, expertise, funds and general timetables for their individual disarmament plans. Legislation would have to include requirements for the immediate initiation of all verification procedures, again with the requisite manpower, expertise, funds and timetables. Lastly, legislation would be needed to set forth the responsibilities of the various nations in regard to the destruction and disposal of all materials included in the disarmament procedures.

The first legislature would also have to pass the laws necessary for the general funding requirements of the World Union. It is expected that the earlier agreement to disarm would include the establishment of planning organs for the development of the procedures needed to conduct a total disarmament and that these results would be the substance of the above legislation. And, the first legislature would need to institute laws or regulations intended to deal with the economic disruptions that can be expected in relation to the dismantling of the industrial/military complex within each nation.

The actual physical procedures to accomplish disarmament and the disposal of the involved materials should be decided and conducted by each nation according to its military institutions. A specialized independent organization would need to be set up to take charge of verification of compliance within each nation and it should contain at least some members from the nation involved. Much of the work included within the above two stages could presumably be conducted by the existing military and scientific communities within the various member nations.

ORDERLY DISARMAMENT

The stages of an orderly disarmament process can safely be assumed to be as follows: First, a safe and effective method of destroying and disposing of the weapons of mass destruction (as well as all other materials involved) must be created. The materials that would most obviously pose a problem in regard to recycling or disposal would be those involving nuclear materials, toxic chemicals or toxic biological materials. A fool-proof method for the disposal of the latter does not currently exist, although some methods are currently being used that have only short term safety capability. The technology probably exists, or could quickly be brought on line, to resolve this issue should the incentives and motivation be sufficient.

There is a question as to whether or not disarmament would include nuclear materials currently being used for what is normally termed peaceful purposes. The answer to this question would in all likelihood revolve around whether or not a safer, cheaper alternative to nuclear power could be obtained in a relatively short period of time.

Second, once a safe and effective disposal plan has been determined, it will be necessary to outline how each nation will collect and deliver the materials for which it is responsible to the site, or sites, where they will be disposed of by the experts appointed for that purpose. This second stage should be executed by each individual nation under the supervision of the general government or its representatives. This second level might also include the transporting of all materials to be destroyed or disposed of. Those nations in which the actual disposal will take place would be responsible for the proper implementation of the procedures set up for such disposal.

Lastly, in the interest of building trust, a system of effective inspection and verification must be put into operation. While this phase could also be left to the responsibility of the various nations, the general government would need to maintain a much stronger hands on approach to insure that the collection, storing, and disposal processes are competently performed. The organization established as mentioned earlier would need to be international and scientific in nature as well as independent of both the general government and those of the nations.

Needless to say, under current conditions it is not possible to even outline the organizations that would be set up to accomplish the different phases of total disarmament. This type of detail can only arise from the actual planning and institution of each phase of the process. What can be stated, however, is that the existing technological and scientific communities are capable of creating a procedure for the recycling or disposal of conventional weapons and materials, as well as those constituting weapons of mass destruction. The experience of both the European Union and the United Nations can be profitably used to guide the World Union towards effective legislation in this matter, especially the inspection and verification phase.

Lack of trust, indeed, appears to be the greatest barrier standing in the way of total disarmament: drafting, much less abiding by, an agreement to, in fact, disarm, will require a very high degree of trust. Should a general agreement to disarm be reached, it is reasonable to expect that it would also be possible to establish a world government to obtain these goals.

Having set forth the necessity of immediate action on the issue of disarmament, let us now take a look at some of the other problems that will face the World Union. Here, we can compare the results obtained by the United States, the European Union, and the United Nations in their responses to similar problems. Where appropriate, we may also look at the experience of other nations such as China, Russia, or India.

19TH-CENTURY LIBERALISM AND "IDEOLOGY"

The method to be used in Volume 2 will revolve around several key concepts. First, it will discuss the importance of 19th-century liberalism. Second, it will discuss the Articles of Confederation of the early United States as well as the Charter of the United Nations in relation to their failure to fully exploit the concepts of that liberalism — or possibly to reject those concepts. Third, it will discuss the United States Constitution and the Treaties of the European Union as a second attempt to incorporate more fully the ideals of 19th-century liberalism. Lastly it will look at the evolution of these organizations in their efforts to more fully conform to or deviate from the principles of early liberalism.

Before entering into detail, let's define the use of the term ideology in relation to the tenets of 19th-century liberalism. First, it must be stated openly that all three of the organizations used as examples in this discussion have in fact adopted these tenets as their basic ideological position.

Under normal circumstances the word "ideology" has a negative meaning; however, it can have a positive meaning if one considers the work of Paul Ricoeur. Ricoeur expresses this first by showing that writers and speakers who use the term go out of their way to make it clear that "ideological thinking" applies to the beliefs of others and not to themselves. In other words, "ideology" is used to represent the belief system or philosophy of others. The term is largely used to disassociate the user from whatever idea is being expressed. On the other hand, Ricoeur shows that ideology represents shared beliefs (actual or mythical), common background, and a common foundation — which are necessary to bring a people into a sustained effort to accomplish common goals. In that sense, it can only be a positive. If the positive meaning is accepted in relation to the tenets of 19th-century liberalism, then it can override the underlying ideologies of the various organizations discussed. It also allows the development of 19th-century liberal concepts to be incorporated into a worldwide system of federalism.

Ricoeur claims that ideologies over time tend to solidify political structures into frozen forms that are incapable of further evolution. When ideologies reach this stage, they are no longer capable of standing as the bond that holds people together in the pursuit of common goals and therefore become repressive of needed changes. It is at the point where ideology becomes frozen that the struggle to maintain the society that was created by it begins. This is merely to accept the fact that any ideology is nothing more than a group of ideals, myths, common historical evolution, etc., and that the struggle for existence is one that entails the prolongation of these common factors.

The struggle for existence (by the group formed from the original ideological factors) is an attempt to artificially maintain the common factors in an environment that has changed. This leads in turn to the repressive nature of ideology at this stage, that is, to maintain the structure's existence it tends to repress the natural changes that are brought about by an evolving environment. The repressive tendencies begin to push the members of the once consolidated group away from each other.

It is at this point where most writers and analysts have begun their discussion of ideology. It is also the point where one can insist that the current system of nationalism has become repressive and obsolete in the pursuit of human rights.

Therefore the remainder of this preface will attempt to identify the main factors that represent the common universal bond that motivated the people of the United States to seek a common goal, by analyzing the Declaration of Independence in detail and by considering the role played by the Articles of Confederation.

CREATING THE AMERICAN IDEOLOGY THAT ENABLED UNIFIED ACTION

Let us first consider the Declaration of Independence that was published on July 4, 1776. This document represents Thomas Jefferson's interpretation and understanding of the tenets of 19th-century liberalism that justified the American Revolution. The Declaration sets forth in detail the injustices of the British king in his acts toward the colonies. In relation to these, Jefferson also sets forth what in his interpretation represents the reasons that such actions were unjust in the first place. A closer look at the reasoning used by Jefferson should clearly establish the first ideological use of these tenets by an existing government, that is, the United States.

The Declaration does represent the sentiments of the Enlightenment but in no way represents the political realities that existed in 1776. This was, in fact, a Utopian project. Had this case been brought before a competent court of international justice limited by the application of the rules then existing in international law, the colonies would have lost on every count submitted, with the possible exception of the apprehension of colonial citizens on the high seas with the intention of impressing them into the naval service of Great Britain. The complaints listed in the Declaration of Independence represent a fine display of Enlightenment sentiments, the most liberal then in existence, but they described an ideal condition that was not represented in reality anywhere on earth. They have, however, become the mythological basis of the political ideology that in fact bound the citizens of the new United States to the pursuit of common goals.

The original thirteen colonies were peopled mostly by immigrants who voluntarily came to find a new home and to escape religious persecution. The British were interested in establishing the colonies for two main reasons, first, to establish their presence on the North American Continent to compete with the already existing empires of Spain, France, and Holland; and second, to be rid of the religious sects that would not accept the Church of England or the English government. For the first hundred and fifty years the expansion of the colonial empire of Great Britain around the world, coupled with a long series of wars in Europe, created a situation in which the thirteen colonies were pretty much left to their own resources for governance. Over this period of time, of course, the colonists essentially came to see themselves as independent of British rule, and when circumstances allowed the British to attempt to tighten the control over their empire the thirteen colonies rebelled. For many reasons, but mainly because they had not been allowed the freedom to evolve, the other British colonies throughout the world at this time did not revolt.

The mainstream ideals found in the Declaration of Independence, whether a part of political reality or just philosophical expressions of human hopes, became the basis of the political ideology of the new United States and provided the bond that enabled the citizens of the US to seek after common goals. Some of the more important of these ideals are as follows.

1. That government is instituted among mankind to provide security for the general welfare of all. In 1776 the "general welfare" was essentially the guarantee that external invasion and internal insurrection would be prevented. In a less defined way it also seemed to express the need of mankind for the rule of law rather than the rule of force.

2. The Declaration expressed the intellectual desire (one could almost say mythical desire) of all people to be represented, either directly or indirectly, in the laws that would control them. In 1776 no people was ruled by a government that allowed the people a say in the laws that were passed to control them. Only the House of Commons in Great Britain gave any hint that such a thing was even possible in real-life politics. It was, however, one

of the ideals that had grown up during the century and one half that the colonists had been left to self-rule.

3. It was expressed that any people, if oppressed beyond toleration, had the right and the duty to rebel and establish a new government. It can only be pointed out that no existing government, then or now, would have accepted this as valid. It was again part of the intellectual furniture that accompanied the growth of the Enlightenment movement in Europe.

4. The Declaration expressed the belief that all men were created equal by a universal creator, and that the same universal creator had given them inalienable rights to life, liberty, and the pursuit of happiness. In reality this would probably qualify as a mythical belief even in 1776. There were very few people, if any, that lived in a society in which all men were treated as equals, and where they had inalienable rights; but this idealistic notion had grown as part of the enlightened outlook of the upper classes in the US by this time.

The Declaration of Independence was not an attempt to set forth a political reality; it was, rather, an attempt to solidify the actions of a group of people (the colonists) towards the achievement of a common goal (independence from Great Britain). In order to accomplish this feat it was necessary to bind the people together by fostering their common acceptance of mythical beliefs in the equality of all men, common historical backgrounds, language, etc. The common historical background was expressed by pointing out all the supposed evil that had been perpetrated by King George III, which was in fact the political reality in 1776. The reality is that in all probability the actions complained of by the colonists would have been seen by an international court as legal, ethical, and moral, with very few exceptions. World opinion, if such a thing had existed in 1776, would have been in favor of Great Britain in regard to the validity of the rebellion, regardless of the statement to the contrary in the Declaration.

The Articles of Confederation were the first attempt by the people of the former colonies to follow through with the common goal of independence and to set up a government that reflected their new ideology. A quick reading of the Articles shows that there was a major conflict incorporated into them between the ideal of individual rights and the rights of governments as corporate entities. The ideal of individual rights was put on the back burner in the Articles by the fact that the states did not give up any of their sovereignty; and the general government was only given power to affect the actions of the states as corporate entities. The government created by the Articles did attempt to incorporate some of the ideals set forth in the Declaration, for example, Article 2 takes the position that individual rights trump those of government. Under this article each state retained the whole of its sovereignty with the sole exception of the powers granted to the general government. The general government, however, was not granted any authority to extend its laws directly to the people but only to the states. Articles 3, 4, and 5 set forth the ideal that governments were instituted to secure the general welfare, that is, protect against external attack and internal insurrection. They also set forth the right of individuals to have unrestricted ingress and egress across state borders; the right to freely conduct commercial activities; the right to the full faith and credit of each other's laws, records, and judicial decisions; and the right to appoint those who would represent them in the general government regarding the laws passed. Through this latter provision each state was allowed at least one representative in Congress and no state would be allowed more than seven. These representatives were appointed by the states legislatures who were in turn elected directly by the people. Each state would be allowed one vote (the whole delegation must vote as a bloc) on all business conducted in Congress. This interpretation of 19th-century liberalism has in very real ways been carried forward into the United Nations and the European Union.

The Articles also denied specific powers to the states, such as the power to receive foreign representatives; the power to conclude treaties or alliances with foreign powers or between themselves; the power to place import or export duties on the commerce that was conducted between them or with foreign nations; the power to maintain a military force in time of peace; the power to declare war without the consent of Congress; and the power to issue letters of reprisal or marquee except against nations against whom Congress had declared war.

In relation to the general defense the states were assigned the following duties. They were responsible for appointing and maintaining all officers under the grade of colonel and to fill any vacancies. They were responsible for raising the land forces necessary for the common defense as needed by the general government. They were responsible for paying all expenses of the general government in relation to executing the public defense. The payments were to be assessed on the basis of the proportion of all the land included within the state. They were given the power to levy all taxes necessary to raise this money. This again has been carried forward into the structure of the United Nations and the European Union.

The general government was delegated the following powers. The congress was given the power to declare war and peace (exclusively). The general government was to have the exclusive right of sending and receiving ambassadors and consuls. The general government was to have the exclusive power to make treaties and form alliances with foreign nations, including the Native American Nations. The general government was given the power to establish the rules regarding captures at land or on the sea and how such property was to be divided. The general government was to appoint courts for the trial of cases arising from piracy or other felonies committed on the high seas. Congress was made the final arbiter of all unresolved disputes between two or more states or between the citizens of two or more states. The judges in the latter cases were to be appointed by the state legislatures of the states involved. If they could not agree, Congress would then pick three judges from each state and the legislatures of the states involved would then reduce that number to thirteen from which congress would appoint five drawn randomly from the thirteen. The general government was given the power to determine the alloy and value of all currency whether issued by the general government or by the states. There were several other powers, but the important point was that before any of these powers could be exercised the action of the general government had to be approved by nine of the thirteen states in congress assembled. Every attempt was made to insure that the Confederacy would not become a true supra-state government. This also has been the intention with the creation of the UN and the result of the evolution of the EU.

This first attempt focused on the rights of the thirteen states almost exclusively. The Articles set forth the standard recipe of the nation state system that each nation was a completely independent sovereign entity and the powers retained by the states reflected this. The general government could only affect the states in their corporate capacity and the citizens themselves were subject only to the laws of the states in which they resided. Any five of the states could in combination veto any action contemplated by the general government. The powers granted to the general government were not sufficient to establish a sovereign government and were in essence a mere treaty of friendship between the states. The Articles for this reason did not incorporate any references to individual human rights as found in the Declaration, as it was understood that these rights remained with the people and their representatives in the state governments. The Articles paid lip service to the concept of protecting the general welfare but were totally dependent on the good will of the states to do so.

Under these circumstances it is not surprising that the Articles of Confederation failed to create a government that could be considered a fulfillment of the common goals demanded by the new political ideology of the early United States. The government created by the Articles did not have the power to secure individuals in their life and property; to guarantee their equal treatment under the laws; to insure that they were represented in Congress regarding the laws that were passed to control them; or to provide them with a means of dissolving the government should it become intolerably unjust. It is understandable that more attention is not paid to the Articles of Confederation as they did not address any of the common goals sought after in the fight for independence. The abiding fear of tyranny in the states after independence from Great Britain is clear from the tenets expressed in the Articles. As discussed in Volume 1, not only the leading citizens of the United States were unhappy with the document; but so were the states themselves along with their citizens. The call therefore went out to reform this document and to bring it into closer alignment with the common goals expressed by the new political ideology. The Preamble to the Constitution directly confirms that this was in fact the main purpose of the Constitutional Convention. The Preamble sets forth the common goals that are intended to be served by the new constitution, that is, to establish justice, to insure domestic tranquility, to provide for the common defense, to promote the general welfare, and to secure individual liberty.

The current system of nationalism can be seen in the same light, that is, that it has failed to promote the main goals of a truly democratic system even at the national level.

It is of the highest importance to recognize that the evolution of the basic foundations of the US political system have continuously been used to justify the growth of not only the United Nations and the European Union, but also the general worldwide acceptance of liberal democracy after World War II. In fact, Volume 1 concluded that enough common background, historical relevance and common political foundation exist to infer that the tenets of 19th-century liberalism have themselves become a common nature in the developed countries, that is to say, the belief in individual human rights, the market system, and a common humanity generally. It is likely that because such a commonality exists many of the problems faced by the early US in initiating its political system will not arise when world government is established. This position is further strengthened by the experience of the United Nations and the European Union. It is even more strongly evidenced by the historical experience of China and India, especially in relation to the market system. The European Union since its beginnings has struggled to become more than a system of friendship through treaties and has to some degree obtained the earmarks of a federal system; but even so does not represent anything akin to a nation state or supranational government. The proposed constitution for world government presented in Volume 1 accepts as valid the argument that the battle over human rights and effective general government that took place early in US history will not occur in the case of an effective world government. Thus the world union will begin its evolution at the same stage the US had reached in 1789.

The constitution produced by the Constitutional Convention accomplished the task set forth in the Preamble as well as in the Declaration of Independence. All of the basic factors involved in the new political ideology of the United States were incorporated into the various articles of the Constitution. The jealousies and fears evident in the Articles of Confederation had been overcome. The first ten amendments, commonly called the Bill of Rights, represented a compromise that allowed the coming together of those who favored a strong national government and those who favored a limited national government to insure the ratification of the Constitution. It can be argued that the prior acceptance of the above ideology made it possible for such a compromise to be concluded.

In following the evolution of the political system of the US, it quickly becomes apparent that the ability of the political ideology to explain political reality is tested continually. It represents every conceivable problem, situation, circumstance, or unintended result that has faced the governments and people of the United States. As will be seen, in many cases the problems which arose directly challenged the philosophy that underlay the political ideology of the United States. In some cases this challenge resulted in the alteration or abandonment of one or another of the tenets that were originally included in the ideological environment created by the Constitution. These alterations and rare abandonments were necessary to bring the political ideology into conformity with the changing political reality. As a result the alteration can best be described as a series of compromises.

A compromise (as used in Volume 2) is an agreement, either temporary or permanent, between the various interests involved or operating with the common goal of solving the issue at hand. The various interests, when the stance taken is a strong one, can bring the process of resolving issues to a standstill or stalemate. In this case nothing is possible in regard to solving the pending problems. The ability to compromise allows each position to take some portion of its stand as a prize but in total allows for a creative solution to the problem faced. Generally speaking the most difficult problems that have faced the US, at least politically, have resulted in a stalemate that could not be resolved even though temporary compromise was obtained. As a result some problems such as economic recession have arisen many times and have been resolved in the short term only to return again in full force later. However, one mark of whether or not the continued pursuit of common goals is still active is to be found in the ability to obtain compromises when necessary.

The historical events that have been chosen in Volume 2 as representative of the effectiveness or ineffectiveness of the US political ideology, as well as that of the United Nations and European Union, are here conceded to be arbitrary. Many others could have been chosen with equal or maybe greater likelihood of expressing the position taken. Some that were chosen may in fact be argued not to be representative at all. This however is justified by expressing the fact that the problems they identify will in all likelihood also face the world government. Each event chosen will first be approached from the standpoint of the type of problems it produced; and then whether the response to the problems produced were overall representative in relation to the individual rights affected and the underlying causes. Lastly, a look will be taken to determine whether the resolution was the result of a proactive or passive governmental intervention and whether or not a compromise was needed to resolve the issue. The result of this inquiry should lead us to the point where a decision can be made as to whether or not the same problems will be faced by the world government and whether or not they should be resolved in the same manner.

Using the US Constitution as a guide is not, in this work, meant to create a new, larger United States. It is imperative that any such fear of the proposed world union be removed. While it may be true that an evolving world union created in this manner will in some degree resemble the current United States, it is not inevitable. It is likely that the evolving union will sidestep many of the decisions made by the historical United States, the historical United Nations, and the historical European Union. It may instead accept some of the solutions that have been used by China and India in the resolution of similar problems in their multifaceted cultures. The premise used in Volume 2 will, in fact accept this likelihood.

CHAPTER 1. THE CONSTITUTION AND PIECE-MEAL SOCIAL ENGINEERING

The first thirty years of operation under the US Constitution can be seen as a time of experimentation. The intent of the US Constitution, as well as the constitution here proposed for the world union, is to create a republican representative democracy. Under this form of government three basic principles apply in a general manner. First, the whole of the sovereign powers of government (at all levels) rests initially with the people. Second, under a written constitution the people delegate some of their sovereign powers to the various levels of government. Third, that there should be general equality before the law.

In relation to the world government proposed, this would mean that initially all sovereign power be retained by the people and that the people through the proposed constitution would delegate (or deny) the powers they wished the various levels of government to exercise.

In the US the people participate in all levels of government through their elected representatives. The same would be true under the proposed constitution for a world government. In some cases under the constitution the people specifically deny one or another level of government the right to exercise a power. Any power not delegated to any level of government or powers that are denied to government are retained by the people. The theory of republican representative democracy is one thing, however, and the practical exercise of that form of government is another.

One general problem faces all republican representative democracies created under a written constitution: If the powers that are delegated under the constitution to either the general governments or the member states or nations are too tightly defined, the various governments can be severely crippled in their ability to act in the interest of the people. On the other hand, if the same powers are too loosely defined, the various governments are given the leeway to overstep the powers intended for them. Under the latter condition, if the general government is able to gather most of the power into its hands, then the government is converted into a national representative democracy or possibly a tyranny. If the member states or nations are able to gather most of the power into their hands, then the government is converted into a true federal organization.

The argument can be made that the US federal government has indeed become an example of a national representative democracy; and that both the United Nations and the European Union are examples of a federal organization.

Under the proposed constitution, as with that of the US, the solution as concerns the general government is the creation of three distinct branches of government each with various checks and balances over each other. The legislative branch would be directly responsible to the people for any actions that it took. This responsibility of the people would be exercised either directly through the power of elections or through the direction given by the people to their representatives at both the general level and the level of the nation state. The House of Representatives would be elected directly by the people. The Senate would be appointed by the national legislatures, which in turn are elected directly by the people, especially if, as with the EU, all member states are required to be democratic in nature. The executive branch would also be appointed by the legislatures of the nations; but would also be subject to the directions issued by the people in the elections of the national delegates to the Electoral College. Only the Judicial branch would be free of direct intervention by either the people or the general government. They would however be initially appointed by the executive branch subject to the confirmation of the Senate. During service, however, they would be free of constraint, serving for life (or during good behavior).

Under the proposed constitution, no powers are delegated to the several nations as is the case with the US Constitution. Instead, certain powers are denied to the several nations. The Constitution does however specifically state that all powers not delegated to the general government will be retained either by the several nations or the people.

In addition the Constitution clearly sets forth the responsibility of both levels of government to acknowledge and protect the human rights of their joint citizenry. These rights include the freedom of religion, the right to develop cultural diversity, and the sanctity of contracts and private property. More importantly the Constitution also sets forth specific protection against enslavement, cruel and unusual punishment, and a list of other protections intended to insure equal justice under the law. These rights were originally incorporated into the US Constitution as a compromise during the ratification process and constitute the first ten amendments. In the case of the proposed constitution for world union they are incorporated directly into the initial constitutions wording.

It is common knowledge that the new US Constitution incorporated several generalized components of the intellectual movement known as the Enlightenment. First, in the economic realm it was intended that the Constitution would guarantee the operation of the economy on the basis of a free play of market forces such as supply and demand. Second, it was further intended that a strict policy of isolation would be maintained in relation to the affairs of other nations. Third, that each individual would be both a citizen of the United States and the state in which he resided and be guaranteed equal protection under the laws of each as well as under the laws of any other member of the union. These concepts have also been carried directly into the proposed constitution for a world union, just as they are included into the basic foundations of both the United Nations and the European Union.

The first challenge to the US Constitution and the new government came during the ratification process. Each of the powers delegated to the federal government was challenged during the ratification process and continued to be challenged for the first thirty years of US history. The first thirty years also saw each power that had been denied to the states contested in some fashion by one or more of the states, with very few exceptions. The challenges, and their solution, took up a great deal of the effort of both the federal and state governments during this period.

The first ten amendments, although they did suffer some minor challenges, were not put under significant pressure during this time period. One of the issues that had been ignored by the Constitution and by the ratification process was the various regional differences that had evolved during the eleven years of the confederacy. During the first thirty years, however, these varying interests were brought to the forefront. In many ways the diverse interests of the various regions of the country were the motivation and means through which the early compromises were reached relating to the processes of government. These issues included, among others, the use and disposition of the US territorial lands located in the Ohio and Tennessee River Valleys; the creation of a uniform monetary policy; the institution of a federal taxation system regarding import and export duties (tariff); the issue of slavery; and the federal powers of regulation in regard to interstate commerce.

Although in theory all of these powers had been delegated to the federal government by the Constitution, there were no practical examples available to guide the actual exercise of the powers. It is the attempt to actually exercise the powers that brought about the challenges, most often based on some specific regional interest. The actual processes of government, particularly at the federal level, had been intentionally left open for resolution in practice during the first years of operation. In fact, it took nearly thirty years to finally resolve these issues.

Although intended to be an essentially unchanging written law, the US Constitution has proven to be an extraordinarily flexible document. It has been both a practical document (in that it solved the most pressing issues facing the thirteen states) and also a theoretical document that proved a fertile ground for interpretation, allowing the solution to problems that had not been thought of at the outset. An intentional effort was in fact made to avoid making it so detailed that it would provide roadblocks to the growth of the new government. The new government was left free to determine the measure of its exercise of the powers that had been delegated to it.

It might be argued that the Constitution had been too liberal in its lack of detail, allowing the possibility of several conflicting interpretations to be possible in relation to each power delegated. In fact one of the first issues that faced the new government was how the Constitution would be interpreted and by whom. This lack of detail, however, over the long run has been a clear benefit to the US in allowing solutions to problems that arose in the future to be formed by interpretation when the time came.

The Constitution was created under a spirit of compromise; it was ratified with the same spirit of compromise; and to a very substantial degree it has continued to operate using that same spirit of compromise. The Constitution was drafted with the intention of solving a limited number of problems that had arisen under the confederation; and the fact that it was drafted in less than four months clearly indicates that those who were members of the convention had a limited agenda. The Constitution was intended to be a practical document; but the quick arrival of unintended consequences also showed that the Constitution was a flexible and very useful tool in the solution of problems that could not have been dreamed of by its drafters.

As we shall see, the continuing commitment of the US to the principles of compromise, piece-meal social engineering, and creative interpretation have contributed to keeping the Constitution a fit object of focus in the solution of pressing social problems. For some two hundred and twenty years the Constitution has accurately reflected the political reality found in the US.

Recently some challenges have been offered, suggesting that the US Constitution no longer represents political reality. In essence this is a claim that the principles of 19th-century liberalism are no longer able or capable of being instituted. The argument is that the above principles represent obstacles to the institution of unified planning. The only way to determine which argument best expresses the political reality of today's world is to take a look at the evolution of the US and other organizations claiming to be democratic and see if they in fact do present an accurate picture of reality. It is still an open debate as to whether the concepts of 19th-century liberalism or those of collectivist planning are the most likely to produce solutions to the problems involved in human rights issues.

Our task will be to attempt to determine the effect these problems and their solutions have had on the US system, especially in relation to its underlying political ideology. The solutions to the problems that will be looked at herein have usually been made official by one of three methods. First, the solution has been codified into law through the passage of appropriate legislation. Two, in some cases the solution has been made official by the proclamation of an executive order by the president. Three, in a large number of cases the solutions were the result of judicial decisions issued by the Supreme Court or regulations issued by the various bureaucratic agencies. These three arenas have been the playing fields upon which the various interest combinations have contended for recognition. The above described method of problem solving has dominated the US political scene from the beginning with the various interest groupings, such as the financial community, in control of one or more of the three branches of government. It is remarkable that the operation of the US government has never led to all three branches being controlled by the same groupings for a substantial period of time — if it ever happened at all. It is also remarkable that various minority interest groupings, whatever they happened to represent, have always been strong enough to limit the effectiveness of the interest grouping in the majority. This is particularly true since the full development of two party politics in the US. Because of this circumstance all three branches, although able to overall increase their power, have never been in a position to act without paying serious attention to the art of compromise. However, recently the use by both parties of a system of planned gridlock seems to have also reduced the ability to look for and obtain compromise.

The concept of piece-meal social engineering is borrowed from Karl Popper.[1] Popper establishes that only piece-meal social engineering can result in a truly open society. This approach requires that each problem that arises be treated as unique onto itself and that the solution be fashioned solely to treat that problem without becoming a precedent for future problem solving. The reader is strongly advised to study Popper's two-volume work as it is perhaps the best modern argument in favor of representative democracy.

In our case Popper's concepts will be limited to the consideration of the specific laws, the specific executive orders and regulations, and the specific judicial verdicts which have operated as experiments in piece-meal social engineering. That is, the laws, orders, and verdicts issued by the various branches of the Federal Government are all factually-based experiments that allow us to determine how well the solutions chosen explain the problem that was faced. The success or failure of any particular law, order, or verdict as a solution to a problem (in the sense of adequately explaining political reality) does not necessarily determine the usefulness of the theory in question. Each experiment only determines whether or not the specific facts presented confirm or deny the ability of the theory to explain political reality in that limited circumstance. If the experiment led to the alteration, rejection, or amendment of those principles, it will be considered proactive in philosophy. On the other hand, any piece-meal experiment which tends to confirm, support, or promote those principles will be considered to be

---

1 *The Open Society and Its Enemies*, two Volumes, Karl R. Popper, Harper Torchbooks, Harper & Row Publishers, New York 1966

passive in philosophy. The overall result of this interplay of factors in US history will allow us to determine whether the proactive philosophy has been dominant to the point where any attempts to alter or reject them have now become frozen and repressed.

CHAPTER 2. THE BATTLE BETWEEN FEDERALISTS AND ANTI-FEDERALISTS

The main goal of those who drafted the Constitution was to create a durable union. This was not a given at the time that the Constitution was drafted. Even such men as George Washington, John Adams, and Thomas Jefferson had doubts concerning the success of the new government. After two hundred and twenty years it is safe to say that the union has proven durable, at least in the short run. Over this period only twenty seven official changes have been made to the original document and ten of those were made as a compromise during the ratification process.

Less concern therefore will be paid to the actual Constitution and the official changes that were made to it, and more will be applied to the unofficial changes that have occurred. These unofficial changes are represented by the laws that have been passed by the federal legislature, the orders issued by the federal executive branch, and the verdicts rendered by the federal judicial branch. In all three cases the only reaction that was allowed to the people at large was an expression of their opinion through unofficial channels. We can begin with the flat statement that at its inception the new government was accepted as an improvement over the confederation by all member states and their citizens. It must also be recognized that from the first assembling of the federal government regional interests became of paramount importance. The Southern states, which included North and South Carolina, Virginia, Maryland, and Georgia, represented one very distinct sectional interest. These states had already formed a common bond based upon the use of slavery, stable crop agriculture, and a sort of aristocratic attitude. They adopted as their political philosophy what we will call in these pages the conservative position, consisting of states' rights, protection of the institution of slavery, a low tariff, and small independent agricultural and industry open to the influence of a free market. This position was led by Thomas Jefferson and was represented by the Democratic-Republican Party. The North (which would now be labeled the Northeast) included the states of Pennsylvania, New York, Massachusetts and New Jersey, and after 1791 Vermont. The position adopted by these states was what we here will call the liberal philosophy. This position called for a high tariff to protect the evolving commercial and industrial interests, the promotion of a strong federal government, and the promotion of a proactive international policy. This section was led by such men as George Washington, John Adams, and Alexander Hamilton who had formed the Federalist Party. A third sectional interest was formed by the states of Rhode Island, Connecticut, Delaware, and New Hampshire. This section of the country was normally neutral in the debate over a strong versus a limited general government but normally sided with the North on issues such as the tariff and monetary policy. The last sectional interest was represented by the territorial possessions located in the Ohio and Tennessee River Valleys. This area was attached to both the North and the South as a major provider of natural resources. It normally identified with the South on issues involving the tariff, monetary policy, and international affairs but identified with the North on the issue of a strong federal government especially on the issue of frontier safety from Indian attack. In our terms therefore for the first thirty years of US history the South can be labeled as consistently conservative, the North as consistently liberal, and the west as a mixture of the two depending upon the issue involved although overall the non-aligned states tended to be more conservative than liberal. Essentially the neutral states represented the first moderate wing of the liberal position.

The early years of US history revolve around the conservative and liberal battle over the control of the processes of governing. This battle was preordained by the vague language of the Constitution and its conscious effort to allow the free development of the central government concerning its actual exercise of power. The two positions of conservatism and liberalism represent the two main interpretations that different camps used in their attempts to clarify the language contained in the Constitution. The issue was of first importance as its resolution would determine the character of the laws, orders, and verdicts that were issued to establish the modus operandi of the new government. Every issue was debated on the basis of the content of the two competing philosophical political positions.

Initially, the executive branch was led by George Washington and John Adams who belonged to the Federalist Party and therefore represented the liberal philosophical position. The Supreme Court was created by the appointments made by both Washington and Adams and reflected the Federalist or liberal point of view. Initially therefore the Federalist position controlled two branches of the federal government. This control was maintained in the executive branch for twelve years and in the judicial branch until 1834. The legislative branch was very nearly evenly split between the liberal and conservative positions. For the first thirty years, however, the liberal position, through coalitions with the neutral states, was able to maintain a slight majority in Congress as a whole.

The Democratic-Republican Party came to power in the executive branch in 1802 with election of Thomas Jefferson as president. Jefferson represented the leading edge of the conservative position and personally was something of a romantic seeking to maintain the US in the position represented by independent agricultural homesteads and small cottage-type industries coupled with a limited federal government. The Democratic-Republican Party held control of the executive branch until 1828.

The Federalist Party, when it lost control of the executive branch, dissolved as an official party although the ideals it professed remained strong throughout the country. By 1828 it had reconstituted itself as the Whig Party. This however is beyond the thirty year period now under consideration. Therefore, as of 1801, just eleven years after the ratification of the Constitution, the conservative position had won control of the executive branch, the House of Representatives, and a strong minority in the Senate. The liberal position still controlled a majority of the Senate and had solid control of the judicial branch.

A short detour must be taken here to establish the qualifications of citizenship and the number of citizens that could exert political privileges at the beginning of the union. The census ordered by the Constitution had determined the population of the thirteen states as about three and one half million persons. The number of people qualified to exercise the rights of citizenship, including the important privilege of the franchise was, of course, much less. Children and women were ineligible to exercise the rights of citizenship and were therefore ineligible to vote. It can fairly be assumed that over one half of the three and one half million counted by the census were either women or children. For our purposes we will assume that they represented sixty percent of the population counted. In addition, 200,000 Native Americans were counted as they were living within the boundaries of the thirteen states, but they were also ineligible to vote or exercise other privileges of citizenship. In addition, the census counted 500,000 African-Americans who were ineligible for rights of citizenship and the vote. There were also a series of state regulations and laws which restricted the franchise through property qualifications and other techniques.

In the end, it is probably fair to say that only five percent of the total population, or about 250,000 men, were qualified to exercise the privileges of citizenship and the franchise when the US came into existence. In addition, it is probably safe to calculate that somewhere around ten percent of those were willing and able to enter into public service at all levels of government. This would be approximately 25,000 persons who in all likelihood had been committed to public service during the late colonial period as well as the period of the confederation. There is a great chance that most of them were at least familiar with one another, especially on the level of the general government. In this sense, the US system can be argued to have been structured much like an ordinary oligarchy.

The people at large, it can be argued, had little or no knowledge of what actions were taken at the state level, let alone at the federal level. At times the interests of large numbers of people in any particular section of the country were adversely affected by the actions of the state and federal governments. People whose circumstances limited their access to communication and travel were very limited in their ability to seek redress for their grievances. This in turn led to frustration and in some cases violent protests. The result, however, whether violent or not, under normal circumstances led to some type of compromise that brought an end to the grievances of the people. It is difficult today to feel the importance that was attached to the various issues that arose during the first thirty years of operation; but they were of the first importance to those who were attempting to determine the limits of governmental actions. This pattern can be seen as the current situation in a large area of the world. There are many areas of the world that today are suffering from what has been called marginalization, i.e., they do not participate in the global economy or in the global political structure.

Between 1790 and 1820, the Federalist Party was the dominant political force. The Federalists, under our scheme, were labeled as liberal in their political philosophy. The conservative forces during the first eleven years were relegated to a minority position in Congress, while the Federalist Party controlled the executive branch, and through that branch had the opportunity to appoint the first judges and justices in the judicial branch. The first two presidents who served a combined total of twelve years filled the major positions of the new bureaucracy and judicial branch with Federalists, including maybe the most important appointment of all, John Marshall, who served as chief justice of the Supreme Court until 1834. Under Marshall's leadership the Supreme Court was probably the most proactive branch of the government. The importance of having the Federalist Party in control for the first twelve years of operation cannot be overstated. In essence this allowed the liberal philosophy to set the standard by which the government would continue to operate throughout US history.

As absurd as it may sound to us today, one of the first issues that came forward involved the proper manner of addressing the president. Several suggestions were made but in the end the issue was settled when the House of Representatives addressed George Washington by his constitutional title as "the President of the United States." It sounds trivial, but when a world union is established and a chief magistrate is placed in office, the same question will arise. It can only be hoped that as simple a solution will be put forward as in the case of George Washington.

A more important issue arose around the fact that the first assembled congress (1789) was faced with the problem of the structure of the new government as it had been outlined by the Constitutional Convention. George Washington and John Adams were the president and vice-president, as noted earlier. The first president immediately invoked the power to create executive departments. The position of secretary of state was given to Thomas Jefferson through Washington's power of appointment and the Senate's power of consent. The secretary of the treasury by the same process was filled by Washington's closest advisor, Alexander Hamilton. Washington also appointed and the Senate confirmed Edmund Randolph as the attorney general. These men were called regularly by Washington to advise him on questions of policy; this was the first example of the cabinet the succeeding presidents would form, even though no specific power to do so was to be found in the Constitution. Washington also appointed John Jay as the first chief justice of the Supreme Court and the Senate again confirmed the appointment. The Congress in the meantime had established the Supreme Court with six justices including the chief justice, thirteen federal district courts, and three federal appellate courts. At this time the Supreme Court justices were known as itinerant judges, that is, they would spend most of their time traveling and hearing cases at the courts established by Congress. The Congress also set Washington's salary as president at $25,000 per year, an amount which greatly exceeded that of all the other officials and probably all but the wealthiest of Americans. Washington responded by always showing himself in the capacity of the chief magistrate of the US, that is, with the utmost dignity. Today, it must be said, the salary of the president has slipped relative to the salaries of other equally responsible levels of management.

As is apparent in the current political environment not only is a stable structure needed in the case of an eventual world government but also in many of the existing nations comprising the system of nationalism. That is to say, some level of direct communication must be established to control the crisis that is continuing to arise in the global financial markets and in the international political arena. For example, the continuing debate over nuclear proliferation cannot find a reasonable solution within the current system of nationalism.

The Supreme Court can arguably be considered the most important, and by far the most active, in establishing the actual operating structure of the federal government in relation to the states and the people. The court became particularly active after the appointment of John Marshall by Adams in 1801. This appointment was part of the first example of a president attempting to "pack" the Supreme Court with justices that fit his political philosophy. In this case Adams was completely successful. Under Marshall the Federalist agenda was fully put into operation, at least as much of it as could possibly be accomplished by the Supreme Court. Marshall immediately established the doctrine that the Supreme Court had the power to review any laws of the United States, the member states, or any local subdivision of the state governments; including the provisions of the state constitutions. In relation to this review power the Supreme Court would exercise its status as the final arbitrator of constitutionality.

In Marbury v. Madison the Court ruled that when a federal law was in conflict with a state law, or a provision of a state constitution, the federal law would be held superior. Marshall and the rest of the Supreme Court established that the Constitution was clear in granting the powers which the Court was now exercising, that is, the right of judicial review, the superiority of federal law, and that the Supreme Court was the final arbitrator of constitutionality regardless of the source of the law. In rendering the first decisions, including the Marbury case, Marshall expressed his intention to interpret the language of the Constitution as broadly as possible. This was, of course, not a power given to the Court in the Constitution but was left for the Court to decide as it officially began operation. In light of the various compromises that were made in the convention, and also during the ratification process, especially the Bill of Rights, this approach was very proactive on the part of the judicial branch. It alone would establish the power of the federal government to expand its power when necessary. The early control exercised by the Federalist went a long way in setting up the opportunities that would be available for the expansion of federal power. It was equally successful in making it very difficult for those that wanted to limit the power of the federal government and who were advocating states' rights.

In response to the control of the early government by the Federalists the conservatives developed a counter policy. This policy generally speaking became known as the nullification position. It was advocated in large part by the Southern bloc of states, especially South Carolina. Under this policy it was proposed that the states either singly or in concert had the power to nullify a federal law or practice (regulation) if it was contrary to the interest of the involved state.

Some even took the position (mainly South Carolina under John Calhoun) under the nullification doctrine that the states individually and collectively had the right to nullify their ratification of the Constitution. This would allow them to voluntarily end their association with the Union and to withdraw. This position seemed to be supported by the right of rebellion claimed in the Declaration of Independence, as well as the fact that withdrawal from the union was not prohibited by the Constitution. The only constitutional provision that might retard withdrawal was that which guaranteed a republican form of government to the states. Even this provision, however, did not speak directly to withdrawal from the union.

This latter position was held by only a small minority of the conservatives during the period under consideration. When the nullification doctrine is looked at from the point of view of a state right to nullify a federal law, the support is somewhat weaker. The Constitution clearly establishes that the federal laws will be superior to the state laws including any provisions of the state constitutions. The Constitution also makes the Supreme Court the final arbitrator of any disputes that might arise concerning this issue. The whole issue of states' rights was bound up in the power of the states to act independently in a situation in which federal action was invalid but still pursued. In the case of an invalid federal law common sense, if nothing else, would point to the right of the states to evade the law essentially nullifying it. If the entire Constitution is taken into consideration, it is clear that the intent was that the union would be perpetual once established; and by inference incapable of being dissolved by independent state actions. It must be noted, however, that the doctrine of broad interpretation of the constitutional language gave a color of legitimacy to the nullification doctrine. The nullification doctrine was consistently used as a threat by the conservatives in their battles against the establishment of a national banking system, regulations involving interstate trade, and the purchase of lands outside the borders of the US by the federal government.

James Madison almost immediately presented to Congress the Bill of Rights (as the first ten amendments were called); they addressed the most serious objections that had been offered by the conservatives (also called anti-federalists). As an author of the Federalist Papers Madison had argued against the need for a bill of rights, however, after ratification of the Constitution he soon realized that such a document was very much needed to insure the durability of the union. In all, the several states had submitted a total of two hundred and ten proposed amendments during the ratification process. From those submitted by the State of Virginia, the home of Thomas Jefferson, Madison selected the first eight, which were all intended to extend protection to the individual rights of citizens. The last two amendments were taken almost word for word from the Articles of Confederation. Thomas Jefferson, if it be remembered, was the author of the Declaration of Independence and one of the leading thinkers in the US at that time. He believed that the individual rights listed in the first eight amendments were crucial to the success of the union.

It is evident that the same problems will be encountered by the first congress assembled in relation to the establishment of a world government. The matter of etiquette in addressing the chief magistrate has already been mentioned. It will be necessary for the executive branch to create a full executive department including but not necessarily limited to the various cabinet positions, the various departments of executive government, a range of judicial appointments, and other executive bureaucratic agencies. The congress will be required to establish the federal court system and to institute the legislation that will put the government into operation. The structure that was considered adequate to launch the US government would constitute merely the bare bones of the structure needed to operate a world government.

The first tasks of this government would include the institution of a plan for total disarmament, coupled with a plan for inspecting the disarmament procedures of each nation, and presenting and implementing a plan for the safe destruction and disposal of the waste created by disarmament. A task that will be encountered at nearly the same time will be the issue of environmental pollution. A program will need to be instituted to determine the types of pollution that need to be handled most urgently and the specific effects of this pollution that need to be addressed.

This program will have to include a massive plan for the cleanup of environmental pollution that now exists and the prevention of any further pollution of that type, with an outline of how these issues can be handled at the national and local level. A large amount of legislation would be required from the first session of the new world congress. It should, however, be limited to the setting forth of the rules of the game. That is to say, the general legislation should only outline the goals that are intended, leaving the national and local governments the task of drafting the specific legislation needed to implement the desired goals. The other departments, agencies, and cabinet positions that deal with the everyday operations of the government can afford to be developed a little slower, but the former two issues must be resolved to allow for any success at all on the part of the world government.

Problems this large and difficult will of course require the full cooperation of all members of the world union and it is expected that that will include all of the then existing nations. The union can use the experience of the US as a guide but will have to adapt that experience to the needs of the then current environment.

One cardinal point that can, without a doubt, be profitably incorporated from the US experience is the early spirit of compromise that was exhibited throughout society. It may also take a good deal of time to chose the world capital, to install the first chief magistrate, and most important of all, to select the first congressional assembly. It is suggested that the congressional representatives be elected during the ratification process so that if the Constitution is ratified they will be capable of immediate assembly. The same procedure might be followed for the chief magistrates, as well as the initial appointments that are to be made by the executive department, including an unofficial confirmation by the Senate; with official confirmation being available immediately after the first congress is assembled. It seems fair to say that one of the main benefits of using the US Constitution and the early history of the US as a guide is that it will allow much of the above preliminary work to be accomplished quickly and probably before or during the process of ratification. If this proves to be an accurate assessment of the circumstances surrounding the establishment of a world government, the process could be accomplished within less than two years. It took the early US representatives nearly two years to construct the new government. This time was spent in creating executive departments, setting up the judicial system, and the other mechanics of government operation. This was true even though the necessary structure was very small in comparison to what would be needed to institute a world government. Once it is established, however, the world government would face the same initial problems as the early US, that is to say, the issues of how to adequately fund the new government; what fundamental laws would be needed to insure the smooth operation of the government; and how to balance the powers, duties, and responsibilities of the central, national, and local governments. The latter of these will be a major issue facing the first world government regardless of the planning that precedes it. In terms of the concepts of 19th century federalism the effort should be made to leave as much sovereignty to the national and local governments as possible.

Returning now to the actions taken by the federal government of the early US to solve these problems, we see that several obstacles had to be cleared. The first order of business was to put the new government on a sound fiscal basis. As secretary of the treasury it was Hamilton's job to see that this was done quickly.

In 1790 Hamilton submitted his first and likely most important recommendations, e.g., first that the national debt (the debt left over from the confederation) be funded by issuing bonds guaranteed by the new government which would be given to creditors in exchange for the worthless old bonds they held. Second, Hamilton also recommended that the federal government assume all of the debts that the various states had contracted for during the Revolution which amounted to $21 million. This again would be funded by the issuing of bonds.

These two plans were decisively in favor of creditors and speculators and hurt the people who were in great need of money. Most people had sold their bonds to speculators for a mere fraction of their face value. When the people found out that these bonds were to be redeemed at face value they pleaded with the government that they be allowed to receive the difference between what speculators had paid and the face value. The government (Hamilton) refused to consider their claims and allowed the windfall profits to fall to the speculators. In Hamilton's defense, the only thing that can be offered is that he was attempting to win the financial community to the side of the federal government in order to give it an incentive to give the government a hand in getting over the fiscal security obstacle. It took several months of debate before Congress accepted this first report and made it law.

Shortly after making the first report law, Hamilton submitted a series of reports. The first requested the imposition of excise taxes on distilled spirits (alcohol). The second proposed the establishment of a national bank. The reports also called for the establishment of a national mint, which was established in 1792. His last report was presented in 1791 requesting that Congress issue a series of import taxes aimed at protecting the infant industries that were beginning to appear, especially in the Northeast. When it became public knowledge that Hamilton intended for the national debt to support a permanent taxation policy, it raised a hornet's nest of protest. Madison again broke with Hamilton and pushed for a substantial payment to the original bond holders as well as the current speculators who actually held the bonds. In Congress, Madison was defeated and Hamilton's program was adopted.

The state debts however created a clear sectional division within Congress. The South had already to great degree paid off the debts they had contracted during the Revolution. The Northeast however had not paid theirs and stood to be almost the sole benefactor of this program. Hamilton, with the aid of Jefferson, reached a compromise with Madison. Hamilton agreed to back the placement of the national capital in the South in return for support in assumption of the state debts. The compromise also included a federal grant to those states that had already paid their debts to put them in a position of relative equity with those that had not paid theirs. This again was a concession to the wealthy influential creditors.

The national bank would be authorized to issue paper money which would provide for a uniform currency throughout the Union. Having paid off the debt assumptions made earlier, through land sales, the new government was now in possession of huge sums of capital that had to be protected with a carefully regulated monetary system. The debate over the national bank again arose because of the opposition offered by James Madison. The bill was passed by Congress over Madison's objections. Washington, who (like Madison) questioned the constitutionality of the bank, called together his cabinet before offering a veto. Here again he found a division based on a strict versus a broad interpretation of the Constitution. Therefore the bank issue also became the first issue involving the constitutionality of a federal law. Washington decided that this bill was the province of the Treasury Department. He accepted Hamilton's broad interpretation of the Constitution and signed the bill into law. Hamilton's program was later upheld by the Supreme Court under John Marshall's doctrine of implied constitutional powers.

Hamilton's request for a protective tariff was passed in part in 1792 but was largely shelved for later debate. It was not however in any manner forgotten. All these reports or bills clearly support the contention that Hamilton was the most important policy man in the new government. In connection with the proactive approach taken by John Marshall and the Supreme Court, the federalist program was adopted almost in total. Hamilton focused his efforts as secretary of the treasury on the development of commercial capitalism (the result of the recent importation of the Industrial Revolution from Great Britain). Hamilton was very astute in his early recognition of the importance of some newly emerging movements, such as the industrial revolution, the growth of capitalism (at this time largely represented by manufacturing interests), and the growing imperialism of Western Europe. Hamilton's goal, and probably his greatest achievement, was to tie the wealthy elite very closely to the federal government in relation to the protection of their wealth. This was of course the same path as was taken in every nation that was in existence at the time. That is say, those who control the monetary system have power, those who have power tend to exercise it, and those who exercise power are in the end those who control the direction and aims of the government in question. Here again it is offered that no type of conspiracy was in operation but rather only the results of the natural course of events.

The split between the Federalists, represented by Hamilton's programs, and the conservative position, led by Thomas Jefferson and James Madison, brought about the first development of a two-party system in the US. Until the election of 1801 the two parties were the Federalist Party and the Democratic-Republican Party, with the latter representing the conservative position that was during this period in a minority. Party politics, however, were slow to develop as the American public had a somewhat adverse attitude. It appears that neither of the party organizations was intending to create a two-party system, or even to establish permanent political parties, but rather they were attempting to consolidate support around positions taken on specific issues.

Initially the constant theme that kept the parties intact revolved around the difference in opinion as to whether or not the federal government should be stronger or more limited in powers; whether the constitutional language should be broadly or narrowly interpreted; and whether the federal government had only express powers or whether it also had implied powers. It is here that we run into the exercise of the doctrine of nullification. Hamilton during the administration of Washington and Adams was instituting the main agenda of the Federalist Party. The Democratic-Republican minority in Congress was successful in blocking an uncontrolled extension of power after the Federalist agenda was passed into law. Even so the Democratic-Republicans were left with little choice other than threatening the nullification of the Union, or at the very least, the nullification of some of the more odious federal laws.

Each of the issues raised above involved the interpretation of constitutional legalities, sectional interests, and the differing philosophies of the slowly evolving political parties. Because of the not yet defined legal status of most of the new federal legislation, and the emotional character of sectional interests, the party positions during this period remained very fluid. In some cases those who were normally aligned with the Democratic-Republicans would side with the Federalist Party on specific issues. Such was the compromise over the assumption of state debts described above. At other times some of those who stood with the Federalist Party would side with the Democratic-Republicans as when the Hamiltonian import taxation proposal was shelved for later action. The spirit of rationally comprehending each specific issue and recognizing the circumstances surrounding such issues as well as the ability to compromise were all very much alive and well. In fact it might be safe to conclude that during the early period of US history that compromise was the operating system used by the new government. The system of compromise however was basically limited to the procedures used by the executive and legislative branches. The judicial branch was very definitely under the auspices of the federalist agenda. In this branch there was no pressure to conform to public opinion (essentially life tenure) and no real pressure that could be applied by either the executive or legislative branch once appointment had been confirmed. Under John Jay the Supreme Court had already clearly established that federal law was supreme even over the state constitutions and that the Supreme Court was the final arbitrator in conflicts between the laws of the central government and the states, or in any case where unconstitutionality was claimed. Chief Justice Marshall was confirmed in his appointment in 1801 and continued the federalist agenda in a very strong fashion. He early in his career established beyond question that the interpretation of the Constitution was to be as broad as possible based upon the Supreme Courts understanding of the intentions of those who wrote the Constitution. He in addition clearly established that the federal government had implied powers delegated in the Constitution; and that the Supreme Court would also be the final arbitrator of what those powers were to be. The doctrine of implied powers was to be invoked whenever the Supreme Court decided that it was necessary and proper. Marshall was to use these doctrines consistently until his departure from the court in 1834. He was able to do so because the Constitution intentionally did not attempt to define the manner in which the judicial system would operate or interpret its duties. It is interesting to note that although the parties disagreed on almost every issue neither of them can be accused of having stepped outside the "intent" of the

Constitution when scrutinized under the doctrine of a broad interpretation of the constitutional language.

There is a great deal of likelihood that the same type of questions will arise from the first wave of issues that will face a world government. First, it is reasonable to assume that if a world government is established that it will be under pressure to assume the duties of the United Nations and other international institutions. It may also be possible that the central government will be under pressure to assume the national debts contracted in relation to the operations of the World Bank and the International Monetary Fund (IMF). It can be supposed that whatever method is currently in place to guarantee these debts will be used to convert them to like debts under the new government. In short, it is likely that the world government will be just as anxious to maintain the aid of the financial community as was the early US. What is unresolved is whether either added any real security to the early operations of government, i.e., did soliciting the aid of the financial community aid also in the success of the early US government. It is at least arguable it did not do anything to contribute to the early success of the government but rather made official the defrauding of the general public of its funds. It would be recommended here that the debts spoken of above be converted to a private contractual status enforceable through the judicial system and not be made a part of the public debt of the new world government. If the national debts related to the operations of the World Bank and IMF are converted to the status of private debt they will stand in the same relation as the debts now outstanding in relation to trade imbalances, commercial deficits, etc. It is likely that the world government through the judicial system will be required to closely regulate the reduction of national debts but it is not recommended that the central government assume any of these debts; or offer any type of bail out if a nation becomes bankrupt. Second, there can be no doubt that the world government will need to be put on a sound financial footing. In connection with this need it is likely that a world mint will need to be created to issue a uniform currency and that a world organization, whether it be a world bank or a world-wide central reserve system (comparable to the US Federal Reserve System), will need to be established to regulate the value of this currency. The experience of the European Union in relation to the creation of the Euro should certainly be consulted in this area. Initially, as with the Euro, the main problems revolve around the actual structure of the monetary system, the redemption rate to be allowed the various existing currencies and the regulation of the value of the new system during redemption. It will also be very useful no doubt to look at the financial repercussions that resulted from the reunification of the two Germanys and the rapid expansion of EU membership. Third, it also seems reasonable to assume that the central judicial system will have to be established as the final arbitrator of the interpretation of the Constitution, as well as, any disputes that arise between the laws of the central government and the national, or local laws, including any national constitutions. In the case of world government the issue is likely to be much larger than mere legal questions. It can be assumed that the world government will have the right to directly affect the behavior of its citizens through the passage of its laws. It is, however, also fair to assume that the same government will be prohibited from unduly interfering in any individual's right to practice the traditions of their religion, culture, or artistic talents. Conflicts that arise under these headings have traditionally led to challenges of constitutionality in the US and may be expected to do the same under a world government patterned after the US. It is likely that the issues concerning the need for a federal bureaucracy (departments, cabinet, and other operational organizations) will be accepted without argument. The same will undoubtedly be true for the issues related to the supremacy of the federal law and the Supreme Court's role as final arbitrator of constitutionality. It is however to be questioned as to whether or not acceptance of the doctrine of board interpretation of constitutional language, the doctrine of implied powers, the doctrine of necessary and proper determination of constitutional intent, among others, should be accepted without debate. As we will see these very doctrines over time have resulted in the question as to whether or not the US federal government has overstepped the intent of the Constitution in terms of federalism. It is expected that in the case of world government a great number of political parties will develop. For example, in the current EU Parliament there are 102 parties. There are also a number of other interest groups and of course the interests of the individual nations. This has not yet caused any insurmountable problems with consensus building in the EU experience.

The broad issues discussed above were relatively quickly resolved in favor of establishing a stronger federal government in the US. The solutions in large part followed the tenets of the federalist philosophy. The debate between the Federalists and Democratic-Republicans now shifted from the operating premises of the federal government to issues involving how much power should be extended to the federal government in relation to that of the states and determining the areas of society in which it was proper for the federal government to act.

It is unremarkable that initially many of the major issues should have revolved around the issue of states' rights. This was, in fact, the first time in history that any such separation of powers had been attempted and there were therefore no real precedents by which the various factions could be guided. The various states, of course, were still very jealous of their sovereign powers and very reluctant to give them up. The same certainly will be true with the nations who become members of the world union, i.e., they will be very jealous of their sovereign power and reluctant to delegate it to the central government. In this case, however, those involved in the process of delimiting the powers of the central government and those of the nations will have an example to go by that can guide them in their decisions. For example, as has been pointed out, the powers settled in the federal government such as the power to regulate international and interstate trade, the power of taxation, the power of supremacy in legal issues, etc., were all imperative to its success. If the states' rights advocates had held their position in regard to these issues it is likely that within a short period of time the federal government would have been as ineffective as the early US confederation. Using this as a guide it would seem reasonable that these powers, or those similar to them, would be established without the need for much debate. Even so, it was remarkable that the debate over federal versus state rights, especially in light of the nullification doctrine, did not early on lead to the dissolution of the Union. This fact alone would indicate that the issues although they sometimes sparked heated debate were not of a vital nature. They tended to be debates on philosophical principles mainly intellectual in import and removed from the emotional interests of the people at large. In short, they were debates over procedures rather than over structure per se. Social issues as we know them today did not arise in the US system until much later. It is just this sort of issues, however, that bring about the emotions that can lead to the failure of government. In the US situation the then existing qualifications for the franchise, the homogeneity of the voting population, and the lack of communication technology were probably responsible for the scarcity of social issues beyond the sectional issues. This will not be the case with the creation of a world government in today's environment. There will be a variety of issues that would need immediate attention and which would result in the failure of the government if not successfully concluded. These would include the issues of total disarmament, global pollution and clean up, the conservation of the world's natural resources, the safe disposal of toxic waste of all kinds among others. All of these issues would affect the interests of powerful nations and the economic welfare of their citizens resulting in a perfect environment for emotionally determined response. The world government would not have the luxury of an extended honeymoon as was the US case in regard to major social and civil rights issues. The EU can also stand as a valuable guide in this area. The EU has successfully faced a large number of civil rights issues during its existence. In addition to these general issues a number of specific issues would need to be faced. First, the political, economic and social chaos found in Africa, The Middle East, parts of Asia and parts of Latin America would need to be immediately addressed. It is likely that creative solutions to these issues would need to be found outside of the traditional democratic models, i.e., the solutions would tend to be found outside the realm of politics. Second, the economic structure related to liberal democracy would most likely need to be tempered in relation to the development of existing marginalized nations, for example, a creative employment program would need to be instituted in these areas to provide infrastructure improvement. Lastly, a creative approach to the existing social problems related to ethic, tribal, racial, gender, and other such issues would be needed. Although many of these issues could be adjudicated, something beyond adjudication needs to be instituted to eliminate the underlying causes of problems such as these.

The most important issues faced during the period from 1789 to 1820, outside the procedural issues, were the sectional issues hinted at earlier. The power of the federal government to set import and export taxes once established was quickly followed by the debate as to whether or not the tariffs overall should be high or low. Those sections with large manufacturing and commercial interests favored a high tariff (Northeast and part of the West) to protect these interests. On the other hand, those states that were dependent upon the purchase of foreign goods through trade of local products favored a low tariff (South and part of the West). The area made up of the Tennessee and Ohio River Valleys was dependent upon the sale of natural resources in both the domestic and foreign markets and was also largely dependent on foreign goods for their day to day life. Although they were not officially states, but rather US territories, they were still interested in there being a low tariff in the US. This issue was heatedly debated in Congress but the Federalists were consistently able to garner enough votes to maintain a relatively high tariff.

The tax imposed by the federal government on alcohol was not debated in Congress but was violently resisted in Pennsylvania. This resistance has become known as the whiskey rebellion. It was an early example of internal insurrection but was not aimed at replacing the federal government. Washington used federal troops to quell the violence generated by the rebellion and set a precedent that is still in force today. Any internal issue that generates a significant amount of violence can expect that the state militia, and if necessary federal troops, will be used to end the violence. The sectional issues although capable of generating considerable passion were also capable of generating the circumstances which could lead to compromise. Except in the case of Native American raids on the frontiers and the whiskey rebellion all the early sectional interests were resolved on the basis of compromise normally joined into by all involved parties.

In the case of British support of Native American attacks on the frontier settlements the issue in 1812 led to a declared war between the two nations. The US was able to gain a pronounced naval victory on the Great Lakes over the English navy but at the same time the British were able to invade and capture the US Capitol. The result of this war was a clear definition of the Canadian and US border from the Great Lakes to Maine. As a result the British were forced to move out of the Ohio River Valley leaving it in the sole possession of the US. The Spanish support of the Seminoles (actually a collection of Native American Nations) who had immigrated to the Spanish possession of Florida led to another military action in 1820. The US government authorized Andrew Jackson to enter into Florida to put an end to the Seminole raids. Although he was unsuccessful in finding the Seminoles he did take possession of the Florida Panhandle to secure Georgia from further raids. At the same time the US government was negotiating with Spain over the boundary that would separate the US and Spanish possessions after the Louisiana Purchase of 1805. The war was used to pressure the Spanish into a settlement in 1821 that transferred the whole of Florida to the United States for five million dollars, and settled the boundary of the Louisiana Purchase as we will see later.

Looking at the solutions accepted by the early US government in its opening stages of evolution it is possible to suggest whether or not the world union should also attempt the same solutions.

1. The acceptance of the fact that the federal laws will be the supreme law of the land should be accepted without debate by the world union as it has been in the EU.

2. The acceptance of the federal power to regulate both the global market and inter-nation trade should be accepted without debate as to the concept itself although debate should be held upon the powers to be delegated in this area.

3. The acceptance of the federal power to create and regulate a unified monetary system using the European Union as a guide should be accepted during the first session of the general legislature.

4. The World Government must accept its duty to adjust any disputes that may arise over common areas and their use. This would include Antarctica, the Arctic, the open seas, outer space, and possibly cyber-space.

5. The World Government must also accept its role as the peace-keeper in relation to internal insurrections, international crime, among other evidences of violence. It is unlikely if all nations join the union that any examples of external invasion will occur but the world union will need to accept its duty to militarily end any such occurrence.

6. The establishment and acceptance of the Supreme Court as the sole interpreter of the intent of those who drafted the Constitution under the concept of judicial review. This includes the power to declare laws unconstitutional, to arbitrate disputes between the laws of the federal government and the states, and to determine what was necessary and proper in the delegation of implied powers should be accepted by the world union but only after debate as to any needed restrictions.

7. The World Government must accept the value of the ability to compromise and to activate the concept of piece-meal social engineering as the foundation of its operational procedure as an example of federalism at its most powerful.

8. The World Union must end all forms of ethnic and economic slavery in whatever form it exists.

9. The World Union must face the fact that there is an immense diversity in relation to political, economic, and social skills

among the various nations that will become members of the Union and focus on creative solutions to the elimination of these inequalities.

10. The World Union should attempt to allow as much independence as possible to the national members in relation to their cooperating in cultural, religious, economic, intellectual and other endeavors by delegating power downwards to the lowest possible level.

The World Union will face issues similar to the sectional issues faced by the early US government. There are currently areas of the world (Somalia, Columbia, Mexico, among others) where illegal actions such as piracy and drug trafficking are accompanied by a considerable level of violence. If the individual nation involved is not capable of controlling this violence and requests the aid of the general government, the violence should be ended by military means if necessary — but not without attention to dealing with the underlying causes. There are also many areas of the world (The Sudan, Iraq, and Chechnya among others) which face violent struggles revolving around ethnic, tribal or national issues and which include cross border raids (terrorism) between different nations. The World Union will be empowered to end the violence militarily but again should not be allowed to do so without also addressing the underlying issues. In both cases the general government should act proactively as soon as possible. The issues that are involved in these conflicts should be brought before the Supreme Court immediately upon its establishment for independent mediation. It may even be found necessary to break up some existing nations, or at least, to allow them to develop some form of federal system within the existing nation. Any attempt to resolve issues of sovereignty within existing nations, however, should be done at the national and local level with the federal government acting as mediator; or in the last extreme, through legal action by the Supreme Court.

The European Union came into being in 1952 with the establishment of the European Coal and Steel Community. At this stage it was only one small organization attempting to set up a transnational regulation of two heavy industries. Six nations had agreed to give up their individual control of these two industries and delegate this power to the European Commission. The six nations were West Germany, France, Italy, Belgium, the Netherlands, and Luxembourg. Even at this early date the leading minds involved in setting up the European Coal and Steel Community (ECSC) had in mind a long term integration of Europe into a federalism similar to that which existed in the US. Over the last sixty years the EU has failed to fully accomplish the hopes of the founding fathers, however, there has been considerable progress in that direction. Today the EU is not truly a supranational government, but it is still much more than just another international organization. There has been a full integration of Europe in relation to its economic construction (single market, elimination of barriers to trade, money, people and goods and a single monetary system); its ability to act as one voice in international agencies, such as IMF, The World Bank, the G-8 and the General Agreement on Tariffs and Trade (GATT); its ability to stand united on issues of security and defense among others. It has however not been able to achieve integration on a political level.

It is at this level that one must look for an analysis of the EU as a guide to world government. In this work it has been assumed that the world gov-

ernment would be established in a manner similar to that used in the establishment of the United States. The EU, however, may be an alternative way
of establishing the world government on either a temporary or permanent
basis.

We'll begin with a description of how the EU is structured and how it
actually operates. The structure of the EU might be most easily understood
by comparing it to equivalent structures in the US. As everyone knows, the
American government is based on a tri-partite division of power between
the executive, legislative and judicial branches of the Federal government.
The EU is not structured in exactly the same the manner, although all three
political functions are to be found. The European Commission and the
Council of Ministers represent both the executive and legislative power of
the European Union. The European Court of Justice coupled with a Court
of First Instance handle the judicial functions of the EU. The EU also has
a parliament but it was given very little power initially, although it now is
gaining some legislative and executive powers. The European Parliament is
the only European level institution that is directly elected by the citizens of
Europe. The Council of Ministers as its name suggests is composed of the
various national ministers. If this organization existed in the US it would
consist of the heads of the various state departments, that is, defense, education, etc, but in the EU is composed of the ministers that act in the same
capacity as the American secretary of state. The European Commission is
appointed by the various nations. Each nation has at least one member on
the Commission and the President of the Commission serves for six months
on the basis of a rotation through the member nations. The judges are also
appointed by the various member nations from a list provided by the European Commission. Unlike the US judicial system, judges are not appointed
for life or during good conduct, but rather for a term of years certain.

The European Parliament now has the power to approve the appointment of the commission but only in total and not to individual members.
The European Parliament has 736 members currently. The members of Parliament (MEPS) are elected through European wide elections for a term of
five years. The Parliament does not have the power to initiate legislation as
does the Congress of the US. They have now however obtained the right to
offer advice and consent to the legislation that is initiated and passed by
the Council of Ministers and European Commission. Therefore the executive and legislative powers of the EU are delegated to the Commission and

Council of Ministers. Parliament, at present, acts more as watchdog rather than as an essential organ of the EU structure having only the power to dismiss the Council of Ministers and render an opinion on legislation. The judicial powers are all located in the European Court of Justice and the Court of First Instance. As with the US Supreme Court the European court has gained the right to hold itself out as the final arbitrator in disputes between the EU and the member nations or their citizens. It has been established that EU law will be superior to that of the member nations although judicial review has not been established as in the US. Essentially judicial review is a legal process whereby the verdict in one case can be automatically carried over to other cases that are parallel to the one in which the verdict is rendered. The Court, however, does not have any method of enforcing its verdicts and must rely on the European Commission and the legal systems of the various members to enforce them. It in short does not have the power to imprison, fine or hold in contempt anyone or any state that does not abide by its decisions.

The above institutions are the only ones that have actually been created by the various treaties that have over the last sixty years established the EU. There are, however, several institutions that were created but were not covered by the treaties initially. By far the most important is the European Council. This institution is made up of the heads of all the member states. It also has its own bureaucracy, known as the Committee of Permanent Representatives (COREPER). The bureaucracy is made up of the various heads of the national departments, such as the minister of education, defense, etc., and a large staff of experts in various areas such as economics, legislative drafting, etc. This bureaucracy was also not created under the various treaties. Essentially the European Council acts as a sub-cabinet of the European Commission. It meets four times a year to make decisions on European level issues that cannot be handled by the Commission. Normally this includes any issues that directly affect national interests or are of such a sensitive nature that a vote of unanimity is needed on the Commission to create legislation. COREPER during the time between meetings of the Council spends its time settling all issues of a mundane nature and getting them ready for a rubber stamp from the Council. This latter process may include even the drafting of the legislation that will be submitted to the Commission for approval. It also has usually already constructed several alternative ways of treating an issue even when it cannot bring it to a conclusion. This allows the Council to actually only debate the few issues that can't be determined by COREPER. The European Council is therefore an example of government by consensus, that is, an example of intergovernmentalism. The European Council is without a doubt a major decision maker in relation to the overall policies of the EU. Both the European Council and COREPER have been officially recognized within later treaties. The EU has also established a European Central Bank that operates in much the same fashion as the Federal Reserve in the US. It is responsible for the establishment of rediscount rates, interest rates between banking institutions, the regulation of exchange rates between currencies and other financial matters. It also was not created by any of the various EU treaties but was recognized in later treaties. Lastly, there is a court that was created to hear all cases arising under the European Charter of Fundamental Rights. This court goes by the name of European Court of Human Rights and is expected to mediate all issues arising within the union concerning human rights violations.

The above represents the most visible institutions involved in the structure of the EU. As stated earlier in combination they execute all of the executive, legislative and judicial responsibilities on the European level. They are all considered to be supranational institutions. They have been created by the willingness of the twenty seven member nations to delegate some of their national sovereignty to the European level. In this sense the EU has many of the earmarks familiar from other existing federal systems. The EU member nations, however, have delegated much less of their sovereignty than is the case in most federal systems such as the United States, The Russian Federation, and the German Federation among others. It is also possible to see the EU as a form of intergovernmentalism as the decision making process is largely reserved to the nations rather than the supranational institutions of the EU. The fact that only the Parliament is elected has also raised concerns over the lack of transparency in EU actions and the almost universal lack of access on the part of the citizens to the EU decision making process. This latter issue is usually denoted as the "democratic deficit." Even though the EU does not seem to qualify as a fully fledged government it has been very successful in some major areas of concern for any world government that might be established.

The establishment of a world government will almost certainly require the creation of a unified monetary system. The EU experience with the creation of the Euro system, its handling of the logistical problems of putting it into effect, and the rapid transition from institution to acceptance will all be a major help for a new world government. The establishment of a single monetary system on a worldwide basis will allow transactions to be made without the cost of conversion from one monetary currency to another as it currently does in the Euro region of Europe. Although Europe established the Single European Market prior to the European monetary system this could be accomplished in a reverse order in relation to the worldwide market. However, through such existing international organizations as the International Monetary Fund, the World Bank, and GATT the global market has come a considerable distance in the direction of a single market. Many barriers to the free flow of trade, goods, money and people have been eliminated. There is in the global market only one real enforcement process and that is the overwhelming military might of the US. This would under total disarmament have to be replaced with a regulatory system similar in nature to that used by the EU. Here enforcement of the regulations is handled by the European Commission through a rather elaborate system of warnings and fines. It appears that this process is much more humane than the enforcement procedure used by the US in Iraq to prohibit Iraqi territorial action in Kuwait.

The EU has also been able to enact and enforce rather strict environmental rules and regulations that have motivated the member nations to clean up pollution and to eliminate further pollution. This has not happened on a worldwide basis although the EU is one of the strongest voices in the environmental movement within the appropriate international agencies. When a world government is established it should seriously consider the work that has been accomplished in the EU in this area. The US has been one of the strongest actors in relation to blocking environmental action on the international level and cannot therefore act as a guide in this area.

The EU has also made the conscious choice based on its intense desire to maintain peace to spend its funds on social programs rather than military budgets. The EU does maintain through its various members a sizable military presence but they use this presence for peace keeping missions and disaster control. The actual military actions outside of Europe are normally left to NATO, which operates under American control. This latter organization is controlled by the US who provides the majority of the soldiers, funding, and equipment. The EU does have one small European level force labeled the European Rapid Reaction Force of some 60,000 soldiers. Here again the US is not really a good source of guidance for development of such a force on the world level as it maintains the old true military structure. Here the German and Russian examples of a small rapid internet-based response to localized attacks should be studied. If we are correct in assuming that most of the work of any military institution under a world government will be for disaster relief, peacekeeping missions and other things of that nature the EU would be a wise choice for guidance in developing that institution.

Although the first thirty years of existence under a world government would include many of the same problems faced by the early US the solutions offered by US history are not necessarily the best that can be offered. In many cases as noted above the EU experience may be much more valuable and lead to a more efficient and effective solution. Having said this it is again time to go forward with the detailing of the US experience.

The election of 1820 marks a rather clear demarcation in US political philosophy. The bitter debate between federal and states' rights had culminated in the victory of the federalists but at the cost of the demise of their party. The Democratic-Republicans had then become dominant and had done what they could to reestablish the position of states' rights. In this they had failed, in fact, in many cases extending the old philosophy of the federalists into new areas both domestically and in relation to international affairs. The election of 1820 represents the public reaction to the policies followed by early party politics. The election begins the advent of two party politics in the US as we know it today. The two parties would soon control not only the candidates that would run for office but also the issues that these candidates would bring to focus for the public at large. The candidates initially at least would be chosen by the parties using what was known as the closed door caucus. This system would be used not only to choose federal candidates but also state and local candidates. The two parties would shortly be disciplined all the way down to the precinct level especially in the large urban areas of the country. The party leaders especially at the federal level operated behind the scenes and were largely hidden from the public eye while on the state and local level they tended to be more open and public. The party leaders of course would change with time, particularly with the change of fortune of the party in the various elections. The leaders, however, were always a small percentage of the total party membership allowing the party system to evolve into a type of oligarchy.

By 1840 the party structure was highly organized and disciplined and subject to a strict hierarchy. This hierarchical structure allowed for very rapid communication between the party leaders and the members on the street. The candidates chosen by the party, as well as the issues selected for focus during any particular campaign, could be closely monitored by the party leaders. In addition, once the election was concluded the party could keep a very close watch on the behavior of the successful candidate once they had taken office. Given the level of communication technology then in existence the party system proved to be the most effective means of disseminating information. It is probably fair to say the two parties represented the first organized well financed interest groups on the US political scene. Under normal circumstances the party leaders were relatively homogenous in their political philosophy, be it conservative or liberal, and the candidates and party members were expected to hold to the party line or platform. There has however been no significant period of time when either party has been controlled solely by one consistent political philosophy, that is to say, each party from the beginning had a tripartite wing structure. The various wings that at times found themselves a minority in the party were still capable of forcing compromises on the wing that was in the majority, and depending upon circumstances the status of the various wings within the party, could and did change rapidly. It is of interest to note that when the moderate wing of each party was in the majority at the same time complaints were heard that there was no significant difference in the positions of the two parties. Recently the Republican Party has been controlled by its ultra-conservative wing, also known as the religious right, while the Democratic Party has been controlled by its moderate or right wing leaving the impression on the part of the public that very little is left to choose from between them. Much more will be said on this issue later.

An interesting point to be considered is how the structure of the parties evolved. Each party tended to produce three internal divisions. In the case of the conservative party, this division was between those considered to be ultra-conservative, those considered moderate, and those considered liberal. In the case of the liberal party, the division was between the conservative liberal, moderate and ultra-liberal wings. These various divisions, however, within the structure of the party were still all liberals or conservatives in relation to the other party. The various divisions led to a situation in which temporary coalitions could be formed which allowed for compromises to be concluded. For example, on a particular issue the liberal wing of the conservatives might have a common cause with the conservative wing of the liberal party and form a temporary coalition putting them in the majority position in Congress. Once in power, however, whether it is in one branch or all three, the party leaders tended to exert pressure to prevent these temporary coalitions from forming. It is a definite credit to the system of government created by the Constitution that neither party has been able to control the political environment for any substantial length of time. The various checks and balances, coupled with frequent elections, and life time tenure in the judiciary all combine to prevent such an occurrence. Even when one party held a distinct majority in both houses of Congress, and controlled the executive branch as well, two factors normally combined to limit the exercise of the power one would expect from such a majority position. First, because of the duration of service of the Supreme Court justices they tend to be out of step with the more rapidly changing philosophy of the other two branches and the people at large. Second, the relatively short terms of the members of the House of Representatives tends to break down majority positions. The people of course are influenced in their votes by the perception they have of the success of any representative, senator, or executive leader to represent their interests. The people of the US very seldom display a homogenous political philosophy whether it is conservative or liberal, but rather tend to lean for periods of time in one direction or another. Later we shall see what the effect of interest groups and parties have had on the voting habits of the people. It is also interesting to note that a two party system evolved from the failure of the original system established under the Constitution. Initially the selection of candidates for all elective officers was to be exercised by the states normally through their legislative bodies. The people voted directly for the candidates chosen to stand for the House of Representatives as were those who were selected to stand as electors in the presidential elections. Both however were selected by the various state legislatures. Senators were appointed directly by the state legislatures and the people only participated indirectly in this choice. The candidates for president and vice-president were selected and elected by the combined efforts of the state electors and again the people only participated indirectly. As a result the states were also largely responsible for determining the issues that the candidates would focus on in their term in office. This system tended to break all three branches into sectional interest blocs. This was especially true of the legislative branch. Initially the party system grew out of rather permanent coalitions of sectional interests within the legislative branch put together to facilitate the obtaining of po-litical compromise. Under this coalition system it was possible for two or more sectional interest blocs to form a temporary alliance to defeat or pro-mote specific legislation, often without the remaining members knowing of the coalition. Just such a coalition was formed, for example, between the Democratic-Republicans and the Federalist to promote the issue of renew-ing the national bank. The alliance was formed on the basis that the South would back the issuance of a new charter for the bank and the Northeast would support a movement to lower the tariff. The alliance was formed to prevent the Western interests, coupled with the conservative wings of both parties from blocking the passage of both pieces of legislation. These alli-ances tended to operate outside the normal political channels and tended to be invisible to the people at large.

The secondary growth of the parties outside the temporary alliances formed in Congress was spurred by the actions of the states themselves. Very early in US history the states began to move away from the appoint-ment of senators and electoral representatives by their legislative bodies. Instead the states began to initiate systems making the senatorial candi-dates and electoral representatives directly subject to the public vote. This simple default on the part of the states removed one of the major checks intended by the Constitution to prevent a tyranny by majority. The politi-cal parties did not lose a step in taking the place of the state legislatures. It soon became evident that the candidates for Congress, as well as, those for president and vice-president would be determined by the two main politi-cal parties. Accompanying the power to select the candidates also went the power to determine the issues that would be promoted during the election process and in Congress after the election.

The party system, as it developed, tended to cluster around the two distinct political philosophies that were already in existence, that is, the conservative and liberal positions. What was later to become the modern Republican Party sought and obtained the consistent support of the large commercial, industrial and financial interests. What later became the mod-ern Democratic Party found its support in the large urban working classes, immigrants, and small farmers and slaveholders. The Republican Party based on its support tended to seek more limited government intervention in relation to regulation, taxation, and interference with private contractual rights (including corporate policies). This was in essence a continuation of the philosophy espoused by the earlier Democratic-Republicans but for a different set of reasons. The Democrats, on the other hand, because of their support base tended to promote a more proactive intervention policy by the federal and state governments. They sought stronger regulation of the economy generally, as well as, more active intervention in social issues, such as, immigrant and workers rights, and in the abolition of slavery. This was in essence a continuation of the philosophy espoused by the earlier Federalist Party again for different reasons. There were, as we shall see, some intermediate parties that developed, either as precursors to the modern parties, or as temporary third party coalitions but they all merged into the modern parties by the late 1920s.

It was only on the issue of slavery, between 1824 and 1860, that both parties agreed to a consistent hands-off policy. The Democratic Party found a large bloc of its consistent support in the South and therefore took a hand's off approach towards slavery. The Republicans took the position that the federal government was not authorized to intervene in a private issue such as slavery and also took a hand's off approach. Because of this stance on the part of the political parties the movement among the public to abolish slavery was forced to take the form of a grassroots protest movement. As we will see later, this unintended consequence had long term repercussions in relation to politics in the United States.

As mentioned above, the two political parties evolved over time, adopting the overall political philosophy of the US but remaining fluid in their philosophical interpretation of those positions. Since 1820 there have been relatively major shifts in the philosophical positions of the two parties, beginning with the demise of the old Federalist Party. That party had been formed for the sole purpose of guiding the initial legislation passed by the government into a track that would insure the success of the union, that is, by creating a government capable of proactive intervention when necessary. It was replaced by a party that accepted the concept of a strong proactive government but their liberalism was focused on social issues rather than on governmental procedures or operational methods. The Democratic-Republicans were formed with the sole purpose of supporting the agrarian philosophy of Thomas Jefferson and the concept of states' rights that was included in it. This party was replaced by one equally conservative but focused on the protection of special interests, such as, the large commercial, industrial, and financial interests rather than on the protection of states' rights. Both parties, however, like their predecessors remained fluid and capable of dramatic shifts in their philosophical positions depending on the issues faced.

In light of the developing party system and the continuing debate fostered by the two parties regarding the limits of federal power a traditional view can be taken of the actions resulting from the major issues that arose between 1820 and 1840. One of the first events to be faced arose in regard to the Creek Nations and their continuing raids into the frontier sections of the State of Georgia. The Creeks, along with other Native American nations, had taken refuge in Florida, a Spanish possession, with the Creeks being settled in what is now the Florida panhandle. The Georgia legislature petitioned the federal government for aid in putting a stop to these raids. Under the Constitution the states had been given the power to invoke federal aid whenever they felt that an invasion of their territory, or the violence associated with internal insurrection, could no longer be handled at the state level. In this case Georgia was being invaded by a foreign nation and had no right to infringe on another nation's (Spain) territory. The federal government responded by commissioning Andrew Jackson to lead federal troops to aid Georgia. There still remains a question as to whether or not Jackson's commission included the power to annex Florida to the United States. Regardless of his actual commission, Jackson was able to defeat the Native Americans easily and annexed the panhandle to secure Georgia from further raids. At the time that Jackson began his actions inside Florida the federal government was also negotiating with Spain on other issues. The meetings being held were an effort by the two nations to come to an agreement on the exact borders separating the Louisiana Purchase from Spanish possessions in North America. Although never officially acknowledged it is believed that Jackson's military success in Florida was used as a bargaining chip in these negotiations. In 1821 the US signed a treaty with Spain that ceded the whole of Florida to the United States in lieu of a payment of five million dollars. In addition the boundary between the two countries was settled. The US obtained the Gulf coast of Texas from the northern border of modern Louisiana as its eastern border to the eastern coastline of Texas as its western border. The southern boundary of the US territory was established as following the Arkansas River to the 42nd parallel and running westward to the Pacific Ocean. Spain retained possession of the rest of Texas, all of Arizona, New Mexico, Colorado, Nevada, and most of California. In essence the US was able to obtain several million square miles of territory, with the prospect of obtaining more due to the sparsely populated territory retained by Spain, for a few dollars and the threat of war. Had the US been a little more insistent it is likely that the whole of the continental United States with the exception of the Oregon Territory would have been in the possession of the US as early as 1821. The only thing that prevented this occurrence was the widespread belief that the areas retained by Spain were useless for human habitation.

The US public greeted the news of this additional territory with enthusiasm, however, the Congress and other political leaders greeted the news with concern over the seeming abandonment of the policy of isolation from European affairs. Both parties ratified the treaty, accepting the consequences of a war they had not the opportunity to debate or approve. It appears that the intervention by the federal government, although requested by a state government, was a calculated policy of imperialism on the part of the executive branch in relation to the territory gained. The calculated imperialism, if any truly existed, was carefully covered up by the fact that no official orders were given to Jackson.

A second major issue of the 1820s that spurred the growth of political parties was the economic panic that had begun in late 1819. A number of domestic factors were involved in this economic panic but the main cause turned out to be a downturn in the economy of Great Britain. At this time the national bank had instituted a policy of easy credit to the state governments in regard to loans for the development of roads and canals. The State Banks in turn had used a significant share of these borrowed funds to support speculation involved in these projects. When the downturn came the national bank tightened credit across the board and began to demand payment in gold and silver on the outstanding loans. The same policy was quickly followed by the State Banks leaving their creditors holding the bag. Neither James Monroe nor John Quincy Adams believed in extending federal aid to private individuals although the State Banks were saved from bankruptcy by the federal desire to maintain financial stability. The end result was that the national bank salvaged the State Banks coupled with the policy of letting individual creditors fall into poverty. This policy for understandable reasons caused a great deal of mistrust to grow around the national banking system. The national banking system had been instituted by Alexander Hamilton to provide for stability in the federal monetary system. The panic of 1819 caused a significant degree of economic chaos especially in the private financial communities such as large scale speculators, contractors, etc., but the national banking system did prove itself in this crisis capable of maintaining financial stability.

The main result of the government's decision not to rescue private individuals was a heated debate in Congress over the renewal of the charter of the national bank. The people as mentioned earlier had become distrustful of the federal banking system generally and threw their support to the election of Andrew Jackson who had declared that he was against renewing the charter. Congress, however, denied the public will and renewed the charter in 1824 on the basis of the compromise mentioned earlier. Jackson, as president, did not accept the decision of either the legislative or judicial branches and ordered that all federal deposits be made in State Banks that had supported his campaign for president. These banks quickly became known as "pet" banks. The result was a vast increase in the assets of these pet banks and a consequent decrease in the ability of the national bank to act as a stabilizer in the economy generally. The State Banks almost immediately succumbed to the temptation to overreach themselves with easy credit to land speculators, land jobbers, and others. This continued to be the mode of operation relatively trouble free until 1836. In 1836 another economic recession this time properly called an economic depression struck Europe. By late 1837 the effects of the depression entered the US with the same response as in 1819. The federal government tightened credit and the State Banks again faced imminent bankruptcy. This time due to Jackson's policy the national banking system was not in a position to bail out the State Banks. The State Banks in their turn were then forced to declare bankruptcy and close their doors leaving the private investors who owned the State Banks responsible for the debts. Many of the private owners of the banks lost their entire stock of assets. Those who suffered most, of course, were small farmers, small merchants, and working people. Andrew Jackson who was at least partially responsible for the result was now safely out of office when the panic struck leaving his successor Martin Van Buren to respond. Van Buren again took the approach that no federal aid would be given to help the private investors during the financial crisis. The people were also denied any type of federal aid leaving them dependent on what could be furnished by churches and other private charitable organizations.

Ironically the panic of 1837 was seen by nearly everyone as a failure on the part of the national banking system to fulfill its function of providing economic stability. As a result the system was totally dismantled and re-placed by the institution of an independent National Treasury. The new Democratic Party which was created under Andrew Jackson solidified its position by stoutly opposing the call for a National Treasury and extensive federal regulation of the monetary system. The old Democratic Party and its successor the Whig Party took the position that the federal government should be proactive and extend aid to private individuals in such a crisis and that this aid should be provided through a National Treasury. The latter were largely responsible for the passage of the legislation creating a Nation-al Treasury in 1840. This act was repealed a year later but was again passed in 1846 and became a permanent feature of the US economic structure.

A third issue revolved around the growing movement to abolish slavery. This issue was again brought to the public's attention by the petition of the Missouri Territory to be admitted as a state. At the time that Missouri ap-plied for statehood there were eleven states that allowed slavery and eleven states that did not.

The constitution submitted by Missouri in its request for statehood would permit slavery to exist. If Missouri was admitted, it would turn the balance in favor of those who favored the continuation of slavery as an in-stitution. It goes without saying that Missouri had already accomplished all of the constitutional requirements to become a state. The debate, therefore, was not based on any constitutional arguments, but solely on the issue of slavery. The debate was centered on the disagreements that had separated the North and South from the beginning of the Union. The South had just recently used the threat of nullification in connection with the battle for renewal of the charter of the national bank; the restrictions placed on the sale and movement of slaves in interstate commerce; and the use of high tariffs to protect the growing commercial interests of the North. The North, on the other hand, had resisted the South on all these issues of great im-portance. The question finally boiled down to whether or not the federal government had the power to declare slavery illegal in all the territories controlled by the United States. Those who claimed the government had this power (North) based their claim on the fact that the Congress under the Articles of Confederation had outlawed slavery in the Old Northwest Territory. Those who took the position that the federal government did not have this power based their arguments on a modified states' rights theory. Under this theory it was argued that the powers not specifically granted to the federal government were reserved to the states. The Constitution was silent on this specific issue and the actions taken under the Articles were not a part of federal law. It was also argued that the 5th amendment to the Constitution prohibited the federal government from taking the life, liberty or property of individuals without the due process of law. This latter argument was countered by pointing out that federal law was not intended to be applied to territories that lay outside the borders of the US by constitutional provision.

The debate was abruptly curtailed by the application of Maine for statehood as a non-slave state. This allowed room for a compromise to be brought forward allowing both Missouri and Maine to become states under the constitutions they submitted but with the further provision that slavery would be prohibited in all the remaining territories with the sole exception of Arkansas, where slave-owning plantations were already common. This compromise, had not other factors intervened, might have over a period of time ended slavery without the need for a civil war. The compromise effectively isolated slavery in what was to become known as the "Deep" South. In this area, the soil was suffering from the effects of single crop agriculture and was already showing signs of depletion. Had this trend continued, the economic advantage provided by slavery would have disappeared, allowing its natural demise. As it turned out, the compromise only put the slavery issue on the back burner for a period of forty years. The debate over slavery helped to define the US political philosophy in relation to human rights and to solidify the opposing positions of the parties in regard to the government's role in defending human rights.

When attention is turned to the institution of a world government it must be considered whether political parties will play as important role as they have in the US. In the political arena, at least in a general way, particularly when a democratic system prevails, all issues revolve around two distinct counter positions. In most cases the positions are clear cut, i.e., one position favors and the other does not favor a specific resolution of the issue. In other cases both sides may favor a specific resolution of the issue but still disagree as to the extent that the solution will be applied and at what level of government. For example, on the issue of conservation of the world's natural resources all of the many varied interests will tend to collect around two positions, i.e., they will either favor the institution of measures to conserve the resources or they will not. Even if all interests favor the institution of conservation measures they still may disagree as to whether the central government, or the national governments, or both should be responsible for the implementation and execution of the measures passed. Even here the issue will tend to be relatively clear cut with one side favoring federal implementation and the other favoring national implementation. As a result this polarization of issues around two general opposing positions favors the evolution of two position politics even in the case of a world union. This result is also affected by the level of technology now available for the distribution of information and the coordination of effort. It can be expected on each issue that central government action is favored in a proactive sense an increase in the bureaucracy will be needed to fulfill the obligation. It will be expected that the central government will pass detailed legislation setting forth the measures to be taken and that a department will be set up within the executive branch to implement the measures passed; and that a central government agency will be set up in each nation to execute the measures and to inspect the actions taken for compliance with the measures. On the other hand, each issue that is resolved in favor of the national governments will require only that the central government pass general legislation outlining the overall goals to be accomplished. The national governments will be responsible for passing the specific legislation, implementing and executing this legislation, carrying out the inspections to insure compliance or again delegating these tasks to their local sub-governments. This method has the advantage of being capable of tailoring the response to the exact needs of fulfilling the desire goal expected; however the federal solution has the advantage of being capable of uniform enforcement throughout the union. In recent years the US experience clearly points to the national solution as being the most inefficient and ineffective on nearly every issue. The EU experience, on the other hand, has shown that European level legislation and regulation is very effectively implemented, inspected and completed on the member state level. Much of this is the result of a conscious effort on the part of the member nations to maintain control over internal projects themselves. Study indicates clearly that this system is just as effective as the US system and more cost effective than the US system.

The US experience has shown even at a very early date that an irrational devotion to one or another of the two positions can and often does lead to a stalemate preventing the solution of the issue. When such a stalemate occurs one of two reactions has normally taken place. Either the issue is tabled for a period of time for later debate or circumstances are favorable for the introduction of a compromise. The history of the party system in the US seems to have been largely responsible for the clarification of positions taken and the resulting ability to find a workable compromise. As we will see later there are also negatives that are related directly to the operation of a two-party system. The point at this time is that it can probably be expected that some type of party political system will develop in relation to the institution of a world government. It is likely that it will be a multiple party system similar to the one holding sway in the EU. Here the Parliament has some 102 parties that have held some seats in the institution. However, four of these parties have been able through coalition to hold enough seats within Parliament to control the needed votes to do business. The evolution of this system is likely to be much different than in the case of the US. It is likely that the national governments will be much more proactive than were the states and that the limitations on the central governments' ability to intervene will be more jealously guarded against. Other factors are likely to be in effect as the party system evolves, for example the existence of already established interest groups, but what their effect will be cannot be predicted in advance. The effect of an early two-party system in the US seems to have been largely beneficial. The disciplined organizational hierarchy of the two parties by 1840 had devolved all the way to the precinct level. This stimulated the political thinking at the grassroots level raising the voting percentage of white males in presidential elections from 26 to 78 percent. The same discipline in the parties reduced the growing chaos in the process of selecting candidates and in focusing the attention of the public on the most important issues. Within Congress itself the parties helped to clarify which issues were truly national in import and which were merely sectional in import. This clarification helped to promote a more detailed ability to balance the various interests and to produce compromises. There is no reason to believe that the evolution of party politics (in the EU sense) would have a different effect in the early history of world government. Although by 1840 it was becoming apparent that the two parties were actually replacing the states in the selection of candidates and issues this would not necessarily be true in the case of a world union. The parties may in fact play the same role on the national level as they do at the level of the central government, i.e., allow for the organization of the national governments in a more efficient manner to accomplish these goals. It is expected that party politics in the case of a world union will be much more beneficial than it has been even in the US experience. There is, however, a growing voice against the use of democracy (especially multi-party democracy) as evidenced in the developing nations. Here party politics since World War II have tended to revolve around extra-political issues such as race, gender, ethnicity, regionalism, etc. This has in many cases, if not all, led to chaos and solutions that involve the establishment of non-democratic regimes. It will be necessary in any case for the world government to establish new solutions to the problems of developing nations, or nations with specific problems such as those set forth above. In many cases the problems are directly linked to poverty and a general lack of education among the people.

During the period between 1820 and 1840, the US Supreme Court remained active. The Supreme Court issued three major decisions that produced little comment at the time but which had significant impact later. First, in the case of *Dartmouth College* v. *Woodward* the court ruled that the states did not have the power to alter an agreement that was valid between the parties to the contract. This verdict was later used to deny the states the right to review the charters of private corporations that had been issued earlier. The decision is important for two reasons: one, it strengthened the contract rights between private parties regardless of their bargaining power, and two, the ruling set forth the concept that corporations were to be treated as if they were private individuals. The decision was nullified later in relation to its main concern by the states incorporating into the original charter the right to review the charter periodically. This made the right of review a part of the original contract and thereby protected from the ruling in the Dartmouth case. This decision did not touch upon the issue of review by a state of a charter issued by another state. A later ruling used the full faith and credit provisions of the Constitution to deny the right of review except in the case of the state that issued the charter; and in this case only if the issuing state had written the right of review into the original charter. As a result corporations sought out the states that offered the most liberal charter provisions to incorporate themselves.

Second, in the case of *McCulloch* v. *Maryland* the court unanimously denied the states the power to tax federal enterprises. The court rejected the Maryland argument that the federal government was an instrument created by the states and therefore subject to be taxed by the states. The Maryland argument was a rather weak attempt to exert the philosophy that stood behind the doctrine of nullification. The court upheld its tradition of consistently providing that the federal laws and authority generally was superior to that of the states. The intent was to more clearly establish the fact that the federal government would be superior to the states in any area in which it was authorized to act. The unintended result of the verdict was to establish the principle that the Supreme Court would be the final judge of where the federal government was authorized to act. The importance of this verdict cannot be understated as we shall see at a later time. The majority opinion written by Chief Justice Marshall once again underscored his intent to interpret the Constitution as broadly as possible and to find implied powers when necessary and proper.

Third, in the case of *Gibbons* v. *Ogden* the court extended the power of the federal government to regulate interstate commerce. The issue decided in the case was of small consequence at the time. The concept delineated in the case over time would evolve into one of the major sources of power granted to the government to intervene in the daily lives of its citizens. The immediate impact of the verdict was to open the door for the development of large scale financial organizations needed to finance the development of public transportation. The opening of canal development to the new steamboat industry as well as later land grants to the railroad industry brought financing beyond the control of the states and spurred both their development and financial speculation. The federal government took a rather laissez-faire attitude towards the regulation of public transportation systems, even though the court had ruled that the states were forbidden such regulatory powers. The result was to spawn the growth of the huge transportation monopolies. The projects themselves were still at this time fully financed by a cooperative effort of the states and private investors. The impact of this verdict was again not felt until many years after its rendering.

The Supreme Court continued to operate under the old federalist political philosophy especially until the retirement of John Marshall in 1834. The court not only supported at every turn the expansion of federal power on the domestic front; but also promoted a more proactive federal presence in the international affairs arena. During the two decades under consideration the capability of the federal government to intervene in areas that had up until this time been untouched grew greatly; but the exercise of that power awaited a more conducive environment.

In the EU experience a much different approach has been taken. The European Court of Justice while it has some of the powers of the US Supreme Court is a much weaker legal institution. It cannot force its verdicts into a position similar to any one of the three verdicts listed above for the US Supreme Court. All verdicts rendered by the European Court are implemented on the national level and are in most cases limited in effect to the two parties involved in the case decided. In short, the legal system as it exists in the EU is not a decision-making power like the US Supreme Court. It can be argued that this system should be incorporated into a world government structure, but it must face the fact that the EU is currently not a supranational government in the political arena. It has also been pointed out that relying on national legislatures to implement and enforce the decisions of the court and on the Commission to impose warnings and fines for noncompliance is both costly and inefficient.

As we have seen the first thirty years of US history was largely a battle over whether the federal government would act in a proactive or passive manner in relation to the issues affecting both the federal and state institutions. The proactive philosophy was able to largely win the day on this issue but was limited to a significant degree by the strength of the opposing view. The federalist or nationalistic philosophy gained the early control of the government and was able to promote enough of its agenda to allow for the gradual growth of federal power throughout US history. After 1803 the anti-federalist or conservative philosophy was able to gain substantial control of the government. The loss of confidence in the national banking system, the loss of support for a high protective tariff, and the rising political consciousness of the voting public had by the end of the period began a movement away from the strict nationalism of the early era. Nationalism was now replaced with a new awareness of human rights and the necessity of proactive state action.

In chapter 4, covering a period from about 1828 until 1865, an attempt will be made to detail the failure of the US to return to any simple rendition of the old Jeffersonian type of republicanism.

There can be no doubt regardless of the party system developed that the world government will face the same issue of balance of power between the central government and the national members. The EU has already faced this issue and has for the time being settled on a balance which favors the national members. If the world government is proactive to the same degree as the early US government the general government of the world union rather than the national members will exercise the majority of power. On the other hand, if the world government is passive in its action the majority of power will be exercised by the member nations. Judging by the US experience it is likely that the world government will need to be proactive on some issues and passive on others. The proactive issues would include among others protection of the environment (toxic waste disposal, global warming, nuclear energy, etc.); the conservation of the world's natural resources (their use, their equitable distribution, etc.); the regulation of commerce between member nations (the global market, global finance, global wealth distribution); and the use of common areas (outer space, the open seas, uninhabited land areas). The fact that the general government must be proactive on these issues does not also mean that it must be proactive in the implementation and enforcement of the laws it passes in relation to these issues. The general government should remain in charge of passing the general legislation needed to accomplish the goals and an overall control of inspection guaranteeing execution of the programs regardless of the balance of power. The Nations should be put in charge of passing the necessary specific statutes, regulations, or edicts that are needed to implement the overall plan and be in charge of executing those specific statutes, regulations or edicts. They should also remain in control of dispersing the needed funds, accounting for the spending of those funds, and for insuring that the work done was efficient and effective. The US experience clearly shows that if the nations do not assert themselves proactively in this area, these duties will go by default to the general government. In the US the result of this tendency has led to the accusation that the most expensive, inefficient way to get something done is to give it to the federal government.

It is at this level that party politics can play its most effective role. In the early US experience the two parties focused on promoting compromises between the various political interests that formed around issues. They also promoted both direct and indirect participation in the solving of the various issues by both the states and their citizens. They could play exactly the same role in relation to the world government. There will be a host of varying interests on each of the issues that arise and these interests will attempt to be heard. These interests will range from the interest of each individual nation, or in some cases groups of individual nations, to those of individual citizens or groups of citizens. It is likely that if the member nations strongly commit themselves to participation in the solution of most issues that they will also represent the strongest interest groupings. The experience of the European Union clearly shows that such a situation can arise, that is, a situation in which the member nations exercise more power in relation to the issues faced than the general government. In the case of the European Union the general organizational institutions are left responsible for drafting the overall legislation for resolution of issues while the member nations are free to implement, conclude, and inspect the projects created by the general institutions.

In many areas, especially those involving ethnic, cultural, religious or individual human rights, it is to be expected that the central government will play a more passive role by allowing the various nations to handle these problems in whatever manner they see fit, retaining only the right to intervene in cases of violence, if requested, and to provide a legal basis for mediation upon petition by the parties involved. In these cases it is not possible for the general government to be directly in charge of their resolution. The actual implementation of the solution adopted will by necessity need to be implemented by the nation or nations involved under the overall supervision of the general government or its representative in relation to the general concern for human rights included in the constitution.

In short, effort must be made to insure that the world union remains a federal political institution to the greatest degree possible. In the case of the US the argument can be made that the decisions made by the various states, the Supreme Court, and the federal legislature early in the history of the US led in exactly the opposite direction. This trend toward concentration of power in the general government might be beneficial for a nation-state but may not be so beneficial in the case of a world union.

In relation to whether or not the world government should be financially organized around a world bank or a world treasury department it would probably be easiest to use the European Union as a guide. The US case was resolved by the establishment of a federal department of the treasury. Again this may be the best solution for a nation-state but may not be so beneficial in the case of a world union. The European Union has created a common currency for a large number of its members and has operated without the establishment of a department of the treasury. The banking systems of the large member nations have however acted in much the same manner as the national bank did in the early US. The issues here as in the European Union would include financial regulation, speculation in hard assets, the development of worldwide infrastructure, and the establishment of specific standards of economic responsibility before members could qualify for central government aid. It may require that a central banking system be created that incorporates the tasks now handled by the World Bank, the IMF and GATT plus those of the various international financial institutions.

Lastly the issue of individual human rights must be approached. This issue includes a list of specifics much too long to be listed in a work such as this one. From a general point of view it appears to be an issue that can be presented in several different lights. Human rights can be seen as largely an issue revolving around equal treatment under the law. This is the point of view that has been used in both the US and in the European Union. In the US this point of view was executed by passing specific laws and then enforcing them through the various court systems. In the European Union generalized concepts of human rights under the rule of law were incorporated unofficially into the standards required before an applicant could be admitted as a member of the Union. On the other hand, the issue can be seen from the point of view that the issue is essentially a universal guarantee that all people are treated as equal. Under this viewpoint each individual is accorded equality in every way, that is, physically, mentally, emotionally, economically, etc., whether they are truly equal or not. This approach has led the US and a number of other nations to institute what have become commonly known as entitlement laws. Such programs and their abuse have brought several of the most highly developed and wealthiest of nations to the point of bankruptcy. There may be no other rational way to handle large issues of equality in nation-states but an alternative approach may be possible under a world union. Such an alternative will probably be found in a stronger federalism possible in the world union. It is important that the warning issued by F.A. Hayek in his book *The Road to Serfdom* be kept in mind. Hayek points out that each time an attempt is made to plan every detail of a national policy, the end result is the loss of the rights the plan was intended to protect.

CHAPTER 4. PROBLEMS THAT HAVE FACED THE US AND THE EU, AND
THEIR EFFECTS ON A WORLD GOVERNMENT

During our review of the events chosen for study we have concluded
that two major trends are revealed in US History as cogent to our consideration of a world union. First, very early the federalists were able to place
their nationalist platform into effect. In essence this platform called for a national government that tended to hold most if not all sovereign power in itself; with the lower governments obtaining their powers by delegation from
the federal government. The Supreme Court especially under John Marshall
worked diligently to put this hope of nationalism into effect. There can be
no doubt that the Supreme Court was successful in putting the legal system on a nationalistic base. Second, Alexander Hamilton as secretary of the
treasury was able to accomplish in the economic arena what Marshall was
able to do in the legal arena. The economy was quickly nationalized through
the establishment of the national banking system coupled with the federal
control over international and interstate trade and taxation. The financial
independence of the federal government was insured through a system of
protective tariffs (which also protected the commercial and industrial interests of the country) and excise taxes on products such as whiskey. These
powers were quickly backed up through the use of military force when necessary, as in the Whiskey Rebellion. The nationalistic platform of the Federalists consistently pushed three planks; the federal control of the monetary and credit system within the union; the federal control of commerce

and taxation throughout the union; and federal control of the financing of large public transportation projects, such as, canals, railroads, and water traffic (steamboat lines). All of these nationalistic goals had been instituted with the exception of the last by 1820. It was not until after 1840 with the development of the Louisiana Territory that the federal government would obtain success in the area of financing public transportation. The economic nationalism of Hamilton had taken a firm hold on the US economy by 1820.

Those who held the early Jeffersonian philosophy of small scale agrarianism and a true republicanism between the federal and state governments were in large relegated to the sidelines of the political arena. It was not until 1801 that Thomas Jefferson who was the leader of the Democratic-Republican Party could capture the executive branch. Once they held the executive branch they were able to hold on to it until 1829. There time in history, however, had already passed. The Jeffersonian way of life had already begun to succumb to the industrial revolution with its emphasis on commerce, industry, and large scale financing. The small independent farmer was beginning to give way to the wage earning worker. Although the Democratic-Republicans were able to slow down the trend towards nationalism they were not able to replace it with their brand of republicanism. The republicanism represented by the independent yeoman, cottage industries, and states' rights became a part of the mythological lore that underlies the US political ideology. It could and still does act as binding cement when the people attempt to exert pressure to obtain a free democratic society as a common goal. Andrew Jackson attempted to salvage this philosophy after his election in 1829 in a modified form.

The question, of course, arises as to whether or not a similar result would be obtained by the establishment of a world government based upon the US Constitution? It can be concluded immediately that under the circumstances that existed during the early history of the US that the failure of nationalism would have also been the failure of the Union. The intent behind the Constitution, as was pointed out in the Federalist Papers during the ratification process, was to establish a government that was a curious mixture of national and republican principles. The fact that the federalists were able to take initial control of the new government swung the balance in favor of nationalism. In the case of a world government, with the knowledge that the central government must be superior to the national governments, the supranational tendencies will undoubtedly be in control from the beginning. It can be expected that the supranational balance will be written into the Constitution proposed here and will almost immediately become dominant; but that does not by any means suggest that the national governments will not play a very important role. A world government will begin with the understanding that its legal system and its economic role will both be supranational with the national members obtaining their powers in these areas by delegation from the central government or through their implementation of the legislation passed by the supranational government. The national governments, however, should remain dominant in the area of social legislation, that is, in the areas of civil rights, pollution control, conservation of natural resources, and any aspect of cultural importance. Even in the legal and economic arenas, the national governments are likely to play a more important role than the states in the US union. It is for example likely that the various nations will need some leeway in interpreting the general laws to preserve the unique cultural traits contained within their borders. This might mean a less uniform enforcement of the central governments laws but on the other hand might allow for a more creative and realistic approach towards generating a voluntary obedience on the part of both the member nations and their citizens. Each case that arose in US history involving a question of constitutionality received its final determination in the Supreme Court; however, the Supreme Court might here be strictly limited to the facts of the case and be less able to institute general political philosophy. In this way although the central legal system would still be superior to the national systems the nations could play a more significant role under principles of republicanism. Indeed in each instance set forth the current EU operates in exactly this alternative fashion. In the EU instead of a true federalism there is a system that has been named intergovernmentalism.

In the economic realm the balance between nationalism and republicanism will be a little more dubious than will be the case in the legal field. The national governments will more than likely need to be included in the early economic decisions in every way possible (probably through some sub-cabinet system as is found in the EU). There will be a need for a uniform monetary system, and a uniform method of controlling the value of the currency created under it. This cannot be done without including the existing nations in the process of creating the original uniform currency system and in the process of redeeming the old national currencies. The most recent example of this process can be found in the conversion of the European Union from the various national currencies to the euro. It is likely that the method used by that union to accomplish a uniform monetary system will also work to smoothly convert the world government to a uniform monetary standard. The existing nations are of course in a much better position to participate in this process than were the thirteen former colonies in the US situation. The same will be true of the effort to establish a uniform regulatory system for inter-national trade within the union. The existing nations must be included to insure that the already existing contractual positions are incorporated into the new system. The member nations will also have to be closely involved in the economic repercussions that will arise from a total disarmament, a world-wide effort to end and to clean up environmental pollution including a beginning of a conversion from dependence on fossil fuels. From what has been said it is likely that in the economic realm the decision making balance will from the beginning be much more in favor of the central government than nation states. Unlike the US experience therefore the world union will probably be essentially supranational in the legal realm and the economic field from the beginning. This does not affect the underlying principles which support the concept of representative democratic republicanism. Unlike the US experience republicanism may in fact play a greater role in the world union. The EU is currently struggling with the issue of a perceived democratic deficit but is progressing in making the supranational institutions more transparent and open to the ordinary citizens. The EU might also be used as a guide for the development of creative methods of balancing wealth distribution among the nations on the basis of long-term projects involving infrastructure. Much of the aid now given by the EU comes with a demand that expenditure be aimed at infrastructure improvement (the reduction of dependence on agrarianism and poverty).

As we have seen earlier, the presidential campaign of Andrew Jackson in 1828 was based on the exploitation of his reputation as a war hero and as a "man of the people." Jackson did, it appears, have some skill as a general that he had displayed in the successful campaign in Florida against the Creek Nation. His reputation as a man of the people, however, if one considers his record while in office as president, seems more myth than fact. Jackson's first administration was faced with two heated controversies. First was the attempt of South Carolina to gain widespread support for its radical nullification theory. The radical version of this theory held that the states as a voluntary member of the Union by way of its ratification of the Constitution could nullify its ratification and voluntarily withdraw from the Union. South Carolina in 1829 through various congressional coalitions was attempting to gain further support for its position. This effort was spearheaded by John Calhoun, who had recently been converted from a nationalistic philosophy to one that promoted states' rights. Economic conditions in South Carolina had brought about this conversion of Calhoun's views. South Carolina's soil was depleted and it was difficult for the cotton industry to maintain itself within the state. As a result many people were now migrating out of the state, aggravating the already deepening depression of the local economy. The depression conditions were brought to a head by Jackson's reinstitution of a policy of high tariffs. Calhoun began his campaign to save South Carolina by getting the state legislature to nullify the high tariff set by the federal government. He was able to accomplish this not only in the case of the tariff law of 1828 but also in the case of the tariff law of 1832. South Carolina began to systematically refuse to collect the tariffs, especially at the port of Charleston. South Carolina then called for a Southern convention to institute a general nullification of the tariff law. The other Southern states at this time rejected unanimously the theory that states had a right to nullify harmful federal laws, leaving South Carolina standing alone. Once this became apparent, Jackson took a stand against nullification. He called it akin to rebellion and said that rebellion was in fact treason. This stand would unintentionally set the stage for the Union reaction to the secession of South Carolina from the Union.

At this time Henry Clay offered a compromise that would allow South Carolina to withdraw respectfully from the box it found itself in; Clay's plan would reduce the tariff slowly until 1842, at which time it would be cut in half on cotton. That was not as much as South Carolina had sought but was reasonable in view of the fact that Jackson had sent troops to enforce the tariff collections at the harbor of Charleston. Calhoun as a face saving measure was able to get the South Carolina Convention to nullify the force bill that had sent the military to Charleston to collect the tariff. The military was no longer needed after acceptance of the compromise, so Jackson ignored the gesture. Jackson's decision to ignore the nullification of the force bill, however, had far-reaching consequences only some two decades later.

Second, in 1824 the charter of the national bank had been renewed after a rather bitter fight. The renewal had been challenged legally but was upheld by the Supreme Court. Jackson upon his election in 1828 made it clear that he did not approve of the national banking system by refusing to allow deposits of federal funds to be made in the national banks. He also refused the national bank the power to make loans to finance the growing public transportation sector. As a result of these two policies the national bank System was denied the assets represented by federal deposits, and the public transportation systems had to rely on state and private financing. This was the prevailing environment until after 1850.

The national banking issue was reignited in the campaign of 1832 when the charter was again due for renewal. In the campaign Jackson did not as was his practice make any commitments on the issue. His personal opposition to the national bank was already universally known. The banks current charter would run through 1836 but the director of the bank decided he could not wait until then and sought to renew the charter in 1832. The new charter was granted in 1832 but without the necessary votes to overturn a veto. Jackson promptly vetoed the bill sending it back to Congress with his objections. Congress as expected failed to garner the votes to overturn the veto leaving the issue in limbo.

Jackson was then elected for a second term by a mild landslide which Jackson took as a sign that the country agreed with his position in regard to the national bank. Despite advice to the contrary, which Jackson had actively sought, Jackson decided to withdraw the federal deposits that had been made to the national banks and place them with state chartered banks. The State Banks were chosen on the basis of the support they had given Jackson during the campaign. The national banks which were privately owned were forced to restrict credit because of the reduction of their assets. The result was the removal of the national banks as a stabilizing agent within the monetary system. The states and the state chartered banks responded to the increased currency represented by the deposits by entering into a wild speculative credit surge. The credit extended by the state bank system was used by the debtors to purchase public lands the sale of which rose from four million acres in 1834 to twenty million acres in 1836. The purchase of the public lands created a large federal surplus which was at first used to pay off the national debt. The surplus continued to grow even after paying off the national debt. Henry Clay called for a distribution of the surplus funds to the several states, but Jackson opposed this plan. A compromise was reached in which the surplus was distributed to the states as "loans." The loans were in reality deposits which were never demanded back.

Jackson through his secretary of the treasury decided to issue a monetary order. Under this order the federal government refused payment for the sale of public lands in anything other than gold or silver. Most speculators, and all farmers, could not afford to pay for the public lands with this type of payment. The distribution bill had the effect of transferring the funds deposited in state chartered banks to the state treasuries. The specie circular also forced the State Banks to demand payment of their loans in gold and silver. The restriction of credit brought on by these two acts was aggravated by the depression which struck both Great Britain and France. Jackson was fortunate that the effects of his policies did not become evident until after 1837 by which time Van Buren had already assumed the office of president. In assessing Jackson in relation to these two issues he appears to be a mixture of sectional and national philosophical traditions. He distrusted the national banks due largely to his Midwestern background but definitely accepted the nationalist concept of federal control of the monetary system. In the case of nullification he rejected the states' rights theory without qualms and stood firm on the principle of a nationalist federal government. In neither issue did he display any real concern for the needs or desires of the people as a whole. His institution of the "spoils" system, i.e., the pet bank system was clearly to aid the party organization and not to benefit the people.

A third issue facing the Jackson Administration removed any doubt concerning his concern for the rights of the "little" man. The South had begun to petition the federal government for the right to annex the lands that had been set aside for Native American Reservations. In order to facilitate the annexation a call went out for the federal government to remove the Native Americans to the "Great American Desert" namely the Oklahoma territory. The issue was essentially isolated to the states of North Carolina, South Carolina, Georgia, Florida, Alabama, Tennessee, Mississippi, and Arkansas. The Native Americans had long ago been driven out of the Northeast and the Ohio Valley including Michigan by force and the problem did not exist in these areas. The Native American Nations that were involved included the Chickasaw, Choctaw, Creek, Seminole, and Cherokee in the states listed above. The Fox and Sauk Nations were also removed from Iowa and Wisconsin to the Oklahoma territory. Jackson accepted the removal plan and between 1832 and 1835 forced the transfer to the Oklahoma Territory. Most of the Native American Nations went without resistance but the Cherokee and the Seminole put up stiff but ineffective pressure against the order. Some of the Cherokee managed to hide out in the mountains of North Carolina and Tennessee and became the eastern band of the Cherokee located on a reservation in North Carolina by the same name. A few of the Seminole were also able to establish themselves in Florida by hiding out in the impenetrable swamps of central Florida. The removal program was without question a direct violation of the treaties that had been negotiated with the Native American Nations. It was also a clear sign of the unabashed greed of the people of the states involved for land.

These issues may seem remote from our espousal of a world union but there is little doubt that the same type of policy could again be instituted. One does not have to look far to see the hatred of people for one another. It is evident in Africa, it was evident in the former Soviet Union, and it is true in the Middle East and parts of Asia today. It is certainly possible that the world government will be called upon to remove people from one area and settle them in another, or that it will be called upon to allow the return of people to areas that they had formerly been removed from. The world government will surely be called any number of times to resolve disputes between peoples who do not trust one another or even who have longstanding hatred of each other.

The Jackson administration is just one example of an executive magistrate in the US who had less than a favorable attitude towards the rights of individuals as opposed to the right of the government to act. This may be nothing more than the expression of a deep seated human condition that will need to be guarded against constantly. Jackson was the last stand of the old Jeffersonian tradition of limited government (at all levels) and concern for the welfare of the people as a whole (the independent yeoman, self-sufficient and capable of providing for all of his own needs without the aid of anyone); however, this "last stand" was more in the minds of the people — as a result of campaign propaganda — than any reality in practice. It can also be expected that the world union will face similar problems in relation to the development of a worldwide infrastructure system especially in the most under developed areas. The same type of speculation, greed, fraud, and other financial misconduct can be expected to arise in connection with such projects. In such large projects as the development of infrastructure the world government will definitely be expected to maintain a strict accounting of funds and an extensive inspection system. Both may be implemented and conducted by the nations involved especially in the areas of labor and service industries. In other words, it appears that speculation, fraud, waste and such improprieties are best controlled at the local level.

The election of Martin Van Buren in 1836 (the first president that was actually born in the US) marked another turning point in the philosophical debate over federal intervention. From this administration forward there would not be even a pretense that the federal government would be limited in fields of action if it desired to enter them. The old concerns about state rights, sectionalism, and republicanism would be replaced with only a concern over how and where federal power would be exercised. Periodic attempts would be made to place some minor restrictions on the actual exercise of federal power but not on the power itself.

The process began with the Van Buren administrations' handling of the recession spoken of above which struck in 1837. The Van Buren response was to put forth a call for the establishment of an independent federal treasury coupled with a bail-out of the remaining State Banks by including them in the treasury system. On the other hand, the federal government would not be allowed to offer any aid to alleviate the suffering of private individuals. Here those needing relief would be forced to depend on their own resources or those of private charitable organizations. This policy of government bail-outs in the corporate and financial sectors of the economy has been consistently followed since Van Buren's use of the technique. The second step was the entry of the federal government into the controversy involving slavery in the District of Columbia. This represented the first time in US history that the federal government had intervened in any area that had maintained the institution of slavery before the ratification of the Constitution. This also created a situation where the Whigs in the South began to depart from the party itself. It was also the first time that the federal government had intervened in a purely social issue within the borders of the Union; a precedent that would not be lost on the various reform movements now beginning to form. A third step was taken in response to the entry of the industrial revolution in full force within the Union. Early inventions in agriculture, such as, the iron plow share and the cotton gin, coupled with the development of a refined steam engine revolutionized agriculture in the US spurring the rapid growth of the Louisiana Territory. The steam engine coupled with the Erie Canal opened up the commercial trading potential of the Great Lakes, the St. Lawrence Seaway, and the Mississippi River and opened up the Ohio Valley all the way to St. Louis. This trade was controlled from the commercial hub of New York City. The Wilderness Road and others opened the Tennessee Valley to large scale development and the beginnings were made to extract the vast amounts of coal and timber to be found there. All of the rapid growth of commerce and industry including agriculture was supported by the federal government's acceptance of an attitude of laissez-faire towards regulation. It was not that the government lacked the power of regulation, which it had won in the Courts before 1820, but that it consciously chose to follow a policy of not exercising the power. This attitude was largely to the benefit of wealthy investors and the growing corporate monopolies.

All three of these pressures will be faced by the new world government. There will be questions arising in relation to just where and how the powers of the central government are to be exercised. This will be particularly important from the standpoint of involving the national governments as much as possible in all areas of the society. It will of course be imperative that the central government in cooperation with the national governments end all forms of slavery now in existence whether it is economic or physical slavery. Lastly, the question will arise as to the amount of regulation that will be necessary to insure the smooth operation of inter-nation trade. There will be pressure applied by those nations that now control the lion's share of that trade to favor their positions over others. It will be necessary regardless of whether they are favored or not to provide for the protection of their economic stability while a transition from international trade is made to inter-nation trading. Again the experience of the European Union will prove invaluable in this area. A failure to exercise regulatory power in this area is not an option; a truly cooperative sharing of the regulatory power between the central government and the national governments is an option worth pursuing. This in fact is the system used in the EU to regulate its' single market. In many ways the global market seems to be developing along the same lines although the development is short of that achieved in the EU.

By 1860 the industrial revolution is estimated to have been responsible for employing over one million people; for the direct investment of over one billion dollars; and for the production of goods worth more than two billion dollars. Most of the increase in employment had come along with a rapid increase in the urban populations of the US. This urbanization in turn was the result of the industrial revolutions tendency to consolidate work in one place. By 1860 urbanization (defined at the time as people living in cities of 8,000 people or more) had skyrocketed from three percent of the population in 1790 to over sixteen percent. New York City, for example, had grown to over one million people by 1860 and was one of the largest cities in the world. The industrial revolution coupled with the rapid westward expansion of the US also spurred a growth in the immigration rate. In 1840 only about one half million people were estimated to be recent immigrants. Between 1840 and 1860 another four million people immigrated to the US in search of jobs or land that they could farm. Most of the immigrants settled in the large urban areas such as Boston, New York City, Philadelphia, and Charleston. By 1860 therefore about fourteen and one half percent of the total population was represented by recent immigrants who were mostly industrial workers. During this period most of the immigrants had arrived from Western Europe and had little trouble integrating into the general population except in the case of the Irish immigrants. Of the four million that came in the twenty year period mentioned 1.6 million were Irish, 1.2 million were German, and half a million were English. The remaining 1.3 million came mostly from the Scandinavian counties and had moved westward to obtain farm land. In addition there were about 1.5 million African-Americans in the country who were not counted as citizens, that is, they were here largely as slaves. It is estimated that there were also about 200,000 Native Americans living within the borders of the US without being granted citizenship. As noted earlier most of the Germans, Scandinavians, and some Irish moved into the Appalachian regions to work in the new mining operations or into the Ohio Valley to obtain farm land. These immigrants did not represent a threat to the existing population; in fact, they were very welcome to those already living in the area. Generally they found it rather easy to assimilate into the already existing society. In the urban areas however the immigrants were seen as a threat to existing workers and existing neighborhoods. In the great urban areas they were met with very stiff discrimination in relation to jobs and housing. This trend would continue throughout US history and still continues today in relation to the African-American and Spanish speaking populations. Those from Western Europe were soon able to organize themselves politically, especially the Irish, and forced the underlying society to allow them to assimilate. The small number of immigrants from Eastern Europe and China found that they could not assimilate and they established separate settlements soon to be known by such names as Pole Town and China Town. This was also a trend that would continue throughout US history.

The world government will be faced with the same problems but from a different source. The old factory system of the industrial revolution has been converted into the hegemonic system created after World War II. This system requires the acceptance of two basic demands, namely, deregulation of the global market and the recreation of production. Under the latter, production is undergoing a division of labor consisting of a core of well-paid and secure employees and an insecure and low paid sector of employees. The core employees are largely found in the industrialized nations and are responsible largely for research and development. The peripheral employees are now organized into flexible work teams that allow for small scale production of a wide variety of products. Production plants have been removed from the industrial countries and have been placed in countries in which large amounts of cheap labor can be obtained. These peripheral workers are usually grouped into classes based upon ethnic, religious, gender, or race considerations. The result has tended to be the creation of a small number of wealthy core nations and a large number of middle power and peripheral nations. The latter have come to be known as the "fourth world" and are essentially unable to exist without poor relief from the core. This has created a demographic trend which sees a large number of people migrating from the South to the North and from the East to the West. A world government will therefore be faced with large scale employment problems both in terms of high unemployment and chronic underemployment. It will also be faced with a massive immigration problem. Neither the current US approach nor that of the EU offers any real solution. The US controls the ideological underpinnings of the global market as set forth above through its hegemonic military power. The EU solution has been to offer huge poor relief programs to the marginalized counties but has come up against popular protest in its' handling of the immigration problem.

Up to this point the most important features of the period running from 1840 to 1860 revolve around the effects of the industrial revolution, urbanization, and immigration. As of 1860 the federal government was still following a policy which kept their hands off these areas of growth. There had been prior to 1860 no attempt by the federal government to limit the amount of immigration into the country. The federal government at that time had also walked away from any participation in the development of urban infra-structure leaving that to the local governments and private investors. Even in the areas affected by the industrial revolution the federal government had opted not to exercise its regulatory powers. This will not in all likeli-hood be the case with a world government. From the very beginning it will be necessary for the central government to exercise its regulatory powers, in cooperation with the national governments, to manage the conversion of the global market from an international favor to one based upon inter-nation trade. It is also impossible to imagine the world government, at least initially, not taking a part in the establishment of some sort of rational im-migration policy, i.e., in the large scale movement of peoples across national borders to find jobs, land, or other sources of livelihood. Illegal immigration is a problem that reaches across the board in highly industrialized nations and will need to be faced by the new world government. It is hoped that in a relatively short period of time the solution will naturally follow, as it did in the early US, although temporary problems of a severe nature can be expected to develop. It is also unlikely that the world government will be able to walk away from the development of effective infrastructure prob-lems that it will face. In many areas of the world the major problems facing their populations is the lack of adequate sanitary facilities, adequate drink-ing water, and adequate transportation facilities. These cannot be ignored if the government is going to attempt to live up to its commitment to provide for the general welfare of the public at large. In the latter area there will be a substantial need for cooperation from national governments in terms of planning, financing, manpower, and economic support generally. In the areas where these needs are the greatest one also finds the most urgent need for jobs, housing, medical care, and population control. In short, the US historical response of laissez-faire should be avoided whenever possible by the new world government. It should be replaced with a true cooperative effort between the world government and its national members. The Euro-pean Union again stands as a valid example of how this cooperation can be managed.

Two other major events occurred during the period under consideration which commands our attention. Both of these events brought the federal government to the point of direct intervention into areas previously un-touched. The first, and arguably the most important, evolved as a grassroots movement directed only tangentially towards the federal government. A very active movement began with the intention of reforming the traditional churches that were operating within the US society. At the time this was labeled as the "great awakening" and somewhat later as the first of several evangelical movements. The movement sought to remove the formalism of the traditional churches and to replace it with a highly emotive personalized worship. The new worship was to be based both upon personal salvation and personal morality. It was believed as a major tenet of this movement that personal salvation could not be obtained unless strict attention was paid to the morality of individual actions. As a result one offshoot of this movement was an emphasis being placed on the immorality of slavery rather than its legality. Other issues of personal morality also began to become evident, such as, the sale and use of alcohol, the abuse of women, the abuse of the insane and criminal elements of the society, and the economic abuse of child labor. It was slavery at this time that most directly touched the federal government. The movement was able during the Van Buren administration to exert enough pressure to obtain the banning of slavery in the District of Columbia. This was the first time that the federal government had intervened in the issue of slavery in any area that had established the institution prior to the Constitution. It was also the first time that the federal government had intervened in an area exclusively devoted to civil rights and the first time that the power of a well organized and financed interest group was demonstrated. Second, by 1860 it became evident to the leaders in the South that the movement was strong enough to call for and ratify an amendment to the Constitution that would outlaw slavery; although no such amendment had yet been submitted for consideration.

The second event involved a series of events that are related to the war with Mexico. A strong popular grassroots movement in what would become the states of Texas and California had developed. The movement appealed directly to the federal government to send troops into these areas to protect the interests of the settlers and to annex the territories to the US. The executive branch of the federal government decided to take an approach similar to the one that had been used in the annexation of Florida. Spain had already transferred all of its colonial powers in these areas to the newly formed government of Mexico. Supposedly the invasion of Mexico was to be a punitive measure for actions taken by the Mexican government in relation to the US settlers in these areas. US citizens, even under the treaty of 1821 with Spain, did not have any rights other than those granted to them by Mexico. The invasion was therefore not even as subtle as that undertaken by Jackson in the case of Florida; but in reality represented an act of naked aggression against a legitimate government. This war marks a series of firsts in relation to the federal government. It represents the first example where the federal government dropped any pretense of maintaining the doctrine of strict isolation in foreign affairs, as well as, marking the beginning of a concern for the unilateral interests of the US in terms of economic expansionism. It also marked the first time that the US had entered onto the territory of a foreign nation by amphibious assault and established marshal law. Lastly, it marked the first use of military officers trained at West Point. All of the generals that were to play a prominent part in the Civil War obtained their first taste of war in this short engagement. The war lasted for seventeen months and resulted in the annexation of the whole of the Southwestern US. As pointed out earlier this territory was sparsely settled by the Mexicans and would probably have become a part of the US without the need for an imperialistic style war. As a result the federal government took its first step in intervening in the affairs of foreign nations for less than reputable causes. In 1853 the US also signed a treaty with Great Britain that gave the US sole control of the Oregon Territory in return for a solid delineation of the US and Canadian borders. The US had now obtained to its continental limits with the sole exception of Alaska.

The period between 1840 and 1860 also defined the major differences between the North and the South. The South by 1860 was composed of a population that was largely native to the area, that is, was composed of citizens who were the direct descendants of the original settlers. The North on the other hand was composed of a rather diverse ethnic complexion brought about by the arrival of over four million immigrants. The South had developed its infrastructure in relative isolation, that is, the roads served mainly communication within the Southern states rather than between regions of the country and its railroad system had been developed using a different gauge of track than that used in the North or West. This had made it difficult for either the North or the West to communicate in relation to trade networks with the South. All trade between them was confined to the use of river and sea traffic which was conducted mainly by the West and North respectively. In many ways economically by 1860 the South had become a sort of economic dependency of the North. In addition the South had placed its future in the development of stable crop agriculture such as cotton and tobacco both of which were dependent upon the continuation of the institution of slavery; and the use of small family owned businesses to provide for the commercial products it needed. As a result the South had essentially been untouched by the industrial revolution that was taking place in the North and West. Ironically it was only in the political arena that the South had been able to maintain parity with the North and West. Until 1860, for example, the South had been able on average to maintain more seats in Congress than the North, and nearly as many as the North and West combined. The Southern states still held the majority of the justices that were sitting on the Supreme Court and had placed more presidents into office than the North and West combined. This was beginning to change even before the beginning of the civil war. The lack of a universal educational system, the depletion of the soil from stable crop agriculture, and the rise of industrial opportunities in the North and West had already begun to draw the poorer classes out of the South into the North, and at this time, especially into the Midwest. This only further aggravated the sense among Southern leaders that the South was an economic dependency of the North.

In regard to the operation of an effective world union this period of US history offers us several valuable lessons. It is very likely that the creation of a world union will release a great amount of economic activity. This activity will range from the surge in employment brought about by programs of disarmament, environmental pollution clean-up, etc., to the expected scramble to obtain a viable place in the global market. Regardless of where and how this economic activity is generated, it is also sure to produce vast disparities between nations and probably whole regions in relation to the benefits obtained. Some areas such as the US, Western Europe, and Japan will be in a position to monopolize these activities unless controlled by the general government. The poorer less well equipped nations and regions will have to exert great effort to even maintain their current position in the global market. The general government must be instrumental in seeing that the distribution of employment, for example, in all projects of global significance such as disarmament and pollution cleanup are distributed equitably between all nations with emphasis being on the areas the most depressed in terms of employment. Such an effort on the part of the general government will require that a massive program of intensive education be instituted to bring the work force up to the qualifications needed to accomplish these tasks. It is likely that initially the majority of this training will be provided by professionals that now operate within the US, Europe, Japan and other highly developed nations. In regard to the global market it is imperative that the general government maintain a strict regulation of the opportunities available for participation in this market. It was during the period under consideration that the US entered the industrial revolution, the world market place, and the attempt to bring about a feeling of nationalism within the society. It is also during this period that one can recognize the failure of the federal government to attempt to equalize the benefits of the industrial revolution in all segments of the society, that is, by failure to regulate the growth of private monopolies and financial aggregation; as well as, failing to regulate the growing disparity within the interstate market. This experience coupled with the more successful European Union approach will direct the world union to a solid approach to these problems. If not, one can expect that huge monopolies such as US Steel, Standard Oil, and American Tobacco; as well as, financial empires, such as, those founded by J.P. Morgan will appear. They will differ in that they will be multinational corporations rather than national corporations. They may even be formed from existing multinational conglomerates that band together under some form of interconnecting directorate to control segments of the market. The European Union was created essentially to counteract the dominance of the US and Japan in the world market as were such associations as OPEC. Both of these attempts have to various degrees been successful. However, the affects that have been created by these forced realignments of the global market have resulted in serious problems such as inflation, stagflation, and monetary crisis. It must also be understood that the US, China, and India in combination represent a large share of the current pollution that is being released into the environment. They are also the very nations that so far have refused to even consider negotiation in relation to this pollution. It will take either a world government, or at the very least substantial, consistent worldwide pressure, to force these nations into a position where they must consider their role as polluters. Therefore, it appears that a large amount of effort will need to be expended by the central world government to insure a relatively equitable distribution of the economic benefits of world union as well as a relative equality of opportunity for every nation to participate in the global market. Lastly, the central government will need to take charge of the worldwide implementation of disarmament and pollution control and clean up.

The question now arises as to whether or not the issues brought up under the doctrine of nullification will face the world union. The issue certainly exists for the EU although to date it has not been tested. In the EU case it is understood that any member can at any time for any reason withdraw from the union. This may never happen due to the vast integration of the current members into the supranational institutions but it is surely possible. It cannot be doubted that at some point the world union will be faced with a dissatisfied nation, or group of nations, that may wish to secede from the union. This could be the case even if there are strict constitutional provisions that prohibit voluntary withdrawal from the union. If a dissatisfied nation or group of nations believes that it, or they, are capable of successfully coping with any pressure applied to prevent their withdrawal that withdrawal is inevitable. For example, prior to the achievement of complete disarmament any number of nations including the US could become dissatisfied with the initial operation of the general government and decide to withdraw from the union. Under these conditions it is likely that such a withdrawal could not be prevented and that the union itself would dissolve.

In terms of economic disruption the same result might be obtained after total disarmament by the voluntary withdrawal of key nations such as India, China, or Japan. If the current military operations in Afghanistan and Iraq prove anything they prove that military action alone is insufficient to force a people to do what they do not want to do. Current conditions also tend to prove that economic sanctions alone do not work either; although it is also true that the economic sanctions are neither rigidly implemented nor strictly enforced. However, if the world union managed to accomplish total disarmament and to institute an effective regulation of inter-nation trade (global market), it is likely that the union could survive the withdrawal of an unspecified number of nations; and that these nations would find it difficult to maintain themselves without the active support of the remaining union. If this turns out to be an accurate assessment then any desired readmission to the union should be made available without punishment of any type. Regardless the world union will more than likely be faced at some time with a nation or group of nations that wish to voluntarily secede from the union. This event should be handled without the use or even the threat of military force; but rather with a sober determination as to whether or not the union can survive and continue to exist effectively without those wishing to withdraw. In any case, where the existence of the union is not threatened by a proposed withdrawal, that withdrawal should be allowed. This is the approach taken by the EU.

The world union will also be faced with conditions in certain nations that amount to virtual slavery or at least as involuntary servitude of one form or another. Currently such systems are supported by the willingness of the wealthiest nations to take advantage of them, i.e., by purchasing the products produced without restraint or by using the system to generate profits by the use of cheap labor and cheap natural resources. All of these systems of abusive labor practices, whether in manufacturing or obtaining natural resources, must be eliminated by the general laws passed by the world government and enforced by the national governments. In addition such discriminatory practices as genocide, such as that occurring in Darfur, Iraq, and other places must be brought to a peaceful solution. It goes without saying, however, that the existing diversity of culture must be allowed to remain in place and to freely develop in whatever direction it can. In other words, it is not the variety of religion, political structures, social customs, etc., that need to be regulated but only the violence that results from the abuse of them in unauthorized ways. The need to allow the central government the power to intervene in these areas indicates that the central government will wield substantial control over the daily lives of the citizens it governs. This will, if modern conditions are any guide to what will occur in the future, be the case in an effective world union. The question does not seem to be whether or not the central government will have such power but rather how that power can be controlled by the national members of the union. The US Civil War points to one type of solution, that is, the taking of complete power by the federal government without allowing for any participation on the part of the involved states. This solution created as many problems as it solved and is not to be recommended in similar situations. The European Union is an example of another type of solution in which power is equally distributed among the various members. At this point that type of solution appears to be working successfully but it has been operating for too short a period of time to make a final assessment possible.

CHAPTER 5. PRE-MODERN DEVELOPMENT OF THE UNITED STATES

The period of US history running from 1865 until 1914 represents a period during which the expansion of the federal government both in relation to its size and its power proceeded essentially unimpeded. This process began with the military suppression of the rebelling states and the unquestioned power of the federal government to deal with them. The federal government under Andrew Johnson and his reconstruction program denied the Confederate States and their citizens all civil rights accorded to the rest of the Union. This was true even though the Confederate States had been returned to the Union by force of arms. The first action taken by the administration of Johnson was to declare military law in the South. The second action was to give the confederate states no choice as to the manner in which they would be allowed to rejoin the Union. They were required through their state legislatures to pass a law asserting their loyalty to the Constitution including the 13th, 14th, and 15th amendments. The Confederate States, however, were not allowed representation in Congress and had not had the opportunity to debate or even to vote on the three listed amendments. The 13th amendment emancipated the African-Americans, the 14th amendment made certain that the African-Americans became citizens of the state in which they resided among other provisions, and the 15th amendment gave the African-Americans the right to vote. Had the South had a chance to debate and offer their views on these issues, even if the result had been the same, the feeling of ill-will would have been avoided at least to a significant degree.

It is believed that Lincoln had a plan by which the South would have received different treatment. Lincoln it appears would have liked to have seen the Confederate States reunited to the Union in such a way as to make it seem as if they had never seceded. He would have, under this plan, treated the eleven states and their citizens as wayward children rather than as criminals. He may even have been planning on offering federal aid in the rebuilding of the eleven states especially in regard to the destroyed infrastructure. It is a matter of debate as to whether or not this plan actually existed. Even if it did not hindsight shows that it would have been the preferable manner in which to handle the situation. Reconstruction was favored by the Union and sanctions were applied to the South which treated them as political enemies. Under this program all of the qualified personnel that existed in the South were denied the right to participate in public service. The Southern educational system, as mentioned earlier, was unable to provide for suitable replacements which led directly to the situation in which opportunists from the North and criminals from the South took control of all political functions after the Civil War. The result was thirty years of political chaos. The real tragedy was the fact that the power of the federal government was exercised without any regard for the civil rights of any individual whether white or black. The African-American population had been given their legal freedom but had been left to their own resources in exercising that freedom, which as it turned out were minimal. A large proportion of African-Americans had no skills other than those related to agriculture, they had little or no economic status and no where other than the South to go.

The poorer classes of the white population, probably somewhere in the range of 70 percent of the white population, were also left to fend for themselves under conditions little better than those faced by the African-Americans. The 30 percent that remained reacted by reinventing the system of slavery under the tenant farm system. Under this system both the African-Americans and the poor whites were reattached to the land. Although this system allowed for some compensation for the labor provided what was received rarely reached the level of benefits given to African-Americans as slaves. In short, the African-Americans and poor whites were worse off economically under the tenant system than they were under slavery while at the same time being equally attached to the land. The South in addition reacted to the domination of the North over their civil rights by again isolating themselves from the rest of the nation. This isolation was most notable in the institution of the legally sanctioned system of segregation. All in all the intended consequences of the reconstruction program were accomplished, i.e., the eleven states and their citizens were properly punished for their rebellion. The unintended consequences, however, were much more important in long term effects. As a result between 1865 and 1914 the South remained essentially a backwater in relation to developments that were occurring in the rest of the nation.

By 1900 therefore the North, the Midwest, and the Far West had greatly surpassed the South in industrial and commercial development. The same was true of educational and cultural development at least from the perspective of modernization of societal concepts. In many ways the South was no better off in regard to civil rights than the Native Americans who were denied civil rights everywhere in the country. There were a few exceptions to this general rule. The textile industry had developed to the point that it could sustain the continued growth of cotton under the tenant system and the American Tobacco Company had managed to keep pace with the integrated vertical growth of corporate structure and had supported the continued agricultural dependence in some areas on the tobacco crop. In addition, Northern industrial interests had begun to open the mining potential of Kentucky, the Virginias, and Tennessee. The latter development was controlled by large Northern corporations who were operating under a totally unregulated system and represents the worse abuse of labor and people in general yet seen in US history. The mining district known collectively as "Appalachia" was one of the poorest, least educated areas of the whole country, and mining company policies tended to keep it that way.

The United States by 1900 was composed of 45 states with only Oklahoma, New Mexico, and Arizona left to round out the contiguous 48 states. Alaska and Hawaii still remained some fifty years from inclusion into the Union as states. The population of the US had grown to over 76 million. During the first one hundred years the US Constitution had been amended only five times with three of the five amendments being ratified in relation to the Civil War. During the same period a series of changes had occurred that are not reflected in the amendments to the Constitution or the public consciousness of the time. First, the US had begun a rapid alteration from a rural society based on small family subsistence farming and cottage industry to a highly urbanized corporate society. Second, the US had become much more cosmopolitan especially in the larger urban areas due to the immigration of some 19 million people. Immigration had been largely uncontrolled prior to 1900 but would come under severe restrictions as another 38 million people would immigrate to the US over the next ninety years. The success of the US experiment in representative democracy can be shown in no more effective manner than to show that some 50 million people who did not live in the US wanted at all costs to get to the US and establish a new life. On the other hand, as would be expected, only 2,200 Africans had chosen voluntarily to immigrate to the US. Third, the Native Americans who had been largely confined to reservations were treated as if they did not exist by the larger society as were, to a somewhat lesser degree, the former slaves. This inherent racial discrimination was widely accepted by the society at large as a normal circumstance of life in the United States. Fourth, the land area of the US between 1865 and 1900 had increased tenfold; while its industrial and commercial capacity had expanded to the point that it was second only to Great Britain. Lastly, between these dates the educational system of the US became one of the most diverse and one of the most effective in the world.

Even when these changes are taken into consideration the US in 1900 was very little changed from what it had become within a couple of decades after its foundation. It was still a republican representative democracy by all definitions. The US still held firmly to its belief in the effectiveness of laissez-faire in the economic realm as well as the belief that all that was needed was for the free play of market forces to be allowed to occur. In addition, its laissez-faire attitude in foreign affairs, evidenced by isolationism, was in effect although as we have seen this doctrine was departed from more often and fully than in the economic arena. Generally speaking the US had shown more concern for the civil rights of its citizens than anywhere else on earth with the exception of Great Britain. The brutal treatment of both African-Americans and Native Americans prior to 1865 does not represent an exception to the rule, as neither of them were legally citizens, although this treatment was a clear violation of the myths supported by the Declaration of Independence. This continued to be true for the Native Americans until 1921; but the treatment of African-Americans after 1865 represents an exception to the general concern for civil rights of citizens. Underneath the tremendous changes that had occurred both economically (industrial revolution) and socially (urbanization) the US was essentially the same as it had been in 1820. The general public had accepted the ideological underpinnings of democracy (equality of all men, equality of opportunity, the freedom of political choice, and the rule of law); and were still under the belief that they were in reality living it. Up until 1900 it is hard to argue that the particular brand of representative democracy created by the Constitution did not represent the best explanation of political reality in the US. Even the severe test of a general Civil War had not eroded the belief in the general applicability of the system of government that had been created. There were, however, some latent signs that various experiments that had been instituted were beginning to challenge this belief in the status quo. The consistent use of a broad interpretation of constitutional language, coupled with the consistent use of the doctrine of implied powers, was beginning to erode the republican foundation created by the Constitution. What the federal government had failed to take in regard to the powers reserved to the states under these two doctrines the states had begun to give up voluntarily. This tended to convert what was intended to be a true federal republican system into a true nationalistic democracy. It was also a concern that the growth of the power of the two political parties specifically, and of organized interest groups generally, were beginning to erode the underlying democratic principles upon which the Constitution had been based. In short, before 1900 the US adhered to the tenets of 19th-century liberalism; but after 1900 began to tinker with the ideas of European-style socialism and other forms of nationalistic democracy.

Beginning with the 1890s two of the major underpinnings of the US democratic tradition started to suffer erosion from direct federal intervention. The first was the economic doctrine encapsulated under the terminology "the free market system." The doctrine of laissez-faire in relation to the economy had led to the creation of vast vertically structured monopolies, which in turn, had led to such abuses as price fixing, unfair competition within industries, and control of natural resources. The public began to demand that something be done to curb these abuses. It was at the time expected by the public that remedies would be found and applied by the state and local governments. However, through a broad interpretation of the constitutional provisions dealing with regulation of interstate commerce, and the doctrine of implied powers, the federal government was able to intervene in the major economic abuses. The federal government took direct intervention both through regulation and law suits. Second, the doctrine of isolation that was applied to foreign affairs also came under direct attack as the federal government proceeded to an aggressive policy that did not pay even lip service to the old doctrine.

In the South a formal attack on the civil rights of citizens was initiated by the local governments. Under the system of segregation, the African-American citizens of the participating local districts were denied equal civil rights in relation to the general population. The policy of segregation evidenced by the so-called Mississippi plan was a direct response to the forcing of citizenship for African-Americans by the federal government through the 14th amendment. As stated earlier, the eleven confederate states were forced to abide by the 14th amendment even though they had been denied the right to debate the issues and had not been given the chance to independently ratify the amendment. The Mississippi Plan by local statute created the need to satisfy a residency requirement to qualify for the franchise. The requirement was that the prospective voter must be a resident of the state for two years and the district in which they wished to vote for one year. This requirement effectively eliminated any person who was involved in the tenant farming system whether they were black or white. A second statute made a set of specific crimes cause for denial of the franchise. These crimes included vagrancy and rent hopping both practices found widely in the tenant farming system. This statute was intended to affect the same people as the first statute but somehow caught those who for some reason were capable of meeting the residency requirement. A third statute was passed which required all taxes including poll taxes to be paid by February 1 of any election year. This allowed ample time for those paying the taxes to lose their receipts. A fourth statute instituted a literacy requirement intended to catch any who had managed to bypass the other three. The literacy requirement made it possible to deny the franchise to anyone who could not read the Constitution. A loophole was allowed white people if they could prove to the election commissioner that they understood the terms of the Constitution even if they could not read them. This loophole was not offered to the African-American community. Essentially these statutes denied the franchise to a large segment of the citizens of each locality that put them into effect. Seven states besides Mississippi adopted the plan through its institution under local law; North and South Carolina, Louisiana, Georgia, Virginia, Alabama, and Oklahoma. The plan itself was based on an 1883 ruling of the Supreme Court that limited the effect of the 13th and 14th amendments to the actions performed by states and prohibited their application to actions of individuals. As a result the use of local segregation statutes was given formal validity under the Supreme Court ruling.

In the other states of the Union the use of segregation was instituted on an informal basis. Through the conscious use of discriminatory practices, especially in housing and employment, the African-American and selected immigrant communities were segregated from the general population. In the case of the African-Americans this led to the development of ghettoes in the urban inner cities; while in the case of the effected immigrant communities it led to the creation of cities within cities such as Pole Towns, China Towns, etc. The unofficial segregation policy of most states, although it accomplished the same goals as the official Southern policy, did not draw the intense attention that was eventually applied to the South.

The situation as concerns Native Americans must be looked at in a different light. The Native-Americans that remained on the reservations were not granted full citizenship until 1924 and prior to that time the vast majority of Native Americans were considered to be non-citizens whether they were on the reservation or not. By 1900 the so-called "Indian wars" had come to an end. In each case the Native Americans had faced an enemy that whenever possible attempted to exterminate them, that is, an enemy that consciously practiced genocide. When all Native Americans who had not been assimilated to the general population (as was the case with the Mohawks in up-state New York) or remained hidden (as was the case with the Seminole, Cherokee, and Apache) were finally removed to reservations a "new" benevolent policy was instituted by the federal government. This policy was a blatant attempt by the government to force the Native Americans to adopt subsistence agriculture and to introduce a system of education that was intended to make the Native Americans "white." This benevolent policy succeeded in suppressing what remained of the Native American cultures that had survived the attempt at genocide. It also, of course, generated a great deal of ill-will on the part of Native Americans for the US and its people. After many decades of repression the Native American nations that are still functional are attempting to revive their native cultures as best they can. On the other hand, while the federal government was attempting to make the Native Americans white they were also taking away the lands granted to them as reservations. Between 1887 and 1934 under the system created by the Dawes Severalty Act the Native Americans witnessed the reclaiming by the US of 86 million acres of the original 130 million acres granted as reservations. Most of what remained was deemed at the time as waste land or all of it would have been reclaimed. The Burke Act passed in 1906 was intended to give a boost to the reclamation process by granting immediate US citizenship to any Native American that voluntarily left the reservation. These abuses were aggravated by a policy of discrimination in employment and housing outside the reservation proper and by the fact that employment was virtually non-existent on the reservation.

In these cases the public began to recognize that the mythical foundations of democracy, i.e., that all men are born equal and that all men are guaranteed equal treatment before the law somehow did not seem to carry over into actual practice. There was no denying that the African-Americans, Native Americans, and selected groups of immigrants were treated as unequal and discriminated against by the law that was supposed to protect them as individuals. They could and were deprived of life, liberty, and the pursuit of happiness without the due process of law not to mention the denial of their property rights, voting rights, and others. Not only these groups but other social classes began to feel this lack of equality, that is, the working class, women, and children among others.

The second area in which democracy was being challenged was that found in the economic arena. The original underpinning of US democracy in this area was based on the Jeffersonian idea of the independent self-sufficient yeoman practicing either subsistence agriculture or a family based cottage type industry and commercial trading. This mythical yeoman was endowed with the virtues of independence from government control of his day to day life that is to say he lived under a very limited governmental structure and was free to choose his employment, religion, and society without interference by anyone other than his maker. This was the mythical foundation that acted as the social cement that bound the US public to seek the common goal of democracy whether it ever actually existed or not. The revolution that brought this mythical state under question was spearheaded by four men: Cornelius Vanderbilt, Andrew Carnegie, John D. Rockefeller, and J. Pierpont Morgan. Under the influence of these four men and the men that they financed such as Henry Ford, Thomas Edison, and Alexander Graham Bell the US was rapidly converted from a predominately rural society, serviced by small local family businesses, into a fully industrialized economy serviced by gigantic corporations. The society quickly became highly urbanized as a result of the effect of these changes on traditional ways of life. The innovations such as the holding company, the hierarchical corporation, the vertically integrated monopoly all contributed to the creation of a true national economy. These innovations were created to cope with the changes brought about by such technological advances as the iron plow share, the reaper, the cotton gin, the refined steam engine, and the assembly line.

The process began when J.P. Morgan created a banking system controlled by his holding company and which emphasized a highly structured investment financing program. This opened the door to the creation of other holding companies that would control whole segments of the economy, such as, the telephone and telegraph industry, the railroad industry, the steamboat industry, and the public transportation industry generally. Morgan's banks would provide the financing to these individual holding companies allowing them to capture their specialized segment of the economy minimizing the effect of free competition in the market as a whole. By 1900 this had led to the establishment of several fully integrated vertical monopolies, that is to say, corporations that controlled the natural resources, the manufacturing processes, and the distribution processes of the specific product of their interest. This process became most evident in the railroad industry (Vanderbilt), the oil industry (Rockefeller), and steel industry (Carnegie). Once this stage had been obtained the abuses that it occasioned also became evident to the public, that is, unfair competition (price fixing, denial of markets, etc.); unfair labor practices (sweat shops, wage control, child labor, etc.); and unfair tax reporting. It was the public reaction to shoddy products, high prices, and unfair labor practices among others that finally shook the federal government loose from its former adherence to the doctrine of economic laissez-faire. The first federal response was the passage of several statutes in the 1890s that were intended to curb the worse of the offending abuses but did not include a system of direct regulation of the business community. The federal government also avoided any intervention in the labor arena. Labor was left on its own to combat the power of huge corporations and did so by attempting to create equally powerful labor unions and the use of generalized work stoppages, known as strikes, to force the companies into a relatively equal bargaining position.

The federal government's second stance involved its partnership with big business in an attempt to control the effects of labor unions and strikes. Both the government and business took the stance that strikes were illegal under the Constitution and that both were authorized to use force to prevent them. The big corporations consistently used private armies such as the Pinkerton Agency to forcefully break strikes; while in very large strikes such as the Pullman Strike the federal government used state militias or federal troops to end the strike.

As in the case of civil rights the federal intervention into the economy brought about a public recognition that the mythical foundation of democracy, at least, in relation to the free play of the market system did not operate as would be expected. Instead the consolidation of power in the hands of a few huge corporations supported by governmental policy made it possible for the marketplace to be totally restrained from free competition. In short, the free market was anything but free.

The economic realm developed in much the same manner in the EU, that is to say, with the creation of the European market industries tended to become larger and more powerful. The EU, however, through the knowledge of the US experience did not have the same reluctance towards regulation. The EU economy is very tightly regulated, some would say even over regulated, and civil rights processes are also highly regulated to avoid the type of abuses suffered by immigrants, Native Americans, and African-Americans in the US. It would not be possible for a system such as segregation to develop within the EU although there is growing evidence of public resentment of immigration and some level of discrimination against these immigrants in relation to employment and housing.

In the global market things are much more like they were in the US after 1900. The economic realm is based on two major principles: 1) deregulation, and 2) the opening of national economies to adapt to the demands of the global economy. The demands of the global economy, that is, that national economies maintain a high rate of unemployment and strict control of monetary deficits to avoid inflation on the global level are enforced in the end game by US military might. The activity of the multinational corporations in regard to the control of labor, manufacturing and resources is very similar to the activities of the monopolistic corporations in the US. The abuse of labor at the periphery both within the industrialized nations and the marginalized countries is occurring at a scale much exceeding that found in the early decades of the 20th century in the US. The world union will be forced into a more active problem-solving stance than that taken by the US in 1900.

A world government would inherit all of these problems and many more. However, an effective world government will have to cope with the problems of various power combinations regardless of the form that they take. It is likely that the central world government will learn from the US experience that a laissez-faire approach does not work in such circumstances but rather creates even larger, more intractable problems. It is true, however, that huge international conglomerates, whether in the form of a private corporation or a national government acting in the capacity of a corporation, have already shown themselves capable of monopoly-type activities especially in relation to the obtaining and control of natural resources. In the Middle East, for example, it is evident that the US international conglomerates, the Japanese conglomerates, and the European Union all have the capability of directing oil production to their private use. It is the control of oil reserves that resulted in the naked aggression taken by the US and its allies against Iraq when Iraq failed to follow the rules of the global market and acted territorially by invading Kuwait. Does the US have any real vital interest involved in the establishment of democracy in Iraq? Is the US interest one of real concern for the political freedom of the people of Iraq? Is democracy merely a name given to the establishment of a control system that will guarantee a continued pliable trading partner in Iraq? Open access to natural resources is one of the vital interests of the US in Iraq and elsewhere, and that access is enhanced by political stability throughout the world. The US is willing to accept the denial of civil rights in Saudi Arabia and other countries as long as it does not hamper access to the natural resources it needs. It is also argued by some that the US is using the wars in Afghanistan and Iraq to prepare bases from which to repel any Chinese assertion of interest in the area.

It is this type of power brokering that will require the attention of an effective world government. These problems are no less open to solution under laissez-faire than were those that faced the US government in 1900. In addition the world government will be unable to compartmentalize people in the fashion that occurred in the early US. All people on the planet will automatically be categorized as world citizens due the democratic guarantees of the right to due process of law in the search for life, liberty, and the pursuit of happiness, as well as, the basic civil rights of the vote, private property, and cultural development. Not only individuals, and by extension corporations, but governments will be regulated to insure that they comply with these basic requirements of democracy. This is of course not the case at this time. The large industrial economies, as well as the most powerful national governments, tend to monopolize the world's natural resources, the production of the world's consumer products, and the distribution of these products to their various markets. As we have seen, this is the definition of a vertically integrated monopoly. At the same time, however, these private corporations and national governments are not under any obligation to determine the quality of life in the countries which they exploit for resources and use as uncompetitive manufacturers and as markets for their own products. In many of the poorer countries the restricted income that comes from the wealthy industrialized nations and corporations is left in the hands of less than one percent of the population, with the rest living in abject poverty. A serious commitment to true human dignity and equality will have to be made by an effective world government with the willing execution of this commitment at the hands of the national and local governments.

The main difference between the US experience and the one that may face the world union can be reduced to the difference in relative homogeneity between the two populations. The non-intervention policy of the US government for the first one hundred and ten years of its existence was essentially driven by the homogeneity of social customs, economic needs, religion and other cultural factors found in the general public. It was only after 1900 that enough diversity had developed to bring about an end to the homogenous character of life in the US. At this point the federal government was forced to abandon its non-intervention policy and replace it with a more active policy of regulation and direct interference in affairs. In short, for most of US history there has been little need or opportunity for the federal government to execute a policy of wholesale intervention. Instead the government was allowed to focus on small piece-meal attempts to fine tune its day to day operations. This one factor more than any other may have resulted in the small amount of change seen in the US democracy over its history. The same set of circumstances does not, or will not, face an effective world union. The union will begin with a very wide diversity among its various citizens in relation to culture, economic need, and other relevant factors. The problems it will face are already well defined and of such a scope that a do nothing, or wait and see what happens approach, will be impossible. The central government will be forced to take a realistic proactive approach to these problems while at the same time attempting to sustain the wide diversity that now exists. This will, of course, require a much higher degree of participation on the part of the national and local governments than was required in the US experience. It will also require that a much higher level of awareness be maintained in relation to the commitment of individual citizens to promote effective government at all levels. It may be that the growing struggle that has become evident in national democracies over the issue of diversity is the result of their attempts to maintain an ideological position that no longer represents the reality of the political environment, that is to say, their ideological position has in the words of Paul Ricoeur become frozen and repressive. The establishment of a world union would allow for a realignment of political philosophy to more accurately reflect the political reality of diversity. In addition, the national and local governments must take a much larger portion of responsibility for the implementation and execution of the programs devised. In the end it is the people themselves that must guarantee the effectiveness of all governmental institutions in regard to their interests. It is of interest to note that such an approach has already been taken by the EU but remains an unfinished project. It would still be a wise decision to give close study to the policies adopted by the EU when consideration is given to these problems by a world government.

Returning to the review of US history the early 1900s brought the possibility of two distinct paths that could be taken by the federal government. First, the policies of economic laissez-faire and isolation in foreign affairs could be reconstituted even though the political environment had changed. This path would have required the federal government to push responsibility for regulating economic abuses and abuses of civil rights down to the state and local levels of government. It would also have required the federal government to withdraw from active participation in international political affairs, probably including participation in international trade and finance. This path was the mainstay of the platform presented at that time by the conservative forces in both the Republican and Democratic parties. This included the rapidly growing progressive movement that called for corporate abuse, civil rights abuse, labor unrest, discrimination, and other social problems to be handled at the lowest level of government possible. The mainstream conservatives however avoided the more extreme position taken by the progressives and sought only to involve the federal government on truly national issues; the problem of course being the determination of which issues were national and which local. Second, the US government could take the path of direct intervention and proactive solution of the problems faced. This path would require the federal government not only to pass and implement the laws necessary to solve the problems but also to create the bureaucracy necessary to enforce the laws and regulations passed. This approach was familiar to the politicians of the day from the use of this path to reconstitute the Union after the Civil War. It would further require the federal government to take a very proactive approach to the promulgation of US interests on the international scene. The legal authorization for this approach to international affairs had already been established by prior rulings of the Supreme Court. This path would not limit the areas in which the federal government would be empowered to intervene, i.e., whether they were social, political, economic, or cultural. It would also allow the federal government to freely determine the circumstances under which it would be empowered to act under a consideration of the public welfare. This path was adopted within the platform of the liberal elements of both political parties. It is fair to say that overall the conservative position called for the federal government to maintain both the underlying democratic and republican principles upon which the nation had been founded; while the liberal position called for the maintaining of the democratic traditions but tended to call for the replacement of the republican principles with those of nationalism. It is also fair to say that by the early 1900s the states had lost or given up most of the powers that had been reserved to them by the Constitution; and the people had lost, if they ever had, any power to affect the operations of the national and state governments. Even at the local level the people in general showed a great degree of apathy allowing local affairs to be controlled by professional politicians and business leaders.

The same paths will be open to the world union if it is established but immediately rather than after a century of operation. It is expected from the EU experience that the national and local governments will be in a better position; and be more willing to maintain, a key role in the issues that will affect mankind. Republican principles would call for the national and local governments to take an active and extensive role in such issues as disarmament, conservation, pollution control, sanitation, provision of potable water sources, enforcement of general governmental laws and regulations among many others. On the other hand the liberal path would require the central world government to take all governmental powers unto itself and then delegate the duties and responsibilities it wished to see handled on the national and local level. We would, therefore, again be at the crossroads where the conservative and liberal political philosophies meet. It can be expected that very shortly after the world government is initiated a conclusion will be reached as to which one of these paths most accurately represents political reality at that time. At this time it certainly appears that the world government would be taking the position of legislator with the national and local governments taking the role of implementing and enforcing the laws and regulations promulgated on the global level.

CHAPTER 6. THE MOVEMENT TOWARDS THE MODERN UNITED STATES

It was stated earlier that two main paths of response were open to the federal government by the late 1890s. One was a path that would have limited federal government intervention pushing that responsibility back upon the state and local governments. The other would have required a much expanded exercise of federal power in the area of regulation and enforcement. Although a choice had been successfully avoided prior to this point circumstances had changed and were forcing an environment where a decision had to be made. This did not quiet the debate that went forward between the advocates of the two distinct paths of action.

The Civil War although not exclusively fought as a response to the call for the abolition of slavery did set the standard by which all future reform movements in the area of civil rights would operate. Initially the reform movements that gained popularity after the Civil War included the movement for women's suffrage, the movement to abolish alcohol, and the movement to better conditions for the insane and criminally incarcerated. The original movements were all grassroots movements and although they were well organized they tended to be somewhat underfunded. The attention of the movements was largely focused on the state level of government as the federal government was at this time not seen as responsible for the areas of interest involving the movements. The right of suffrage was controlled at the state level, that is, the qualifications for voting were a matter of state statutory law. It was also felt at this time that the federal government should not be involved in legislating morals such as the ban on the use of alcohol. In the case of the insane and criminals the institutions that held them were all with very few exceptions built, operated, and owned by the state or local government in which they were located. In addition the early Supreme Court ruling limiting the effect of the 14th amendment to the states forced the movements to focus their attention at that level to incorporate the concept of a due process of law. Using the 14th amendment allowed the various movements to concentrate on the standardization of the response to their concerns across the Union. They also hoped to influence enough states legislatures to favor the extension of the franchise to women in order to force a constitutional amendment. These turned out not to be easily won battles as the ban on the use of alcohol was not passed until 1918 and the franchise was not extended to women until 1920. As we shall see there were other issues that had begun to come to the attention of the US public such as workers rights, immigrant rights, racial and ethnic discrimination especially segregation and corporate abuses of all types.

It is in the latter area that the federal government was first forced to intervene in an issue involving individual civil rights. The federal intervention after the Civil War had affected individual civil rights but this intervention was not directed towards individuals but rather against the states and their public officers. As mentioned in the last chapter the US had begun to make itself heard in relation to specific corporate abuses, i.e., shoddy products, high prices, labor practices, and restraint of trade. Under the leadership of Theodore Roosevelt and the newly formed progressive party the public anger was recognized and brought to a point of action. The Clayton Anti-Trust Act that had been passed in the mid 1890s had been largely ignored up until 1901. Roosevelt used the act to attack several large corporations, in particular, the American Tobacco Company through the institution of administrative lawsuits. In the case involving the American Tobacco Company the full intention of the act was followed and the company was forced to break up its vertical monopoly. It is of interest to note that the American Tobacco Company was the sole example of a vertical monopoly indigenous to the South. Whether that fact had anything to do with the especial vigor with which the Anti-Trust Act was applied in this case is a matter of speculation. However, it was not applied with the same vigor in the other cases involving Northern vertical monopolies. In these cases the Act was used only to obtain leverage in forcing the corporations involved to discontinue their most abusive practices. The federal intervention in cases of corporate abuse was authorized not only by the Clayton Act but also by the earlier Supreme Court ruling that gave corporations the status of private individuals. In this latter sense the federal intervention was directed against the actions of private citizens. The actions taken by the Roosevelt administration were successful in eliminating the most obvious corporate abuses but no attempt was made to stop or even slow down the process of consolidation that was taking place in the business community. Roosevelt had acted aggressively enough to divert the public anger away from a focus on corporate behavior. Roosevelt personally believed that the time for the continuation of a rural US society serviced by small to medium sized businesses had passed into history. He accepted the need for the economy of scale represented by larger and larger corporations. He carefully avoided the breakup of any corporation under the Clayton Act with the one exception noted above.

The Roosevelt administration and the federal legislators did not fail to recognize the importance of what had happened. The public concerns had been effectively allayed without any serious action being taken to upset the growing economic consolidation. The Clayton Anti-Trust Act had at the same time been successfully reinterpreted to eliminate the intended breakup of any company found guilty of violating the monopoly provisions of the Act. The reinterpretation would now allow government regulation of corporate activities to replace the breakup of such companies. This was an innovative use of executive power by the Roosevelt administration and was justified by calling attention to the executive duty under Article II of the Constitution, i.e., that the executive branch had the duty to enforce the laws passed by Congress. Within the scope of this duty was the power to create agencies, bureaus, and other bureaucratic institutions to actually carry out the enforcement duty. This early standard would set the manner in which federal intervention would enter all areas dealing with the civil rights of individuals.

A second area in which the federal government made an early attempt to intervene was in foreign affairs. Once again the attempt was masterfully handled by the Roosevelt administration by means of an innovative use of executive power. Although the public continued to accept the myth of isolation from world affairs until after World War I the political leaders definitely proved that isolation was just a myth. By 1900 the US had taken the lead in establishing the economic forms that would over time dominate the world. In connection with this innovation the US also took its place as one of the leading economic powers in the global market place. The innovations included the introduction of mass production; the introduction of large scale investment banking; the introduction of the modern corporation; the introduction of mass transportation and distribution systems; and price and wage controls both governmental and private. By 1900 there was no question that J.P. Morgan was largely responsible for large scale investment banking throughout the industrial world. By 1900, the US had as a part of its commercial expansion in the global market taken a serious stand in relation to the unofficial Monroe Doctrine. The US action in Cuba and Mexico had effectively prohibited any real involvement by European countries in Latin America. In 1853 the US navy had taken unilateral action against the empire of Japan and had opened this Island Empire to trade. The US military had also taken part in the actions spearheaded by European nations to carve up the Chinese empire into spheres of trade interest gaining for itself a favored nation status in China. The US, unlike the European nations, did not attempt to establish colonies in the true imperialistic sense of the time. The territories that they had taken from Spain and Mexico in the wars against these nations were treated as follows: First, in relation to Florida and the Southwestern portions of North America the US incorporated them directly into its Union as direct dependencies or territories. Even at the time that they were obtained it is likely that everyone intended them to become future states which by 1900 most of them had as we have seen. Second, in relation to the Pacific Islands and the Caribbean the territories were treated as US dependencies but not as colonies. The main reason for the persistence of the myth of isolation from world affairs, at least in the minds of the US public, is the fact that most history prior to 1900 was written from a Euro-Centric point of view. From this point of view the US presented an ideal that set forth the intention to remain neutral in European affairs, especially European wars, which was fairly consistently followed up until World War I. This intention was denoted as a policy of isolation from the European point of view. From every other measurement, however, the US role in international affairs had been growing rapidly and was continuing to grow. Under the guidance of J.P. Morgan the US was the recognized leader in investment financing and commercial fiscal transactions; the US was second only to Great Britain in the value of products exported and imported; the US had used its military power aggressively making it one of the most powerful in the world, although still essentially unproven; and lastly, the US had taken in more immigrants than any other country on earth giving credibility to its success as the representative of democracy.

One of the most distinctive trends during the late 19th and early 20th centuries within the US was the development of education. The trend began with the removal of education from the sole responsibility of religious institutions and private educational institutions making it the responsibility of the state and local governments. Education in the US became a mass public institution. Initially this was made evident by state statutes requiring that every child receive a minimum education consisting of graduation from elementary school (the equivalent of a sixth grade education in the US system today). In return the state and local governments would finance the building and staffing of elementary schools. From the beginning this financing was accomplished by the implementation of taxes on real property. The states entered the operation at the level of higher education making grants of land for the establishment of agricultural and teaching colleges. The educational system was designed by the leaders in education to closely follow the models that had been established earlier in Germany. The school system was also affected to a significant degree by the social interpretation of the theories of Charles Darwin. By 1900 the US public education system had obtained to its distinctive character, i.e., a through mixture of liberal education (in the sense of the well rounded scholar) and technical education (training in the trades such as carpentry, masonry, etc.). In the area of higher education, which was still largely in the hands of religious and private institutions, the US by 1900 had already adopted the elective system, that is, each student was required to successfully complete a core program but was also allowed a significant degree of choice in elective courses. This allowed a degree of flexibility in choosing a final life career whether it was in engineering, science, or some other field. In addition, the US had set up a system of professional schools such as law schools, medical schools, architectural schools, etc., that were required to practice the profession. In conjunction with the professional schools, the states also passed statutes that required an examination to obtain a license to practice in the professions. The state licensing requirements also brought into being the various professional organizations to police the practice and ethics of those working in the professions. Together the licensing requirements and professional associations were intended to limit the number of people who would be qualified and capable of practicing any particular profession, which in turn made those practicing able to increase their status in society and the money they received in compensation. It was in fact something of a professional monopoly. It is of interest to note that the professional organizations represent in the US today the most solid bastion of the conservative ideals.

The influence of Charles Darwin was of a qualitatively different sort. In the educational system per se his theories were interpreted as being an important step in the scientific understanding of human reason and its use in training young students. The interpretation of Darwin by US educators, and the use they put it to, shouldn't be underrated. It was used to question the hold that religious authority still held over the majority of the US population. Specifically it was used to replace religious dogma as a training tool and to institute a more objective approach. In short the theories of Darwin began the US emphasis on shifting the education of students from the production of the "universal man" to one that produced a more narrowly educated professional. This process has become even more intensified in the current US educational system especially in the areas of science and technology. It has also become the educational choice of other countries such as Japan, China, Germany, India, and many others. Darwin's theories also had a social interpretation that would become very influential in the US. This interpretation became known as "Social Darwinism" and emphasized the popular understanding of the theories of Darwin such as "the survival of the fittest" and "evolution." In the case of one segment of the business community known as the "robber barons" the survival of the fittest doctrine was used to justify their brutal business tactics. The large corporations owned and operated by the robber barons were quickly labeled as the most fit to survive and therefore any regulation of their activities would tend to support the survival of the unfit. Any attempt to artificially save smaller organizations whether they were businesses, farms, churches, or professional organizations was seen as an attempt to go against the natural order of things. Occasionally this line of argument was taken to the extreme position of claiming that monopolies were the "will of God." Social Darwinism was also active on the political front claiming that government had only two functions: the elimination of poverty and the education of citizens in the sciences. The Social Darwinists protested against any government regulation of business, intervention in social customs, the providing of public sanitation and water systems, the graduated income tax (adopted in 1913), providing public housing or any other public service that could be beneficial in allowing the unfit to survive. This was extended to rejecting any type of civil rights programs or laws that would promote the technical equality of all people before the law. They saw these as simply another attempt to promote the survival of those who would otherwise perish as unfit. Social Darwinism was therefore used to justify the treatment of the Native Americans, the African-Americans, and all unwanted groups of immigrants. This attempted justification of racial and ethnic discrimination was quickly converted into a generalized sense that the people classified as unfit were somehow less human than the native Anglo-Saxon white population. In short, Social Darwinism in the US was not all that different from the Nazis ideology established in the 1930s in Germany in relation to the "Aryan" race. Although these ideals have slowly given way in the current environment they still remain hidden barely below the surface. One only has to look at the platform of the Libertarian Party or the writings and actions of Neo Nazis, Survivalists, and other cult groups to verify the accuracy of this statement.

It is within this larger background that the battle between the essentially laissez-faire conservative philosophical tradition, which had essentially dominated federal governmental action prior to 1900, and the newly established liberal philosophical tradition based upon the promotion of individual entitlement to civil rights took place. Very early the Supreme Court would again establish itself as the guardian of the liberal philosophical position. The conservative elements including the Social Darwinians wanted a continuation, if not an outright radicalization, of the old hands off limited government that had been originally favored by the states' rights position. The liberal position took the approach that the best method of obtaining and protecting individual rights against erosion was to place them in the care of the federal government. In doing so they intended to empower the federal government to intervene in any area of the society deemed necessary. The liberal position found itself focusing intensely on such issues as a woman's right to vote, the abolition of alcohol, the rights of workers and immigrants, and the rights of criminals and the insane. The conservative position opposed the use of federal law as well as federal power in these issues giving their preference to the handling of such problems, if they were in fact problems, at the lowest level of government possible. As might be expected the first line of debate was formed around the federal governments treatment of corporate abuse.

The Supreme Court represented a large part of the federal government's reaction to corporate abuse. As pointed out the executive branch had begun by bringing a series of lawsuits under the Clayton Anti-Trust Act. This very quickly involved the Supreme Court as the cases were brought to its attention. In the case of Santa Clara County versus The Southern Pacific Railroad the Supreme Court clearly established the principle that corporations at least legally were the equal of private citizens, and therefore, beyond the power of the state and local governments to regulate. By default this decision shifted the whole burden of regulation of corporations unto the federal government in particular on the executive branch of the federal government. This empowerment would be protected under the constitutional provisions granting sole authority to the federal government to regulate inter-state commerce. In the case of Chicago, Milwaukee, and St. Paul Railroad Company versus Minnesota the Supreme Court solidified its earlier ruling by specifically prohibiting to the states the power to judicial review of railroad rates set by state law. In combination these two rulings had the unintended consequence of undermining the earlier Supreme Court ruling that the 14th amendment could only be applied to the states and not to individuals. The Supreme Court would now interpret the 14th Amendment, if it found it necessary, as applicable also to actions committed by individuals, especially in the denial of due process of law. The Supreme Court, of course, would remain the final arbitrator of whether or not due process of law had been violated. Initially, these rulings made it very difficult for the state and local governments to institute any type of regulatory system in relation to corporate activities within the state and later to the actions of their citizens as well. This aspect of the debate had boiled down to the question of where the general power to regulate would be settled and the decision was clearly that it would be settled in the federal government either through legislation or creative use of executive orders. The Progressive Movement was first put into the national spotlight concerning this issue. This movement took the position that if regulation was needed it should be created and enforced at the lowest level of government possible as it was there that the problem would be best understood. This approach would also allow a great deal of flexibility to be incorporated into regulatory practices based on the differences of conditions that existed in differing environments. On the other hand, settling the regulatory powers in the federal government would allow for a standardization of rules throughout the union making the conduct of business simpler. The above two rulings of the Supreme Court put an end to the debate and over time eliminated any real regulatory power in the state and local governments as concerns corporate activities. The failure of the Progressive Movement to reinstate responsible state and local government in this case also extended to the issue of federal intervention into other areas involving civil rights.

The two major political parties were also forced to take rather defined stands on the issues involving civil rights. The Republican Party tended to take a highly moralistic stand on issues such as a woman's right to vote, the use and sale of alcohol, federal support of education provided by religious institutions, a high protective tariff, and civil rights in general. In most cases the party took the stand that the federal government was not authorized by the Constitution to act in these cases; that the power to handle these problems, if they were problems, was reserved to the state and local governments, or to the people at large. In short, the Republican Party favored a private rather than public solution of these issues. The Democratic Party, on the other hand, took the position that the federal government was not only authorized by the Constitution to act in these areas but was under the duty to protect the general welfare. It was the duty of the federal government under the due process provisions of the 14th amendment to protect the rights of workers and immigrants, women's rights, and the underprivileged generally. It was the duty of the federal government to protect the public welfare from fraud, abuse, and violence from corporate entities or any other source of threat to the public welfare through strict enforcement of regulatory actions. Both the parties adopted the use of political patronage on the state and local level to support the positions that they favored.

The Republicans who held a majority in both houses of Congress and also the presidency passed the McKinley tariff at the time the highest across the board tariff system ever instituted in the US. The Republicans were also responsible for the fact that the Clayton and Sherman Anti-Trust Acts had lain dormant for almost a decade. Lastly, the Republicans had passed the Sherman Silver Act which made paper money redeemable in either gold or silver greatly enhancing the position of creditors. It was in this atmosphere that the debate was to continue during the early 20th century. The Democrats when they held power attempted to undue, mostly unsuccessfully, the legislation that had been passed by the Republicans. The result was not a stalemate, at least a serious stalemate, but rather more of an unspoken agreement between the parties do no more than was necessary to satisfy the public on the issues at hand. Neither party attempted to seriously debate, or resolve, the issues that had arisen between the end of the Civil War and the turn of the century. This allowed for a dangerous expansion of worker unrest in relation to working conditions and wages; political corruption at all levels of government; ethnic and racial discrimination (especially in the private sector outside the South); and in the agricultural crisis that had struck the US. Both parties tended to react only to the issues that caught the public attention and then only to the extent necessary to restore public calm. In the end both parties tended to protect industry and commerce with high tariffs; to support the continuation of the gold standard; to repress reform movements (especially those that targeted government corruption); and to support the growing industrial/urban complex. In short, both parties accepted the reality of unrestrained capitalism and attempted to do very little to remedy it.

The first issue as we have seen was the handling of the issue of corporate abuse. The resolution was definitely a compromise to appease both political positions. The breakup of the American Tobacco Company was intended and succeeded in appeasing the conservative elements who were calling for a strict enforcement of Anti-Trust legislation. Roosevelt was able to convince both sides that the proper way to handle corporate abuse was through the creation of a vast federal regulatory system which in essence was a direct appeasement of the liberal position that was calling for government intervention. It is likely that Roosevelt's assessment that the time had passed for the US to return to an agrarian society serviced by small to medium sized businesses was correct. It is less obvious whether he was also right in his belief that the problems could be most effectively solved by federal regulation. It is at least arguable that the state and local governments would have been as effective if not more effective regulators especially in the area of corporate abuses. Today it would be insane to argue against the need for economy of scale in many industries such as micro processing equipment, aircraft manufacturing, and others. It would be equally difficult to argue against the use of price and wage control systems in the regulation of the overall economic system. It is merely an idle dream to seriously advocate a return to agrarianism in today's environment. The resolution of this first issue therefore resulted in the marriage of big business and big government.

Big business and big government advocates were both solidly behind the programs initiated by President Roosevelt. They both realized that regulation if properly conducted would result in less competition rather than a truly open market. The same approach was advocated by the leaders of big business and the liberal persuasion generally in the resolution of other issues of social import such as the conservation of natural resources, labor unrest, unemployment, old age security, and the protective tariff. Still seen as issues best resolved at the state and local level or by the private sector were the providing of sanitation and water systems, the availability of electrical power, and the use of public transportation systems. It is hard to assess the initial affects of the marriage of big business and big government on the underlying principles of democracy at this time. The power that had been somewhat transparent in the hands of men like J.P. Morgan, John D. Rockefeller, and Andrew Carnegie was now to become hidden behind such technical shields as interlocking directorates, holding companies, investment banks, and the use of public stock. These shields allowed the undetected use of vast sums of money for both legitimate and illegitimate purposes. The corporations, who acted for the controlling interests, could and did affect the manner in which political decisions were made by the political parties. They in essence became the second level of interest groups behind the political parties. The marriage also seemed to fit well with the ambitions of such men as Theodore Roosevelt, Woodrow Wilson, Herbert Hoover, and Franklin D. Roosevelt all of whom played a key role in the promotion of unrestrained capitalism both at home and abroad. The most fragrant corporate abuses were regulated by law but the power remained with the largest corporations. Theodore Roosevelt began the technique of bypassing the need for formal legislation in the field of regulation by his creative use of the power of executive order. The executive branch was given extensive powers by the Constitution to create agencies, departments, and other bureaucratic aids for the enforcement powers granted the executive branch. For example, the Constitution gave the executive branch the duty to enforce all legislation passed by Congress in relation to the regulation of interstate commerce. In order to enforce the statutes and Supreme Court decisions already on the books Roosevelt created the interstate commerce commission. The duty of the commission was to directly regulate the compliance of corporate citizens with the existing laws and edicts concerning interstate commerce. In doing its duty the commission tended to usurp any regulatory powers that were already being applied by the state and local governments. Roosevelt, who believed personally in the need for larger and larger corporations to take advantage of the economy of scale preferred the use of federal regulation rather than the need for specific federal legislation to handle corporate abuse, i.e., he wanted to handle the problem through the use of executive orders rather than statutory law. As a result he created a large bureaucratic structure to handle the problem headed by the Bureau of Corporations. He let the corporations know that he would not bring suit under the Anti-Trust laws if the corporations would cooperate with the bureau. Most did, but Standard Oil failed to respond to a bureau request and suit was brought against the corporation resulting in its eventual breakup in 1911. The use of executive order in this manner was a creative use of executive powers granted under the Constitution. It took a rather broad interpretation of the relevant constitutional language by the Supreme Court to authorize this usage. The Supreme Court had earlier ruled that the large corporations were subject to the regulations of interstate commerce if their products or services were actually in more than one state. It does not appear that Roosevelt's actions were unconstitutional in any manner but they were definitely a creative use of executive prerogative. The executive powers are of course subject to periodic revision by both the passage of counterbalancing legislation or judicial rulings that make the actions unconstitutional. This manner of using executive power, regardless of the occasional interference of various checks and balances, today remains one of the most used and important powers of the president. The use of executive power to create a huge unelected professional bureaucracy has caused some experts to declare that the US is no longer a republican democracy but a national democracy. The bureaucracy is used essentially to delegate power downwards to the state and local governments rather than leaving them with the power to initiate their own powers. It can be argued that the use of executive orders, the creation of a professional bureaucracy, and the loss of initiative at the state level has indeed tended to subvert the original intention to separate the powers of the federal governmental branches.

Roosevelt also at the same time as he expanded executive prerogative attached himself to the progressive movement. Roosevelt was above all else a practical politician, and as we will see in the next chapter, the progressive movement was very practical in its demands. His attachment to the progressive movement was fueled by his belief that the environment that had created the call for a free competitive market had now passed. Competition within the economy generally would now be controlled either by large corporations capable of establishing vertical monopolies or by government regulation or a combination of both. His belief had brought him to the position where he actively supported the marriage of big business and big government working together in a cooperative environment. Roosevelt was so successful in his attempt to promote this marriage that no objections were raised to it at the time nor have any serious objections been raised against it to the present day. Hands off government had been replaced by a planned interventionism without a public murmur and with the full support of the business and financial communities.

The lessons set forth by the Roosevelt administration were not lost on the various reform movements then in existence. The most important reform movements shifted their focus from the state and local governmental level to that of the federal government with the exception of the progressive movement which bucked this trend. The reform movements had taken to heart the concept that the only effective way to obtain standardized reform throughout the Union was to force the passage of constitutional amendments. The reform movements had also learned that when amendments, or even federal legislation, could not be obtained the same objective could be achieved through the use of executive orders and federal regulation. For example, the woman's suffrage movement, as well as the movement to abolish the use of alcohol, both took the stand that a constitutional amendment was both needed and possible. The reform movements that were seeking more rights for those incarcerated for insanity or crimes took the stand that all that was needed was an executive order and federal regulation. Yet again those reform movements that sought enforceable rights for workers, immigrants, and others soon recognized that the federal government was going to refuse to intervene in any manner in these issues. The various civil rights movements therefore were left with the choice of pushing for these rights at the state and local level (which is exactly what the progressive movement did) or handling the problem themselves (which to a great degree was the method selected by the workers through the creation of labor unions and the use of the strike). The federal government as well as the state and local governments, however, chose to intervene when the workers used work stoppage (strikes) to force acceptance of the labor unions (collective bargaining) by authorizing the private and public use of force to break them up.

Even in the area of foreign affairs Roosevelt consciously attempted to overthrow the old conservative position of isolation. His policy in foreign affairs can best be summed up in one of his own pet phrases 'remain quiet, yet carry a big stick'. His policies in relation to the affairs of Europe as well as his handling of the Panama Canal issue exemplify his approach to world affairs. Roosevelt clearly committed the US to a major role in the world market although he would not become involved in shooting wars. In the Panama Canal issue Roosevelt simply had the US take over where the French had failed. He finished building the Panama Canal and pressured the Panamanian government into granting a long term lease of the Canal to the US. This action alone would indicate that Roosevelt understood the practicalities of the US position in world economics.

The same types of issues that have been discussed above will also face an effective world government when it is instituted. There can be no doubt for example that huge international corporate conglomerates already exist and have the capability of acting in a manner comparable to the vertical monopoly. Indeed it is very likely that some of the largest, especially those associated with the so-called global market, already do control resources, manufacturing, and distribution systems that operate as monopolies. It is also true that some nations such as Japan are attempting to put together coalitions for the same economic purposes. There can be no doubt that the European Union represents one of the most successful examples of such a coalition today. There are already complaints being brought forward that price fixing, wage control, production quotas and other devices are being used abusively against non EU nations by the European Union to protect its member's economies. The US response was to preclude the state and local governments from playing a significant role in the handling of such problems. It is also arguable that this approach has failed to result in its intended purpose. It is necessary therefore that the World Government promote an effective role for the national and local governments in the hands on implementation and enforcement of its laws and regulations, as is currently being done in the EU. This would not only be true in the area of economics but should also be the method of choice in issues of political and social reform and individual civil rights. Even if a decision was made to create a large central bureaucracy for enforcement of general regulatory statutes and orders this bureaucracy should be located and maintained at the national and local level. It would be in the end responsible solely to the central government but would be maintained and operated at the national and local level. It is also possible that the regulatory responsibilities would be handled on a concurrent basis, that is, both the central government and the national and local governments would have regulatory responsibilities. This would of course require that a relatively comprehensive division of the specific responsibilities be made to prevent a large amount of duplication of efforts. This approach has not yet been tried but there does not seem to be any reason why it should be any less cost effective and efficient than the existing national systems and probably will prove to be more so. The European Union has adopted this approach but the lack of a true central government in the Union makes it doubtful whether that approach is working successfully.

Under the influence of the rapidly growing progressive movement and the innovative approach of the Roosevelt administration it appeared that the liberal philosophy had clearly won the day. Although a Republican Roosevelt belonged to the most liberal wing of that party and the progressives were considered to be the most liberal faction in the country; Roosevelt in fact was so liberal in his actions that he finally was forced to give up his membership in the Republican Party and became a leader of the new Progressive Party (he actually headed a third party called the Bull Moose Party). His successor William Taft, however, was a conservative president and this had an effect on the liberal movements of the day.

CHAPTER 7. THE EFFECT OF THE PROGRESSIVE MOVEMENT IN THE US

The Period between 1900 and 1917 is commonly known as the "Progressive Era." It received this designation for several reasons the most important of which was the public reaction to the financial crisis that struck the US in the late 1890s. Those who became known as progressives believed that two main reasons could be given for the financial panic. First, the corporations had been allowed to evolve without any type of restrictions being placed on the manner in which they operated. This had led to serious financial malfeasance on the part of the largest corporations, that is, the vertical monopoly. Second, there had developed a large scale corruption in government at the state and local level especially in relation to the large urban centers. The two in combination had resulted in the financial panic of the late 1890s. The solutions offered by the progressive movement amounted to a real attempt to institute piece-meal social engineering. The intent was to curb both the power and abuses of the corporate community (especially the policies of the Robber Barons) and the corruption that was found in the state and local government (especially the city bosses). The catchphrase used by the progressives was "a greater democracy." The two main planks of the progressive movement's platform were the regulation of business activities and honesty in government. In this the progressives were closely associated with the various reform movements that were in existence at the turn of the century. This association coupled with the fact that the progressives targeted the state and local governments qualified them as a grassroots movement. In connection with the reform movements the progressives called for a large scale expansion of the role of the federal government in overall regulatory responsibility; but at the same time called for the greater involvement of the state and local governments in the implementation and enforcement of the needed regulation. The progressive movement unlike the other reform movements had the full support of the business community which realized that regulation, especially if instituted at the federal level, would mean less rather than more competition. The progressives also called for a large scale popular initiative to end corruption at the state and local levels. The earlier government reform movements, such as the Popularists, had based their platforms on the Jeffersonian tradition of agrarianism and small scale industry. Although essentially the same programs were offered the progressive support was based on the governing classes and not the people per se. The progressive movement therefore tended to be more conservative in its demands although more liberal in its results. In each case in which a reform movement was adopted by the progressives it was swiftly converted to a very business-like efficiency. Even though proactive in its outlook the progressive movement was largely practical in its methods. Under the influence of the progressive movement governments at all levels were being called upon to provide a wide range of services. These demands included more and better schools; more and better roads; realistic conservation methods; public health and safety laws; more and better care for the handicapped, insane, and criminally incarcerated; direct loans to farmers to end the agricultural crisis; and more focus on the rights of workers and immigrants. The progressives were the first to accept the full consequences of the program initially offered by Alexander Hamilton in 1789. As a result the progressives were willing to give up any dependence upon the concept of limited government in return for efficient and honest government. The progressives consistently pushed for an expansion of government services especially at the state and urban levels coupled with a high degree of honesty in government service. In many ways the progressive movement was a foreshadowing of the coming conversion of the US to a state capitalism.

One of the most interesting early experiments called for by the progressives pushed a return to direct democracy. As will be remembered direct democracy is a system whereby the people not only retain the sovereign power but also directly exercise it. Most candidates for office at this time were chosen by closed party caucus. Under this system a small number of leading party officials would select the candidates for office without any participation from the public. The system offered by the progressives consisted of altering the caucus system and allowing for the selection of candidates by means of primary elections. Under this system the party would select several candidates for the office that was open and these candidates would then face each other in a primary election where the people would select the one that actually would run for the vacant office. Each party would have its primary election and the result of the primaries would be that two candidates would face each other in the general election for the vacant office. The intent of course was to return the selection of who would run for office to the people. This system is still used in a number of states especially in relation to the candidates who will run for the office of president from each party. In this case the candidate that wins the primary election of the state under consideration receives that states vote in total for the Office of President in the convention of the party involved. In the general election however under the current system each State's electoral votes are controlled by the candidate that receives the greatest number of votes in that state at the general election. A second reform offered by the progressives was that of the initiative and referendum. Under this program any issue that strongly affected the public sentiments could be put to the test by popular vote. The issue could be put on the federal, state or local ballot by obtaining a specified number of signatures on a petition from duly qualified voters. This was the initiative stage of the process. Once this was accomplished the issue would be placed on the appropriate ballot and if passed by the voters at the election would become law. This was the referendum stage of the program. After passage of the 17th amendment the primary system would also apply to the election of senators, and is applied in many cases to officials at the state and local level. The progressive idea of initiative and referendum is still active as the recall of Gray Davis in California and the referendum votes in the EU clearly show. However, during the early 20th century both the primary and the initiative and referendum programs in the US showed themselves subject to widespread manipulation and the public lost interest in these programs as a means of promoting reform. The EU, however, still in some cases allows the use of the referendum to determine national policy, e.g., the Norwegian referendum on EU membership.

The issue of a renewed commitment to honest public service by the progressives was approached by instituting a method of accountability based on the use of strictly controlled budgets. This system was first introduced into urban government and after success was seen at this level in curbing corruption was quickly adopted at the state level. The federal government did not follow suit until 1921 when the Office of the Budget was created. This attempt at corruption reform on the local level quickly led to the institution of the commission system, later called the city-manager system, in most large and medium sized cities. The new system quickly spawned a new level of trained and professional politicians. This system could not be incorporated into the state level due to the constitutional guarantee of republican government. Instead under the leadership of the progressive movement legislative reference bureaus were created. The reference bureau's sole task was to provide the needed research materials and wording to promote effective state legislative initiatives. This part of the progressive movement is not widely recognized today due to the fact that it was directly incorporated into the state civil service program, i.e., it became a part of the federal and state civil service bureaucracy.

A qualified and professional bureaucracy will be needed in the case of the initiation of an effective world government and no better model of such a bureaucracy exists than that created by the progressives during the early 20th century, especially in relation to the modern version being used by the EU.

The issue of governmental regulation, not only as it applied to the specific case of the Robber Barons but also to the economy generally, was by far the most controversial of the programs offered by the progressives. In the context of our project the social programs offered by the movement appear much more important. However, at the time of the movement itself, the focus was on the abuse of monopoly. The progressives felt that the Clayton and Sherman Anti-Trust Acts had been unsuccessful in accomplishing their intended goals and offered several alternative approaches that revolved around four distinct positions advocated by various wings of the movement. The ultra-conservative wing of the progressive movement advocated the return to the old doctrine of laissez-faire with a minimum of federal regulation. This alternative was given little or no consideration by the movement as a whole. The ultra-liberal wing of the movement was calling for a full scale national planning project in the tradition of socialist and communist movements found in Europe. This alternative of national ownership was seriously considered but in the ended rejected by the mainstream progressives. The rejection of socialism by the mainstream was based mainly on its distrust of violence as a legitimate means of political action. During the early 20th century, violence had become almost the sole political tactic of the socialists in both the US and Europe. Socialism is based in large part on tenets identical with those of modern liberal democracy but the use of violence turned the political leaders in the US against it as a solution to the problems then faced. The moderate conservative wing of the movement called for a faithful execution of the Clayton and Sherman Anti-Trust Acts and a real breakup of all existing monopolies in favor of a true open market. This alternative was also not seriously considered — most likely due to the adoption of the moderate liberal position by Theodore Roosevelt, then the sitting president of the US. The moderate liberal position (by far the most popular position within the movement) called for the strict regulation of the economy at all levels of government. This was the alternative selected by the movement, especially after its endorsement by the president. This alternative as interpreted by the president resulted in the creation of a greatly expended bureaucracy. The president as we have seen created a very large regulatory bureaucracy to affect the reforms called for under the progressive program. The question then became one of who would regulate the regulators? The agencies created by Roosevelt at this time under the reform pressures exerted by the progressive movement were the Interstate Commerce Commission; the Securities and Exchange Commission; and the Bureau of Corporations, later known as the National Labor Relations Board. The Bureau of Corporations was created to allow the voluntary participation of large corporations in the elimination of abuses to avoid legal prosecution. Many large corporations such as US Steel and International Harvester quickly came on board. Those who did not, such as Standard Oil, found themselves subject to later prosecution and breakup. This lesson was not lost on the business community and quickly led to the marriage of big business and big government. In the end, the most important legacy of Theodore Roosevelt may be his recognition of the true import of the grassroots concerns of the Progressive Movement and his ability to turn it to account in the protection of big business and professional politicians in the United States.

The focus of the progressive movement in specifically social issues was on the attempt to involve the state and local governments in the direct solution of these problems. This approach was received with the full support of both the liberal and conservative elements within and outside the movement itself. This support, however, was limited to the public and did not flow also to the professional politicians that held public office especially on the federal level. The major issues undertaken by the progressive movement included the promotion of child labor laws; the promotion of a shortened work day; the promotion of health and safety legislation affecting the work site; and the promotion of unemployment and disability compensation, as well as old age pensions. The attempt by the progressives to involve the state and local governments directly in these issues was defeated mainly by actions taken at the federal level. The state and local governments were very interested in playing a key role in these issues as is shown by the widespread passage of child labor laws, health and safety acts, and the shortening of the work day to eight hours. The Supreme Court, however, through its decisions, made it impossible for a consistent local legislation to deal with the problems of unemployment, disability, and old age pensions, ruling them to be an invasion of the federal duty to regulate interstate commerce. Federal legislation also prevented an aggressive stance from being taken at the local level. As a result, the momentum of the progressive movement shifted from the state and local governments to the federal government, especially denoted by the formation of a national progressive party. The gains made in the areas of child labor, health and safety at the work site and a shortened work day were all incorporated into federal legislation. But action on unemployment and disability compensation and old age pensions was put on hold until the advent of the Great Depression. It remains an open question, one that will need to be answered by an effective world government, whether or not republican principles can successfully resolve major social issues. Equally open to debate is whether republican principles will be more effective in solving these problems than has been the case with the use of the welfare state (state capitalism) principles. It is beyond doubt that the lack of federal support for the republican approach initially brought forward by the progressive movement forced the solution of the involved social issues in the US into a systematic state capitalism rather than a republican format. The point is that individualism is opposed to collectivist planning and the risk is that individualism will be lost (as pointed out by Hayek).

The administration of Theodore Roosevelt represents most clearly the contesting philosophical positions in relation to the progressive movement. While many of the reforms advocated by the movement were found to be acceptable on all levels of government the proactive bias of the movement was to a large degree contested by the conservative elements within and without the movement. At the state and local level the conservative bias was especially strong and acted as a cautionary factor in the establishment of the reforms that were actually accepted from the movement. In short, the manner in which the liberal reforms promoted by the movement were eventually accepted represented a compromise between the extreme positions within the society at large. The compromise was of course the result of the influence of moderate liberal and conservative elements on both sides of the issues. All in all it is arguable that the progressive movement represents party politics at its best, i.e., reason seemed always capable of fashioning a workable compromise leading to real reform where needed.

It has come to be accepted that Theodore Roosevelt was not a true reformer at heart. His personal philosophy was pitted against the use of legislation, particularly at the federal level, for the solution of social issues. His practical nature apparently led Roosevelt to feel that all flexibility in handling such issues was lost when they were reduced to statutory law. As a result his administration relied on the use of executive order to gain the flexibility he desired. His case-by-case approach in the use of the executive order put him in lock step with the Supreme Court which also used a case by case approach. Both approaches, however, tended to disrupt the one advantage of handling these issues on the federal level, that is, the standardization of the solutions attempted across the Union. It is also true that overall standardization in many cases is not needed, indeed, can even be harmful. In this connection Roosevelt's reputation as a "trust buster" is a case in point. In his first administration, which in fact was the completion of McKinley's term in office after his assassination, twenty five cases were carefully selected as representations of earlier anti-trust violations or specific interstate commerce violations. The first case was against the Northern Securities Company a large railroad trust which had been charged with rate fixing and other anti-trust violations. In this case the trust was broken up but quickly reformed itself under a different form of corporate linking. In total out of the twenty five cases brought the vast majority were settled by forcing the companies to cooperate with the federal government in curbing the most noticeable abuses. This cooperation was brought about by the creation of the Bureau of Corporations under executive order. It is interesting to note that his reputation as a trust buster was based upon the one instance in which a company was broken up even though that company re-formed almost immediately. In fact, outside of the American Tobacco Company mentioned earlier Roosevelt did not attempt to break up any companies for violation of anti-trust violations; but did in the case of Standard Oil break one up for failure to cooperate with the Bureau of Corporations. A second issue revolved around the settlement of a long standing coal mine strike. Roosevelt through his threats of regulation under the interstate commerce commission, another body created by means of an executive order, forced the mine owners and striking miners to accept federal mediation of the dispute. Neither side got all that they had fought for but according to the words of Roosevelt the settlement was a "square deal." In the only other case that led to the dissolution of a company the Supreme Court reversed its former position in regard to what constituted business in interstate commerce. A suit had been brought against Swift and Company (a meat packing monopoly) for violation of interstate commerce rules. Prior to this case the Supreme Court had held that if the manufacturing process of a company were all conducted within the borders of one state that company was not subject to the interstate commerce regulations. Swift did in fact conduct all of its manufacturing processes within the border of one state; but the Supreme Court held that since the products manufactured by Swift traveled in interstate commerce that the company was subject to interstate commerce regulation. Roosevelt as a direct result of this decision created by executive order the Department of Commerce and Labor within which was the Bureau of Corporations.

The progressive program especially as it was applied to state and local governments is a clear example of how republican principles can operate under the US system of government. On the federal level Roosevelt's personal preference for federal control brought the grassroots aspect of the progressive movement to a dead end. A later example of a progressive type of republicanism can be found in the European Union. The EU began as a singular attempt to unify decision making in one economic area, that is, the coal and steel industry. Six nations joined in a treaty that allowed a common regulation of the activities occurring in this industry. It turned out to be a huge success and later treaties expanded the union into areas involving all levels of economic activity. This was done at the national and local level and even today does not involve a true federal (central) government. It remains a modified federal system with the central authorities having no real power over the member nations. The central authority operates on the basis of a general administrative organization that is responsible for overall planning in the areas of economic policy, international diplomacy, military actions, issues involving human rights, and issues involving social welfare. In these areas it is not only responsible for overall planning but also for the enforcement of the rules accepted by the member nations. The plans, however, once accepted are enforced locally by the members that wish to participate. A good example of how this system operates can be found in the establishment of a unitary monetary system under the Euro. The general administration established the plan for the conversion of the local currencies into the common currency known as the Euro. The participating members however were left to execute and accomplish the actual conversion in the manner best suited to them individually. Some members, such as Great Britain, did not adopt the Euro as a replacement for their national currency but did adopt a system whereby the national currency could be indexed to the Euro. Some non-members, such as Russia, converted to the use of the Euro almost to the extinction of their local currency.

It seems very likely that the world union due to the size and complexity of the issues involved will be forced to accept similar republican strategies to those used by the progressive movement and the EU — especially in the economic and social arenas. The question of course remains as to whether a world union could be operated on the basis of a modified intergovernmentalism similar to that in operation in the EU. The member nations have to date been very reluctant to delegate their individual sovereign decision making powers in the political arena. This power is still nationally exercised on the European level through the European Council. Currently it is becoming clear that the use of the supranational agencies of the EU as decision makers in the economic and social arenas is also putting greatly increased pressure to also include the political arena. The EU did in fact attempt to draft and ratify a Constitution that would have created a true federalized government. However the Constitution was defeated mainly due to a concern about loss of sovereignty. It is unlikely that another attempt will be made in the near future although the current system remains somewhat awkward and the citizens of the EU are complaining of the lack of transparency and access to the European level.

Whether the world union is organized as a true federalized government or on the basis of a modified intergovernmentalism the use of progressive ideals could be seriously revisited with the expectation that their use would give the world union the transparency and access that is lacking in both the US and EU systems.

CHAPTER 8. THE BEGINNINGS OF UNRESTRAINED CAPITALISM

The first Wilson administration saw the passage of several portions of the progressive or new nationalism platform. First, the Underwood-Simmons Tariff Act of 1913 reduced the tariff across the board to twenty four percent — one of the lowest in US history. This was as we have seen one of the major planks in the progressive movement's platform. Second, the revenue lost due to the reduction of the tariff was replaced by the ratification of the 16th amendment in 1913 establishing the first income and inheritance tax in the US. This amendment had been introduced during the Taft administration and had more to do with Roosevelt than with Wilson. It established a seven percent tax on all incomes over $500,000. Third, the Congress passed the Owen Federal Reserve Act of 1913. This legislation established twelve regional banks that were privately owned by the member banks. All nationally chartered banks automatically became members, while state and locally chartered banks could voluntarily join the system if they chose. The system was intended to provide a pool of available capital as a reserve to be used to flatten the financial cycles which had erupted in the economy. Each member bank was required to subscribe six percent of its capital to the Federal Reserve Bank to which it belonged. The member banks were also required to maintain a certain percentage of their assets with the Federal Reserve Banks. The Federal Reserve Banks in turn were only allowed to conduct business with their members. They were strictly prohibited from doing business in the private sector including direct business loans.

The chief business of the Federal Reserve Banks was to discount the member banks loans that is the member bank loans were taken over by the Federal Reserve Banks at a discounted rate; and the member banks were given Federal Reserve Notes (essentially paper money) with which they could make new loans. The Federal Reserve Notes were based upon a forty percent evaluation against government gold in Fort Knox; and sixty percent on commercial paper (the promissory notes taken over from the member banks by the Federal Reserve Banks). The rediscount rate was set by the Federal Reserve Board which was composed of three members chosen by the federally chartered banks and six members chosen by the remaining member banks. The rediscount rate was intended to be the tool that would either expand or deflate credit availability as needed. The higher the rediscount rate the more restricted would be the general availability of credit and vice versa.

This system was the progressive platform's attempt to relieve the financial concentration on Wall Street in particular the financial monopoly of the J.P. Morgan holding company. It was also intended to bring stability to both the monetary and investment banking systems. This system is still in place today in the US and represents one of the most important economic tools available to the federal government. It is debatable whether or not it has had the desired effect in reducing financial concentration in Wall Street. The two or three largest banking institutions in the US have been able to consolidate under their control a large share of the banking institutions within the US. They are based on Wall Street and are still controlled to a large degree by private family interests such as the Rockefeller family. It is true, however, that the system has brought a great degree of stability to both the monetary and investment banking systems.

Fourth, the Wilson administration initiated an aggressive program in the area of anti-trust. It began with the creation of the Federal Trade Commission (advocated by Roosevelt in the campaign) intended to act as a watchdog over illegal restraint of trade. The Commission replaced the Bureau of Corporations and its reliance on voluntary cooperation by the private sector companies. In short, Wilson attempted to divorce big government from big business and to end the earlier marriage that had been made between them. The Clayton Anti-Trust Act of 1914 specifically listed the actions that were to be prohibited including price fixing, tying agreements, interlocking corporate directorates, and corporate acquisitions of competitors stock. The effect of the legislation was immediately watered down by riders attached to the bill at the time of passage. These riders made it difficult to enforce the provisions of the act and made it possible to appoint directors to the commission with less than a burning desire for regulation. This became the standard legislative tactic to reduce the effectiveness of executive power especially in relation to the use of the executive order. The use of riders was also effective in reducing the power of the executive to force legislation through Congress when his party held a majority in both houses. Labor had initially won a victory by having itself exempted from coverage under the Federal Trade Commission rules but the Supreme Court shortly repealed the exemption and brought the labor movement under the Act. All of this legislation pointed to the fact that the liberal wing of the Democratic Party was now in the majority, but on the other hand, it also pointed to the fact that the conservative wing of the Republican Party had enough strength to water down most of the legislation passed. Today it is true that the various regulatory agencies, departments, and bureaus are still dependent for their effectiveness on the quality of the directors appointed (by the president) to head them. At times the directors are aggressively in favor of regulation and pursue that objective with vigor; while at other times they are solidly against regulation and do not attempt to enforce the legislation that is on the books. Unfortunately the people at large have little or no say in who is appointed to run the various regulatory institutions. This latter fact has resulted in some serious economic and social problems within the US society. During the remainder of the Wilson administration this legislation was essentially a dead letter.

The progressive movement obtained its zenith under the Wilson administration through the Democratic Party's ability to win over the remains of the Bull Moose Party. The liberal takeover of the Democratic Party resulted in a rapid passage of the above legislation but also began the trend towards each party's platform tending to look identical to each other. This tended to be true regardless of the wing that held the actual majority in each party. In relation to this trend the progressive movement had already begun to show signs of its limitations. For example, the initiative and referendum movement, that were intended to expand the publics' participation in politics, had become noticeably infected with political manipulation by professional politicians. The public also became aware that the progressive measures had allowed professional politicians, especially in urban governments, to take power without the benefit of public elections or public control. The conservative call for limited government is due in large part to the recognition that those in power are often not accountable to the public at large. The early debate between the two philosophical positions was put on the back burner with advent of World War I.

In relation to foreign affairs the personal moralistic idealism espoused by Wilson set the tone for US participation in World War I. Wilson apparently believed that it was his personal duty, as well as the duty of the US, to advance the cause of democracy and justice as he understood them throughout the world. He began by being influenced by his Secretary of State William Jennings Bryan who had scrapped the dollar diplomacy instituted by Taft. Dollar Diplomacy was replaced by a policy of active intervention whenever possible. In Mexico, for example, the Wilson administration under the urging of Bryan intervened militarily in a civil war to "insure" that a "proper" government was installed. The "proper" government would not be the usual Latin American dictatorship but would be a democratic system based on the US model.

This type of intervention in Mexico, and in the region generally, did bring some degree of stability to the area; but it also brought with it a good deal of animosity on the part of Latin Americans towards the US. It would seem that the US has still not taken heed of the lessons learned early in the Wilson administration. The US continues to intervene on exactly the same terms especially in the Middle East and Africa. It must be pointed out that this policy was not an official policy of the government of the US during the Wilson administration but was merely the reflection of the personal policies of the president and the secretary of state. Today the policy has become a part of the US foreign affairs ideology and the official policy of the government as part of US military hegemony. More will be said concerning this policy when we look more closely at the current state of affairs in Africa and the Middle East.

This approach would carry over in the US response to the outbreak of World War I. Wilson in line with his idealism did everything in his power to isolate the US from involvement in the shooting part of the war. The world however had already become much too interdependent to allow a major player to sit on the sidelines. Even though the US managed during most of the war to evade participation militarily it did have to commit itself to the allied cause. Prior to actual military involvement the US was a major contributor of money, military equipment, and consumer goods to the allied forces. It is one of Wilson's most important personal contradictions that he sought to remain outside the war militarily but wished to be a major factor in the establishment of peace. As it actually turned out, the military involvement of the US, although coming very late in the war, proved to be a major factor in the defeat of the German forces; while the US played a very minor role in the establishment of the succeeding peace negotiations. Although early in the war the US attempted to keep the seas open to neutral trade against depravations by both the British and German navies she was largely unsuccessful. With the withdrawal of Russia from the war after the Bolshevik revolution in October of 1917 both the British and Germans tried to avoid US shipping in an attempt to influence the US to favor their position. The vast significance of the Russian Revolution was underplayed at the time but soon would enter into full world recognition. By 1917 it was apparent that the US was not going to be able to avoid military involvement and a feverish attempt was begun to provide the arms, equipment, and men that had been stubbornly refused prior to this point. This was the first time that such a large scale propaganda campaign was used to justify the US entry into war. There had been deceptions practiced, such as the behind the scenes maneuvers in the war in Florida against Spain, and the war in Texas and California against the Mexicans, but now such openly propagandistic moves reached a new level. Wilson branded the Germans the natural enemy of liberty, and in Wilson's own words, "the world must be made safe for democracy. Its peace must be planted upon the tested foundations of political liberty." The US has used similar vocabulary in relation to the Gulf War and in the invasion of Iraq as well as the general war on terrorism.

The war brought with it some severe changes on the domestic front. First, over four million men were withdrawn from the work force to serve in the military. Their place in the work force was taken by a massive recruitment effort by the Northern industrial complex in the South. These efforts resulted in the migration of 400,000 African-Americans to take jobs in the North. This was a very large and very rapid, as well as a permanent, shift in population demographics in the US. It is of interest to note that the willingness of African-Americans to migrate north to fill the jobs was both economic and patriotic especially considering their reception when they arrived. The success of the recruitment efforts was in large part due to the feeling of patriotic pride in the African-Americans in response to the propaganda campaign of the federal authorities. In return however they were met in the North with serious discrimination both in the working and housing environments. In addition, one million women entered the work force, however, most of these recruits were single and with the end of the war they returned to the home. As an aside, by 1930 the number of African-Americans living permanently in the North and Midwest was five times the number that had lived in these areas in 1910. Second, the economy came under a much more strict regulation as a result of the war than had been the case with the progressive legislation that had been passed. The Wilson administration created the War Industries Board, which was given the power to fix wages, prices, and production in all industries that produced war related products. It was the most intrusive invasion of the government into the private sector in US history up to that time. Third, it is interesting to look at the public reaction to the federal use of propaganda. One should note the similarity of the reaction to that which has been unleashed in response to the war on terrorism. The federal expression of propaganda was quickly absorbed by the public and became evident in the following reactions. The public schools dropped all German language instruction; symphony orchestras dropped the works of Beethoven and Bach from their repertoires; but the public reaction stopped short of interring Americans of German ancestry. On the lighter side, sauerkraut became "liberty cabbage"; German measles became "liberty measles"; and dachshunds became "liberty pups." The same type of reaction occurred when the French government refused to allow US planes to fly over French territory to attack Libya during the 1960s; French fries became "liberty fries" (later re-dubbed freedom fries) and the French kiss became the "liberty kiss." On a more serious note, the federal reaction included such actions as the passage of an Espionage and Sedition Act which made it illegal to do or say anything that could be interpreted as against the administration policies concerning the war. Even the Supreme Court took an extreme position on the issue in the case of Schenck v. The United States. The court ruled that it was constitutional for the government to suspend the right of free speech during wartime if such speech presented a clear and present danger. In this case the "clear and present danger" was the circulation of anti-war leaflets among the armed forces. In Abrams v. The United States, the court upheld the conviction of a man who was distributing pamphlets opposing intervention in the Russian Revolution. This type of reaction, although it has never been successful in accomplishing its goal, was seen again during the Viet Nam conflict; and most recently in connection with the official policy related to the war on terrorism as exemplified by the passage of the Patriot Act and the institution of the Department of Homeland Security.

The US under the Wilson administration had taken the first steps toward the creation of unrestrained capitalism, that is to say, the system that became known as unrestrained capitalism came about with the environment established at the end of World War I. The production capacity of the US had been greatly increased to provide the materials and goods needed by the allies in the actual shooting war. They were increased even further when the US made its short entry into the war.

If a world government were to be instituted in the near future several regional issues would need to be resolved before any serious discussion of total disarmament could take place. In relation to Eastern Europe the issue has become moot with the inclusion of the nations associated with the former Soviet Union into the European Union. However, there is still local concern in this area over the future of Russia. NATO is still in operation however it has been converted to more of a political tool than a military one. The EU, as well as the US, saw reasons to keep NATO intact, although its purpose has lately become less clear in relation to its former rational. Whatever national self-determination issues remain should be submitted to final arbitration either within the European Union or by an outside power at the request of the Union.

In relation to the Middle East, the situation is nowhere near as well defined. The ongoing question of Arab-Israeli relations; the military actions currently underway in both Afghanistan and Iraq; and the issues of sovereignty in the area appear to defy resolution. The first requirement will be the full withdrawal of all US military personnel from both Afghanistan and Iraq. If peacekeeping troops are still needed in these two countries, then they should be provided under the auspices of the new world government. The next step, regardless of the outcome, will be to allow these two nations to determine the type of government that will rule them and whether or not they wish to join the world union. Although many factors will be involved in this choice of government, it is likely that both peoples will make their decision based on their own needs and their own understanding of the world environment. Some type of arbitration system within the world government will need to be installed to deal with the issues of self-determination in relation to the Kurds, the Palestinians, and other minority peoples in the area. The removal of foreign troops would likely reduce the use of violence by insurrectionist groups. Once the right to self determination has been assured, any such violent insurrections would be treated through the use of global level mediation and military action if necessary.

This would be in line with the policy that all insurrection under a world government would be handled at the national level unless help is requested from the general government. This may also be the approach that needs to be taken in relation to international crime, such as drug trafficking. These problems are complicated and multi-faceted but they are by no means incapable of resolution. These problems may initially be the most pressing as well as being the most complicated. This will be especially true if for whatever reason the nation involved does not request help from the central government. In that case, if violence is involved, a procedure for ending the violence will need to be put in place.

In the case of the Korean Peninsula, the issue again boils down to a case of national self determination. It appears that the people of both North and South Korea would over time support a reunification of the country. The question, of course, is how? The problem is very similar to the one that existed between East and West Germany. As long as opposing political ideological stands are taken reunification will not be possible. With the demise of the Soviet Union, the opportunity arose to discuss the possibility of a reunification of East and West Germany. After much effort the two Germanys were in fact reunited and seem to be on a stable path to joint success as a nation. As long as the same ideological polarity exists on the Korean Peninsula the reunification of the two Koreas will not occur. However, with the removal of international pressures, a solution to this problem along reunification lines may become possible. It is possible also that the current separation of the peninsula will be permanent even under a world government, but that choice must be made by the Koreans themselves.

When one looks at the situation on the African continent the solution to the existing problems is not immediately evident. In most areas of the continent the problems are not only man-made but natural. The natural problems caused by draught, disease, and other calamities can be handled through the provision of large scale and effective aid programs instituted by a world government. The man-made problems, however, are not solvable through the offering of money, equipment, or advice. They are in their own way problems of national self-determination written large. The vast diversity of tribal, ethnic, religious, and customary distinctions that are recognized on the continent make the construction of a traditional nation-state almost impossible, especially under an immediate establishment of a liberal democratic government. However, with the institution of a world government the size, composition, and economic viability of a nation will be less important than the stability of the government in control and its effective fulfillment of its social role. Although not completely accurate the nations within the world union will be in much the same position as the current states of the US and the national members of the EU. Their importance as state and local governmental units is not truly national but rather in the role they play in providing for the immediate welfare of their citizens. Africa for many centuries has been treated as not much more than a huge natural resource mine. The people, and their societies, were treated as strict dependencies and denied their right to natural development. As a result the problems will only be solved by massive programs aimed at the elimination of poverty and ignorance. These programs will need to target widespread poverty, widespread communicable diseases, the lack of permanent infrastructure, including sanitation and potable water, conservation of natural resources, and widespread educational programs. These programs will need to utilize local labor in every way possible to provide for long-term meaningful employment and self-esteem. In essence this is the type of aid now being distributed by the EU. The EU is currently the largest donor of foreign aid for developmental purposes. In the end, however, Africans will need to resolve African problems, whether they be poverty, disease, or political self-determination, regardless of whether in the short term the solutions include the establishment of a liberal democratic government. Some system such as the one used in the EU may have to be instituted to qualify those who wish to join the Union, i.e., applicants may be required to be operating under a democratic government and to have got control of their economic institutions.

The history of the US up to this point seems to point to several policies that might need to be reconsidered in relation to world government. First, a reconsideration of the role played by regulation of the economy, civil rights, and governmental expenditures should be taken. It seems to be accepted that the overall planning and legislative needs of a successful regulatory scheme should be instituted at the highest level possible. This means that the central government should be responsible for determining the overall need for regulation in the economy, civil rights, and expenditures, among others, and that the central government should be responsible for putting the legislation in place that will accomplish these goals. However, unlike the US experience, it is also generally accepted that the implementation and enforcement of the regulations themselves should be accomplished at the lowest possible level of government. It is at this level that the problems are personally known to the regulators in place, and where flexibility in interpretation and enforcement of the rules on the books should take place. It is at this level that the public, if this is possible at all, can be most involved in who does the regulating. It is, in fact, the only place that they can effectively take place. In our case the world government can take advantage of the already existing regulatory institutions at the national and local levels greatly reducing its own bureaucratic needs and costs. Second, the use of any type of civil rights abatement laws, such as, Sedition Acts, Detainment Acts, or others must be avoided whenever a problem solution is attempted. Such actions not only fail to obtain the end intended but they also deter the implementation of the most creative and successful solutions to the problem. The most recent use of such laws in the US was the passage of the Patriot Act in response to the attack of terrorists on New York City in 2001. Third, a clear recognition of the vital interplay between government, religion, customs, and manners must be obtained through a comprehensive program of education. It is vital to the success of world government that a real acceptance of diversity in religion, culture, customs, manners, and other human adaptions be fully accepted and promoted. Indeed, the one aspect of regulation that must be avoided is the use of collectivist type planning if individual human rights are to be protected in the most sensitive areas. In the most troubled areas of the world, it may in fact be most cost effective and efficient to promote the development of the prerequisites of democracy before requiring the institution of a democratic government.

CHAPTER 9. THE UNILATERAL GROWTH OF UNRESTRAINED CAPITALISM

The importance of the labor and civil unrest that occurred in the early post war period can be found in the fact that they represent a reaction to the progressive programs implemented during the preceding two decades. The regulation policies of the progressive movement, at least in the eyes of the workers and their unions, had not succeeded in alleviating even the worst abuses committed against labor. The squalid conditions in the steel and meat packing industries would seem to attest to the accuracy of this feeling. The same general perception was seen to be an accurate assessment of the attitude of those suffering from racial and ethnic discrimination. The government attempt to blame communism was seen by all three groups as something of a bad joke. Those involved in the labor unrest, the violent acts of racial discrimination, or the equally open discrimination against immigrants knew that there were no communist involved in their actions; although some of the tactics used by the Bolsheviks in 1918 may have been consciously adopted. In fact it was widely believed by all three groups that the violence and emotionally charged strikes were the result of the failure of the government to enforce progressive programs and a general sell out by the government of their rights. This general combativeness was to change quickly once the economy began to rebound.

The fact that social problems generally, and civil rights problems in particular, tend to become lost in periods where everyone is benefiting from a vibrant growing economy should be noted. With the onset of a boom economy after 1921 the urgency of the labor and civil rights unrest faded into the background in the public awareness although all of these issues had remained unresolved. The reason for this phenomenon seems to rest on the fact that during periods of booming economic expansion the position of the lower classes, and probably the lower middle classes, seems to improve more rapidly than does that of the upper classes. This improvement tends to be credited to the policies of the political party that is in power at the time that it occurs. This appears to be true even though the former conditions remain unchanged or even become worse during the boom period. Under the conditions that had been in place from about 1913 until early 1922 the public had felt significantly repressed; but with the release of the economy they reacted with unbounded elation. This was the basis of the period between 1922 and 1930 becoming known as the "era of good feelings" or the "roaring twenties." That is to say, there was a widespread feeling that everyone's position in life was rapidly improving and would continue to improve indefinitely. Two important social movements of long lasting significance began with the era of good feelings. Both tended to underscore the conservative attitude that accompanied the public belief in their improving status. The first was a grassroots movement labeled "nativism." Generally speaking the nativism movement gave public expression to the Ultra-Conservative (fundamentalist) bias within the general conservative philosophy. In this case it spawned such right wing activities as the Ku Klux Klan and other such groups. The Klan had been in a fifty year decline from its earlier violent attempts to suppress the African-Americans, Catholics and Jewish peoples. It was given a second life by the nativist call for a return to our Anglo-Saxon roots. The majority of the movement, however, was much more moderate than the Klan fringe. The moderate portion of the movement was able to force the passage of very strict immigration laws; the removal of federal restrictions against racial discrimination in housing and labor at the state and local levels; and the general discrimination against immigrant right to work laws. This subtle brand of discrimination still exists within the US and to some degree throughout the world. It can be effectively countered only by removing the causes that determine an individual's prejudice against another based on perceptions of fear, mistrust, and sense of belonging. These factors are most easily applied when the person one is prejudiced against has a different colored skin, language, religion, or other obvious cultural differentiation. The second movement came generally to be known as militant

Protestantism. It, like nativism, called for a return to a more primitive belief such as that espoused by the early Pilgrims and Quakers. This movement centered on the teaching of the theory of evolution in the public schools. The movement called for the replacement of the teaching of evolution with the creation story as it was told in the Bible. In relation to the teaching of creation the movement called for a complete ban on the teaching of evolution in the public schools. The Supreme Court reviewed the conviction of a teacher in Tennessee for violation of a state statute banning the teaching of evolution in the Tennessee public school system. The Court upheld the conviction of the teacher following the dictates of the militant Protestant movement. The movement in this case had won the battle in court but lost the war. The trial had brought worldwide attention to the case; in particular, it had focused attention on the fundamentalist claims made by the movement. These claims included a statement that the Biblical stories of creation, as well as, those involving Jonah and the Whale, the Garden of Eden, and others were literally true. This stance caused a great deal of ridicule to be brought against the movement not only in the US but worldwide. In other areas the movement was much more successful. The movement's strong incentive for the prohibition on the sale and use of alcohol resulted in the 18th amendment. This amendment made it illegal to produce, distribute, or use alcoholic beverages anywhere in the US. Here again the movement won the legal battle but lost the war. Although the amendment was a dead letter almost from the time of its ratification its importance cannot be underrated. The amendment coupled with its evasion can be credited with a generalized willingness to break the law on the part of the public at large. It also led to a great deal of strengthening in the position of organized crime who sought to benefit from evading the law. The intent of the 18th amendment was to act as a piece-meal experiment in removing one moral cause of a weakening morality in the US as perceived by the fundamentalist fringe. Its actual result was exactly the opposite, that is, it led to a greater willingness, without remorse, to break the law and a general lowering of esteem for authority. In the end the amendment was repealed with the passage of the 21st amendment in 1933. In combination these two movements were responsible for a general decay in religious intensity and obedience to authority within the society as a whole.

The rigid programs promoted by the movement back to "nativism" and "primitive religion" had the opposite effect in the environment that existed in the 1920s. They brought the public awareness to the point at which questions were asked about the very fundamental aspects of life in the US. During the "roaring twenties" a massive shift occurred in the public attitudes towards several general areas of traditional values. First, in relation to the arena of human sexuality, sex became a topic of everyday conversation rather than something that remained hidden behind closed doors. Many of the traditional roles of parenthood were transferred to the factory (child care programs), the school (inculcation of traditional morality), or the government (a substitution of personal for corporate responsibility). The shifting of responsibilities away from individuals allowed for the growth of a greater personal socialization for both men and women. One aspect of this new awakening was the realization that a real dichotomy existed between the social attitudes found in the urban versus the rural environment. This dichotomy was expressed in the open distaste in the urban environment for the traditional values espoused within the more rural segments of society. This distaste is best described by the derogatory names given to those who lived in the rural areas, i.e., "hicks," "bumpkins," etc. The rural areas expressed their dislike of the open virtues of the urban areas with equally derogatory names, such as, "city slickers" and "city dandy." In statistical terms the dichotomy was best expressed by the increasing freedom of expression on the part of women coupled with the rapidly increasing rate of divorce in the urban environment. On the other hand, those in the rural areas offered the continuation of the attitude of woman as homemaker coupled with a reliance on religion. The trends begun in the 1920s, including the US love affair with contracting debt and evading the implications of authority, were temporarily put on hold by the advent of the Great Depression and World War II.

One nascent movement that began during the twenties was not dampened by the depression and war, that is, the public interest in science commonly designated as the "new modernism." This movement was inaugurated by the popularization of scientific theories, especially those of Albert Einstein. New Modernism was a movement revolving around the breakdown of traditional authority comparable to what occurred in the Italian Renaissance in the 15th century. It included the development of atonal music by such composers as Alton Berg and the development of abstract art such as the work of Pablo Picasso; and also the even more exotic stream of consciousness writings of men like James Joyce. In each the individual was glorified in their ability to handle the non-rational aspects of daily life. For a short period (until 1930), creativity was driven by a desire to work outside of the paradigm of standards found in traditional creativity. It seemed as if the goal was the establishment of new rules that were in direct opposition to those that had become traditional within the various arts affected.

Once again, the Great Depression and World War II would blunt the public interest in these movements, although they continued in select circles to be appreciated and developed. For the general public the primary effect of the progressive movement between 1895 and 1930 seems to have been the development of a more liberal attitude and a shift away from traditional standards in a variety of fields. The phenomenon was worldwide and gathered strength as time passed. On the down side, many people seem to have concluded that the individual is not personally responsible for his or her actions — that such actions are determined by some immutable law of nature, some greater social processes — that is, government in the field of politics, science in the field of morals, evolution in the field of social customs, and randomness in the general development of the universe as a whole. It came to seem that none of these processes were within the control of human individuals or even within the control of mankind itself but rather were determined by events within the universe. The result was a public (at least large segments of the public) acceptance of such social and economic programs that diminished respect for the individual, from Soviet Communism to German Nazism, Italian and Japanese Fascism, and unrestrained capitalism that all soon showed what they could do to the individual.

As far as our concern with a world union or world government it may be difficult to see the relevance of the public reaction to World War I and the Roaring Twenties. There is, for example, no way in which a prediction can be made as to the specific events that will occur upon the establishment of an effective world government. However it is very possible that large scale economic repercussions will accompany such programs as general disarmament. It is also very possible that another widespread devastation of human life will occur, similar to that occasioned by the Spanish Flu. Pandemics are a modern fact of life. The world government will have to relieve to the best of its ability the effects of such events.

It is also likely, on the other hand, that a proactive response by the world government to pandemics and other natural disasters as well as to the effects of disarmament and pollution clean-up will unleash unprecedented economic activity. It will be the duty of the world government in this case to ensure the equitable distribution of this activity among the world's peoples. In the less developed areas of the world this increased economic activity could lead to a reaction similar to that of the Roaring Twenties, that is, a lessening of reliance on traditional beliefs found in religion, tribal customs, ethnic prejudice and other social customs — and their replacement with a more objective, practical approach. This response could and should be supported, if it occurs, through the institution of long-term projects aimed at eliminating poverty and ignorance. It is with the establishment of a firm economic and social foundation that one finds the basis for stable democratic government.

It certainly appears that the world union will also be faced with a generalized lack of respect for traditional authority bases, such as government, religion, and customs among others. This problem can only be approached on the basis of education and the establishment of authority worthy of respect.

The processes that allowed unrestrained capitalism to expand during the 1920s came to completion during the 1930s. In the US the first sign that all was not well in paradise arrived with the stock market debacle of October 1929. The weakness of the US economy, and the world market as a whole, was based on the fact that a long period of excessive profits had been generated by the repression of wages and costs. Coupled with the generation of excessive profits and the colonial monopolization of the world's natural resources the profits were invested in the uncontrolled growth of production. This in turn resulted in a glutting of the world's markets with goods that could not be sold at any price. The investment practices that were followed were supported by an irrational belief that production could never keep pace with demand. By 1929 production had far outstripped demand causing the industrial nations to respond by setting high tariffs, aggravated savings programs, and tax policies aimed at stimulating the purchasing power of the public. These policies in total brought the various industrial economies to the point that a serious depression was inevitable.

The collapse of the US stock market was a rather late sign of the trouble facing the world's strongest economies. President Herbert Hoover seemed not to understand the significance of this sign in relation to the industrial economies of the world. He felt that a short-term regional action by the US industries most seriously involved was all that was needed, that is to say, Hoover felt that it could be resolved through voluntary private-sector actions. He called upon private industry to keep their businesses open, to maintain the current level of wages, and to spread the work load among their employees to relieve the effect of unemployment. Hoover consistently resisted any direct intervention by the federal government towards rectifying the suffering that was beginning to appear within the US society at large. All of Hoover's requests were ignored by both the business and labor communities.

In hindsight, the Hoover policy appears to have been a rational one. It is open to debate whether or not a strong acceptance of the Hoover policy by the business and labor communities would have alleviated the most devastating effects of the depression, at least in the US. It is likely that a voluntary cut in rates of production coupled with a resistance to wage and cost increases would have allowed the US economy to adjust to the new levels of production needed. This approach would have meant that the industrial sector would have had, for a period of time, to use its excessive profits to maintain their existing employment base and to revamp their production facilities for a more realistic production capability. It would also have meant that, for a period of time, the labor unions and the workers themselves would have had to accept a freeze on wages and additional hiring. It is probable that these actions would have been at least as effective as those actually taken and in the long run would have been much less expensive.

When the private sector, both business and labor, refused to act voluntarily in response to Hoover's request, he instituted several direct federal intervention programs. Hoover instituted a rather modest expenditure of monies on public works projects. However, at this early stage in the depression, the spending increases at the federal level were offset by an equal or greater reduction of state and local spending in the same areas. The result was that unemployment and the existing programs to aid those suffering from loss of jobs remained about the same. Hoover next turned to the Federal Reserve in an attempt to loosen credit. This, as may be remembered, was to be one of the major functions performed by the Federal Reserve System when it was created. The Federal Reserve due to a sustained period of lax regulation during the 1920s was not in a position to respond to Hoover's request. The credit system had already become swamped in relation to its assets on hand, i.e., both the business and consumer sectors of the private economy had gone on a credit binge for over a decade and this credit could not now be paid. The situation was made even worse by the fact that all levels of government had also joined in on the credit binge. The Federal Reserve could not reduce the discount rate any lower than its already existing level which was too low in relation to the existing economic conditions. Lastly, Hoover lowered taxes in an attempt to stimulate spending but this measure failed to produce any spending beyond the purchase of necessities.

The Hoover administration's reaction to the economic downturn all seem to have been within the traditional response mechanisms that were at that time in place. All the previous legislation that had been passed intending to flatten the economic cycles was being tried one after another. Due to the defective implementation and enforcement of this legislation the attempt to use them to counteract the depression was an abject failure. As a result the Hoover administration being the one in power had to take the blame for the fact that the depression had not been stopped; and that the suffering caused by it had not been relieved. The midterm elections of 1930 returned a solid majority for the democrats in the House of Representatives and a large minority position in the Senate. This was enough to block any further attempts by the Republicans to pass legislation to counter the depression. The mid-term elections also gave the democrats a solid majority in the executive and legislative branches of state and local government. The Hoover administration had become a "lame duck" and quickly retreated to its position of calling for private sector action, i.e., in accepting a do nothing position in relation to the depression. Public expenditures were greatly reduced during 1930 and 1931 as a result.

The federal expenditure reductions beginning in 1930 seemed to have been responsible for a rebound of the US economy in 1931. However, at the same time the worldwide significance of the depression became evident with the collapse of the Austrian economy. The failure of the Austrian economy led directly to the failure of most of the economies of Eastern Europe. The US attempted to counter this economic disaster in Eastern Europe by forgiving those governments reparation payments established at the end of World War I. This reaction had the unintended consequence of forcing Europe to abandon the gold standard and to begin to dump US securities. The result as could be expected was a quick depression of the rebounding US economy.

Prior to analyzing the conditions brought about by the Great Depression and World War II it will be profitable to look at the accomplishments obtained by the progressive movement prior to 1929. The first thirty years of the 20th century represent a real desire to obtain a reasonable level of financial responsibility, economic regulation, and personal honesty in public service, as well as, a growing concern over the abuse of civil rights. This was not only indicative of the mood in the US but in the industrialized world generally. By 1920 the progressive movement had been successful especially at the state and local level in bringing about a higher degree of personal honesty in public service, a relatively rational approach to economic regulation, and a real concern for both private and governmental financial responsibility. It can only be surmised as to the effect that this legislation would have had in relation to not only the spending binge of the 1920s but also the most devastating effects of the depression. As it was, however, this legislation was stillborn due to its lackadaisical implementation and very conscious non-enforcement. It is arguable that had the regulatory legislation in particular been properly implemented and enforced that the worse results of unrestrained capitalism in the US would have been avoided, that is, excessive profits, overproduction, and abusive wage and cost control. This in turn would have had a large although completely unknown effect on the economies of other industrial nations. It can, at least, be recommended that an analysis of the relevant factors be made in relation to the rational regulation of the global market upon the institution of a world government especially in regard to any large scale economic upheaval due to disarmament or other factors. In fact, the current world- wide financial crisis has many earmarks that are similar to the factors that led to the Great Depression of the 1930s.

The failure of progressive programs to produce their intended results is complicated. The movement had produced a series of agencies whose responsibilities were to oversee the economy and level out the financial fluctuations as well as to cleanse the economy of corporate abuse. After installation of the agencies, however, the government particularly the federal government appointed only those directors who would hinder the operation of the agencies in their designated fields. This promoted a situation where the US economy was allowed to maintain the status quo in relation to financial irresponsibility and corporate abuse. The corporations were still allowed mainly through monopoly type actions to control wage and cost factors as well as to fix prices at an artificially high level. This resulted in a relatively long period of excessive profits that were reinvested in an irresponsible manner. The movement had also been responsible for a widespread effort to make state and local governmental expenditures more accountable. This had led to the institution of a strict budgeting system (especially on the level of urban government) and efficient expenditure of the funds collected (increase in professionalism represented especially by the city manager system). This program worked well in the highly organized urban environment of the large and medium sized city; however, it could not be directly incorporated into the less dense governmental systems at the rural, state and federal levels. The rural areas at this time could not afford the cost of professional managers nor could they institute a truly accountable budgeting system. The state level, of course, was mostly made up of elected officials. This system could not be changed due to the constitutional guarantee of a republican form of government. In this case professional groups were created outside the formal governmental system that could advise the elected officials. This development was soon incorporated into the civil service system which if desired could be as easily manipulated as any other closed system. It was not until several decades later that the real effect of the budgeting and professional advisor systems became apparent and became a part of the everyday operation of government at both the state and federal level. The bringing of professionalism to both financial responsibility and legislative competence may be the most lasting accomplishments of the progressive movement. By the end of the 1920s the general public had lost interest in the movement as it appeared to them that the programs failed because they were inherently unworkable. Manipulation of voter sentiment by those in power led to the public perception that the programs were faulty rather than that the implementation and enforcement of the programs was faulty. A common failing of the open democratic system must be recognized here, i.e., that legislative intent (in many cases representative of public preference) is capable of being sidestepped through lax implementation procedures and improper attention to enforcement.

In today's world the progressive programs may still have importance in relation to the operation of a world government. It would be worthwhile for example to reconsider the use of the initiative and referendum system — altered to fit today's conditions. It would be expected that such a system would be most efficient at the national and lower levels of government; but might be just as effective at the general governmental level. In some senses this is the manner in which the current general assembly of the United Nations operates, i.e., the general assembly has only the power to initiate demands with the Security Council having the final approval. The same seems to be true of the operation of the European Union, i.e., the general authority has the power to initiate legislative proposals but lacks the final power to implement and enforce them. The power of implementation and enforcement remains with the member nations. The failure of the initiative and referendum system in the US may be directly attributed to the lack of experience and finesse in using it. With a more sophisticated implementation procedure and a stronger control over possible manipulation there is no reason to expect that this type of direct democratic participation would not be successful in reducing the so-called "democratic deficit". It would also be worthwhile to seriously reconsider the city-manager system at all levels of government. This system was intended to provide professional political management at the urban and rural levels of government allowing the replacement of essentially untrained personnel. It was also adapted to the state, national, and general governmental levels by providing professional assistance in the researching of specific problems and the drafting of appropriate legislation to resolve these problems at the higher levels of government (those dependent upon elected officials). In the environment that exists today it is probable that a significant benefit could be derived from the specific training of these professionals under a university discipline. There are currently several nations, including the US, that have specific departments within their university systems for the training of political professionals. In many countries it is already only the highest levels of governmental service that are not occupied by professional politicians. The miserable record of these leaders especially in the recent history of the US makes this a matter of the greatest concern. A system based on the production of well-trained, well-paid, and honest professional politicians subject to the final control of the public through election, particularly at the highest level of government, seems to be the most effective way of guaranteeing competence. This would of course include a budgetary system at every level of government regulated by a professional staff situated outside of the government that it served. It would be a private sector organization again subject to the public scrutiny through compulsory independent audit and periodic reappointment by the executive branch of the government concerned. It is also possible that large private, independent, and professional organizations would be needed to supervise and inspect for compliance in the case of disarmament and pollution control. Such agencies under appropriate public control might also be instrumental in the conservation of natural resources and the use of outer space and cyberspace. All of these professional agencies and agents would be subject to periodic audit of their activities and subject to either reappointment or reelection based upon their resumes.

It is worthy of note that the US has still not adopted the rational outcome of the progressive programs but still relies on a system that creates ad hoc agencies, etc., to belie public demand and which can be left to wither on the vine once public attention has been diverted. This result is usually obtained by the appointment of directors to the agencies created that have less than an ardent desire to accomplish the aims for which the agency was created. This type of response to public concerns is exactly what must be avoided when a world government is instituted. The progressive programs in the US had two contradictory results, that is, they first provided the environment that led to a sustained economic boom in the US economy; and secondly, their inadequate implementation and enforcement failed to institute the intended economic brake which allowed an unrestrained opportunity for reckless corporate growth.

The mood of the public had also changed due to the influence of wartime shortages and controls, as well as, the post-war suffering involved in economic dislocations related to an unplanned demobilization of four million soldiers. The public not only lost interest in the progressive reforms but with the ideal of reform generally. The public was not in a mood to be cajoled into personal moral or ethical action either in their businesses or their individual lives. The public reaction after the end of World War I was to reject the concept of government regulation, as well as, the regulation of the individual by traditional institutions such as the church. The Republican Party's recent adoption of an overall conservative bias was more in tune with the public mood than that of the Democratic Party (in relation to the public's attitude during the decade of the twenties). In addition, the Republican version of conservatism was holding out the vision that the US had entered upon an age of permanent economic expansion. As a result a laxness in both personal and public responsibility began to evolve. As we have seen, the Republicans once elected failed to appoint persons interested in implementing the intent of the progressive legislation allowing the corporations to amass excessive profits and to reinvest them in an irresponsible manner; while at the same time further allowing the private and public credit sectors to slip into financial chaos. The Republican response to the chaos created by their policies was to institute high tariffs and faulty taxation systems. The result of the governmental policies of irresponsibility coupled with the public avoidance of personal control resulted in the worse depression yet felt in the US.

It appears that many of the same faults can be found in the operation of the current global market system. The basic tenet of the global market is deregulation, that is, to allow the unrestrained operation of the open market. The result has been the growth of huge transnational corporations which control most of the world's trade, manufacturing, and financial transactions. The current economic woes being felt around the world such as high unemployment, declining manufacturing bases, difficulty in maintaining social programs, and difficulty in maintaining fiscal responsibility are eerily reminiscent of the late 1920s and early 1930s. It is at least probable that these economic ills are the result of the same irresponsible behavior of multinational corporations and nation states in connection with both their profits and the reinvestment of those profits as occurred in the pre-depression period of the 1930s.

It is worthy of note that the EU has again attempted to institute a regulatory regime that will require a more responsible approach to doing business within the EU single market. It has also been economically strong enough to force many of its regulations to be observed by companies outside the EU, that is, many US corporations doing business in the EU have adopted the EU regulations in markets in which they don't apply. On the political front, however, the EU has shown itself to be subject to the same corruption that the progressive movement fought against in the US and for the same reasons. A world government, like all governments, must accept the fact that corruption will appear wherever it is allowed to exist. Unfortunately the only means of controlling corruption is one that requires strict auditing of all activity in areas where corruption is likely. The rational use of regulation within an essentially open economic system appears to be the best way to obtain individual responsibility in all areas of action within a society. The EU, while more strictly regulating economic activity at the private business level, has been unable to control the debt structures of its members. As a result public debt has grown beyond the ability of members to repay without general government bail-outs. This is causing a serious strain on the EU system and according to some experts will lead to an economic collapse as great as, if not worse than, the one in the 1930s. In short, in the US and in the EU, lax implementation and enforcement of rational regulation proce-dures has led to a situation where corporate abuses (faulty home mortgage procedures, faulty investment procedures, etc.) coupled with another mas-sive increase of public and private debt (financial irresponsibility) has set the stage for a new depression. If this depression arrives in the near term, the opportunity for establishing a world government capable of instituting rational recovery programs may have gone by the board.

CHAPTER 10. THE FAILURE OF UNRESTRAINED CAPITALISM AND THE GROWTH OF THE WELFARE STATE

The public perceived the policies instituted by the Hoover administration in response to the growing depression as a complete failure. As has been speculated these policies, if allowed to freely operate within the circumstances that prevailed, could have been successful at least hypothetically. In the end, if nothing else they were prophetic of the changes and the policies that were actually adopted. Regardless, the election of 1932 placed the Democrats in solid control of the federal, state, and local governments. Franklin D. Roosevelt was elected president for the first term of what would turn out to be four terms of office. His campaign had been based upon blaming the Republicans for the depression and promising the institution of a new governmental response labeled the "New Deal."

The "New Deal" when analyzed as a total package represents a radical departure from the traditional values that underlie the Republican Democracy created by the US Constitution. The New Deal programs were the first US experiment with the concepts of Socialism as developed in Western Europe. The US under the New Deal programs accepted the Socialist political concept of the welfare state (the public provision of private needs) as compared with a state that merely aided the private sector in providing for private needs. The depression by 1932 had progressed to the point that aggressive federal action could no longer be safely avoided (in the opinion of most experts). Franklin Roosevelt, like Theodore Roosevelt, was an ultimately practical politician. He was not only capable of accepting non-traditional solutions to existing problems but was capable of forcing such programs through Congress when necessary. Unlike Theodore Roosevelt, however, Franklin was also capable of scraping a non-traditional program if it did not work to his satisfaction. Under these circumstances he was the perfect person to introduce a program of collectivist planning along the lines of European socialism. Early in his first administration he set up what became known as the "brain trust"; a group of university professors from the now defunct Progressive movement which would act as his advisory panel concerning programs to counter the depression. The brain trust belonged in large part to the most liberal wing of the now defunct progressive party and had imbibed the philosophy adopted by European socialists. All in all, the New Deal is a good example of how difficult it is introduce and operate collectivist planning while at the same time preserving the underlying principles of liberal democracy. That is to say, new approaches were taken in relation to the depression with a clear understanding that they were experimental in character. The approaches taken were then carefully monitored to determine if they were performing their function as expected. If so they were left to operate with only some fine tuning; if not, they were either redone or scrapped for a new approach. Roosevelt's first term concentrated largely on the promises he had made during the campaign. The programs submitted by the administration were intended to be effective in three main areas. First, a number of programs were introduced with the intention of relieving the worse effects of unemployment. Second, a number of programs were introduced with the intention of aiding the general economy back to recovery. Third, a group of programs were brought to the forefront with the intention of reducing the crisis that was gripping the agricultural community. The brain trust located at Columbia University drafted the programs they submitted to fit the demands of the campaign promises; but also filled out the programs in considerable detail with the manner in which the legislation should be drafted and the programs put into operation. Roosevelt as a practical intellect took the programs as submitted by the brain trust and molded them to fit the realities of the depression. The brain trust having received their political training in the Progressive Movement under the tutelage of Theodore Roosevelt was very liberal in political philosophy and anxious to implement the more extreme suggestions of the Progressive Movement. Under the system inaugurated by Franklin Roosevelt the brain trust was allowed to operate behind the scenes, that is, without the benefit of public sanction and did so with the full support of the federal government. It was in all likelihood the first time in US history that private citizens had been in a position to exercise that amount of influence over a president.

The administration laid the blame for the depression on the actions, or more correctly, the inaction of the Republican Party with some degree of credibility. The public was now clearly ready for more aggressive action to take place in providing remedies for their suffering. Roosevelt, as mentioned earlier, was a practical intellect and therefore a cautious man. He intended for the programs to be instituted more or less as half measures of what had actually been advanced by the brain trust. The Farm Aid Program, for example, was set up to please the farmers; but was limited to the degree necessary to prevent alarm being raised in the urban communities. In addition Roosevelt had been careful during the campaign not to take a stand on the tariff issue leaving him free to act in this area as he saw fit. During the campaign he had promised to try and balance the budget, but he made it clear that he would continue deficit spending if necessary. He had also promised to repeal the prohibition amendment, which was accomplished in 1933. He promised to more closely regulate the new public utility industry while at the same time greatly expanding the availability of electric power. In short, the campaign had promised an end to unrestrained capitalism, which was to be replaced with a form of national planning.

The public accepted the campaign call for radical government intervention programs to relieve the effects of the depression. The desperation that had overtaken the US public would have allowed the institution of nearly any political agenda that was offered. If one looks closely at the conditions that existed in 1932, everything was in place as required by Marxist-Leninist thought to allow for the implementation of a socialistic program or, for that matter, any program that otherwise might have seemed antithetical to the "American way of life," as long as the new system promised relief from the disaster. From 1928 to 1948 there was even a Socialist candidate running for the presidency, although the action of the Roosevelt administration to implement social welfare programs diluted this pressure. The programs instituted by Roosevelt, however, were confusing in that they were promoted to end certain conditions within the economy while at the same time expanding them. The tariff had been left unchallenged so as to avoid offending certain interests. In the end the campaign offered a great deal of change from traditional approaches but gave very little information as to how that change would be managed.

The first one hundred days of the Roosevelt administration was a flurry of action that would stamp the public's view of the New Deal permanently. Quick action had been promised and quick action had been taken. Fifteen major proposals were submitted to Congress by the administration all of which were passed essentially unchanged during the first term of office. They are most easily comprehended by listing them and then looking at each one separately. The fifteen major proposals are as follows:

1. The Emergency Banking Relief Act
2. The Economy Act
3. The Civilian Conservation Corps Act
4. The Abandonment of the Gold Standard Act
5. The Federal Emergency Relief Act
6. The Agricultural Adjustment Act
7. The Tennessee Valley Authority Act
8. The Emergency Farm Mortgage Act
9. The Federal Securities Act
10. The Gold Repeal Joint Resolution
11. The Homeowners Loan Act
12. The National Industrial Recovery Act
13. The Farm Credit Act
14. The Farm Credit Administration Act
15. The Glass-Steagall Banking Act

Within seven months the Farm Mortgage Act coupled with the Farm Credit Act both of which operated under the Farm Credit Administration Act had made available over 100 million dollars in farm loans. This was four times the amount of farm loans made available the year before. This measure was balanced with the Homeowners Act that operated through the Homeowners Loan Corporation. This program made available an equal sum of money for loans to the public for home ownership. This is one example of the manner in which Roosevelt attempted to balance the intervention of the federal government in the various sectors of the society to avoid riling up anger in any major voting bloc.

The Glass-Steagall Banking Act established the Federal Deposit Insurance Corporation (FDIC) that was authorized initially to insure deposits up to 5000 dollars. This program was intended to restore the public's confidence in the banking system and to stimulate individual savings if possible. This act also intended to put an end to the earlier uncontrolled speculation in the banking industry by separating the investment and commercial banking operations. Both of these banking operations were placed under the regulatory control of the Federal Reserve System. Along the same lines the Federal Securities Act created the Federal Trade Commission (which later became the Securities and Exchange Commission) designed to regulate the offering, sale, and ownership of stocks, bonds, and other security instruments. It was felt generally that the economic collapse was largely the result of financial irresponsibility in both the banking and securities industries and this new regulatory system was intended to end it. Also in relation to the banking industry the Emergency Banking Relief Act was used to collect all of the US gold reserves into the Federal Reserve System by dropping gold as the authorized payment for both public and private debt under the Gold Repeal Joint Resolution Act. The federal government finally followed the European trend and abandoned the gold standard altogether under the Gold Abandonment Act, which was also called the Gold Reserve Act. This was both recognition of the current financial reality as concerns the world economic situation, and a method of collecting a large share of the world gold reserves in the US. Roosevelt set the price of gold under the Abandonment Act at thirty five dollars an ounce. This was somewhat higher than the free market price on the world market. As a result the US was able to draw a large share of the world's gold reserve into the US where it was deposited in the vaults created at Fort Knox, Kentucky.

Up to this point in our analysis all of the programs mentioned were intended to become a permanent part of the federal economic bureaucracy. There had been nothing even remotely similar in the expansion of federal power in prior US history. The programs represent an intentional intervention into areas of daily life that had before never been breached. It is at this time hard to imagine the fear and the mindset that would allow Congress to pass such sweeping legislation in such a short period of time. It is evident that little or no debate was conducted within the two houses of Congress concerning the long term effects of these programs. It is likely that very little debate was had even on the short term effects they would have on the US society.

The next programs that will be considered were intended to be temporary measures designed to affect specific targets within the general economic structure. The largest of the temporary programs was the Civilian Conservation Corps Act. This program was intended to provide jobs for unmarried men between the ages of 18 and 25. Over three million men passed through this program before it was terminated. It is of interest to note that it was operated under a strict disciplinary program copied from the military. Like the military therefore it was also a segregated system. Most of the work performed by the Corps was dedicated to the National Forests, National Parks, National recreation areas, and soil conservation. Some of the Corps projects were also tied into the programs initiated under the Tennessee Valley Authority.

The Federal Emergency Relief Act operated through the Federal Emergency Relief Administration. This program was originally intended to be a grant program aimed at funding the state and local governments in distributing aid to the needy. Needless to say this program was intended to be a temporary stop gap. Through its director Harry Hopkins this program attempted to establish state and local work programs in the areas of education, student aid, rural rehabilitation, and itinerate labor. Both Roosevelt and Hopkins favored work programs over giving out money as direct grants; but the state and local governments favored the grant programs as they could be more easily instituted and gained direct favor for them from the public. In the end most of the monies distributed under this program was given in the form of direct grants. In relation to this program Roosevelt also created by way of executive order the Civil Works Administration that distributed another 900 million dollars in "make work" projects. Some of these make work projects provided real jobs in relation to road building and teaching positions. This program was abandoned after only one year of operation.

The remaining programs were intended to act as measures that would replace the temporary programs when they were brought to an end. These programs were intended to eliminate the economic causes of the depression and to put into place steps to prevent the reoccurrence of a depression. The brain trust was as mentioned before essentially a cadre of professionals from the "New Nationalism" campaign of Theodore Roosevelt. They believed in the trend towards a stronger marriage between big business and big government. They also accepted the Progressive philosophy that strict regulation at the federal level was needed to control this concentration of business activity. They had also studied the recent changes that had taken place in Western Europe and had adopted the popular socialism of the day. Many European countries, in particular Great Britain, had adopted socialist type long-term planning programs to end the abuses of unrestrained capitalism. Many of these programs had been very successful in accomplishing that goal. In every case these programs had introduced a degree of national planning at the highest level of government. The brain trust was to incorporate some of the lessons they had learned from these programs in the projects submitted to Roosevelt. The main difference between the European model and the US was the duration of the programs. Most of the New Deal programs can be classified as socialist in form, but were implemented on a short term rather than long-term basis, that is to say, for a period of one year or less rather than as a five year or more plans.

The first step was taken in a national planning program intended to artificially control both farm production and farm income. This program was known as the Agricultural Adjustment Act. This program called for the radical reduction of production of farm crops and animals. In return the farmers would be paid a subsidy to offset the loss in income resulting from the cuts in production.

This was a direct attempt to replace the concept of a free market in the agricultural sector. At first, the program seemed to be working as production fell and income rose; but after the initial surge farm prices began to fall again reducing farm income even further. This program coupled with the severe drought that struck the Midwest and Southwest led to two major consequences. Production fell even more than was expected under the artificial stimulus of the program resulting for example in the slaughter of six million piglets. The two together also essentially eliminated the tenant farming opportunities in the South as well as the small family farms in the rest of the country. This resulted in the displacement of some two million farm related workers greatly adding to the unemployment problem. During this period 400,000 Mexican Americans lost their farm related employment along with another 200,000 African-Americans. With the loss of family farms in the Midwest and southwest another 800,000 farmers and white farm workers also lost their employment. The federal government faced this problem by deporting the Mexican Americans back to Mexico and leaving all the rest of the unemployed to fend for themselves. A large number of these unemployed workers migrated into new areas, especially the western coastal areas, in search of new lives. They became known as the famous "Okies." They were met on the west coast by stiff resistance from the native citizens in relation to job and housing discrimination. The discrimination was so severe that it caused nearly one third of those that migrated to return back home. The Supreme Court added to the suffering in the farm industry by ruling the Agricultural Adjustment Act unconstitutional in 1936. The act included a tax intended to fund the cost of the subsidies granted. This was the aspect of the act that the Supreme Court found unconstitutional as against the provisions prohibiting the federal government from direct taxation. This ruling accomplished nothing more than the conversion of a self-funding program into one that would now be funded from tax-payer contributions. In short, the Supreme Court ruling created the first federal governmental entitlement program as we know that term today.

The National Industrial Recovery Act was intended to provide temporary stimulus to the economy through government spending on public works projects. Through the Public Works Administration and the Industrial Recovery Act three billion dollars was spent on the construction of public buildings, highways, flood control, and other internal improvements. The program from the beginning was intended to be more than a mere make work project. The government consistently let the projects out to private contractors providing work for both the companies and their employees. This same approach is still used today in the letting of contracts for public service work. A second major thrust of the Industrial Recovery Act was to establish a system that mandated fair competitive practices, equal opportunity employment, defined standards of labor, and an overall increase in the level of wages. The fair competitive practices mandate required all contractors (working on government projects) to limit their work week to eighty hours; while the labor standards mandate required the contractors to limit their employees to a forty-hour week. It also mandated that no one under the age of sixteen could be admitted to the work force. The business community stoutly resisted these mandates and in 1935 the Supreme Court ruled them to be unconstitutional on a number of grounds. First, the court found that the labor standards mandates had been unfairly applied resulting in price fixing, wage control, and restraint of trade. It also found that the government had illegally blocked the operation of a freely determined labor market. All of these charges had been partially substantiated by an earlier congressional hearing called to investigate the operation of the mandates. The Act was also unpopular with the public due to the issues involved and no one was much concerned when it was ruled unconstitutional. It is interesting in our case to note that the Act was ruled unconstitutional due to the method it was implemented rather than on its unconstitutionality per se.

The purest program of national planning was incorporated into the Tennessee Valley Authority Act. The Act was not only intended to be another way to combat unemployment but was also intended to be a permanent part of an ongoing national plan to complete the industrialization of the US. It would, if operated as planned, contribute to soil conservation, flood control, and inexpensive electrical power. By 1936 the TVA had completed six dams and had finalized plans for the construction of nine more. The TVA dams successfully fostered soil conservation, flood control, and even produced an experiment in the production of fertilizer. Its main effect, however, was the production and providing of relatively cheap electrical power throughout the Southeast of the US. The further electrification programs of the rural US was taken over by the Rural Electrification Administration which had been created by executive order to oversee the distribution of the electric power produced by the TVA dams. The TVA, which is still in active operation, is perhaps the most successful of the New Deal programs. Today the problem facing the TVA program is the conversion of its coal fired steam plants to some form of cleaner fuel such as nuclear power. This option was not available to the government in the 1930s, forcing the reliance on coal fired steam production. Some advances have been made in the alleviation of this problem but progress has been very slow in coming, mainly due to excessive costs.

The Economy Act was intended to give the executive branch the power to cut salaries for federal employees, to eliminate payments to veterans for non-combat related injuries, and to reorganize various agencies in the interest of the economy. The agencies that were created by executive order to oversee the implementation and operation of the programs passed into legislation were all created under this act, i.e., the Rural Electrification Administration, the Home Loan Association, etc. This act was not strictly necessary as the power of executive order had already been established by

Theodore Roosevelt but this act gave official sanction to what had prior to it been an unofficial executive policy.

The first Roosevelt term of office was successful in dropping any reliance on the conservative approach offered by the Republicans, e.g., dependence upon voluntary private action and regulation at the state and local level. There was no longer any question about the handling of the problems created by the depression. They would be handled, if they were handled at all, by pro-active federal governmental intervention. The fifteen programs that have been looked at can be argued to have been strictly necessary to combat the worse public suffering caused by the depression; but they were in fact a conscious effort to alter the underlying principles upon which representative democracy is based.

The attempt to restructure the underlying principles of democracy was resisted stoutly by the decisions of the Supreme Court and the general conservative attitude of the business community. In contrast the bias created by state and local support of the New Deal Programs undercut the conservative efforts. In areas where the state and local governments did attempt to become active the Supreme Court quickly ruled their efforts unconstitutional. The essential impossibility of state and local participation in New Deal programs left the vacuum to be filled by the federal government and the brain trust was quick to fill it with federal intervention.

In its first term in office the Roosevelt administration was able to create and pass into law programs directly affecting agriculture, the private housing markets, industrial development, public utility growth, commercial and investment banking, the public securities market, and social welfare. Some of the programs, as has been pointed out, were intended to be temporary but both the public and the politicians quickly recognized the real import of the programs and came to claim their status as permanent parts of the new more nationalistic (welfare) state. The very end of the first term in office coupled with the whole of the second term in office came to be known as the second new deal. Five new proposals were submitted and passed into permanent legislation. They would become the high point of the New Deal Program as a whole. The Acts although few in number were of major importance not only as new programs but also in relation to the future evolution of the federal government in the US. The five acts are as follows:

1. The Wagner National Labor Relations Act

2. The Social Security Act of 1935

3. The Banking Act of 1935
4. The Wheeler-Rayburn Public Utility Holding Company Act
5. The Revenue Act of 1935

The Labor Relations Act was intended to officially recognize the right of labor to organize and collectively bargain with their employers. Unions met with stiff resistance in their efforts to organize unions especially in Detroit, Chicago, and Harlan County Kentucky. Although resistance was consistent the movement was largely successful by the early 1940s. Without the assistance of the federal government the armed resistance by big business and state and local governments would have been capable of defeating the union movement. Without the right to use force, however, which had been allowed by the earlier federal stance labor could not be denied. This was one example of how the US would use socialist economic programs to support political agendas, that is, labor rights.

The Social Security Act of 1935 was specifically designed to be a welfare program. It provided for a subsistence level standard of living to be furnished by the federal government to those who were chronically unemployed, disabled, or beyond the age of employment. As we shall see the act came later to include many other types of disabilities and disadvantages that were not contemplated in the original bill. This program represents the most successful of the New Deal programs in respect to the initiation of what have become known as entitlement programs.

The Banking Act of 1935 placed the control of the nation's money supply under the control of the Federal Reserve System. It was now possible for the first time in US history to assert with accuracy that the whole of the gold reserve and the money supply was in private hands. The placement of the monetary policies of the US in private hands was intended to be controlled by means of federal regulation. As we shall see later this turned out to be something of an illusion.

The Public Utility Act was intended to end the wild speculation that had evolved with the expansion of electrification of the rural US. The result had the unintended consequence that the public utility industry became concentrated in the hands of a few large public utility monopolies such as the Edison Companies and AT&T among others. In short, the act produced the first instance of the nationalization of industry in US history although the actual operation of the utilities was not actually operated by the government as it was under the European nationalization systems.

The Revenue Act of 1935 was clearly intended to increase federal revenue in an attempt to keep pace with the increased spending required under the New Deal Programs. The Surtax rates were now applied to all incomes over 50,000 dollars and a sharply increased graded income tax was applied ending with a 75 percent tax on income exceeding five million dollars. The act also intended to sharply increase the rate of taxation on estates, gifts, and corporations. The riders that were attached to the bill essentially made the legislation passed the highest tax ever implemented on the incomes of the middle and lower income tax payers in US history. The wealthy and the corporations were provided with enough loopholes to avoid much taxation. The same process was followed by the state and local governments to allow them to pay their portion of the new welfare programs. The taxes after the riders took effect were blatantly regressive and put an almost intolerable burden on the lowest income tax payers. As has been the tradition within the taxing policies of the US the middle and lower tax payers assumed the largest share of the burden of paying for the welfare programs instituted to relieve their economic hardships. The Social Security Program was intended to be implemented and operated as a self-funding program, i.e., the taxes paid by those who were still members of the work force would cover the benefits distributed to those who were unemployed, permanently disabled, or too old to work. It was a unique welfare program at the time and for awhile remained a completely self-funding program.

The presidential election of 1936 resulted in the largest landslide vote in US history. There can be no doubt that the election represents the widespread satisfaction on the part of the US public to the actions that had been taken over the last four years. It was also clearly a mandate for Roosevelt to continue its radical experimentation in regard to US politics. Even though the second term resulted in the above five programs being instituted there were also several counter trends that became evident which made a full use of the mandate given by the public impossible to use.

First, the Supreme Court as we have seen in a couple of instances had ruled several pieces of the New Deal legislation unconstitutional. The Second New Deal programs involving Social Security and Labor Relations were also awaiting Supreme Court rulings on their constitutionality. The expectations were that the Supreme Court would also find them unconstitutional. Roosevelt empowered with what he felt was an unconditional mandate in the election attempted to block the Supreme Court by a radical reorganization of the judicial system. He sent a bill to Congress that would have raised the number of Supreme Court Justices from six to twelve; and would have created fifty new federal judgeships. The bill would also have required the mandatory retirement of any judge who had reached the age of seventy and who had served ten years on the bench. The bill was resisted by the Congress for a period of time long enough to render the point moot. The Supreme Court suddenly shifted its legal philosophy in relation to the New Deal and ruled both the Social Security Act and the Labor Relations Act constitutional. As a result a vote was never taken in Congress on the judicial bill submitted by Roosevelt

Second, although the economy showed clear signs of recovery in late 1935 and throughout 1936, it went back into a slump in early 1937. The Keynesian economic philosophy which had been faithfully followed by the brain trust called for a continuous program of high government spending coupled with a tight federal regulatory system. Roosevelt during the period of recovery attempted to restrict federal spending in an effort to balance the federal budget (a campaign promise from the first term in office); as well as abandoning the more strictly enforced regulatory programs that were a part of the New Deal. The result seems to have been an undercutting of the economic revival, although it is likely that other factors contributed more than Roosevelt's program to the new slump. The administration reacted to the new slump in 1937 with a massive increase in federal spending coupled with a serious emphasis on anti-trust activities. This shift in emphasis was not given a chance to counteract the new economic slump due to the outbreak of World War II and a shift of emphasis on the part of the administration.

Prior to the outbreak of World War II a last series of proposed legislation was submitted to the Congress. These included a second Agricultural Adjustment Act that called for the permanent placement of subsidies for curtailment of production to be put in place; the Food, Drug, and Cosmetic Act; and the Fair Labor Standards Act all of which were placed on hold due to the outbreak of war. The Fair Labor Standards Act did establish officially the forty hour work week and the minimum wage system still in effect today.

The confusion of the US public was evident in the mid-term elections of 1938. The landslide conditions of 1936 had been completely reversed by the public's reaction to Roosevelt's attempt to pack the Supreme Court and the return of worsened economic conditions during 1937. The attempt to pack the Supreme Court had resulted in a difficult to heal split within the Democratic Party. The loss of public confidence was made clear by a sizable reduction in the size of the democratic majorities in both houses of Congress and in the state and local governments. The seats gained by the Republicans in 1938 did not give them a majority in either house but did give them a strong enough minority position to block any New Deal legislation brought forward. The New Deal as a result slowly ground to a halt during late 1938 and early 1939.

A general review of the New Deal Programs reveals some very interesting points. First, and possibly most important, is that a hard long look had been taken at the solutions offered by European nationalization programs in the economic arena but these solutions were adapted to some degree to the US environment. This adapted form of implementation was forced on the brain trust and the federal government by the US public, the business community, and the labor unions through their resistance to the programs. Even the state and local governments had looked at the offered economic solutions but had also been forced to reject them as unworkable under existing circumstances (mainly the lack of the capability of state and local governments to implement long term planning). If ever in US history a time was ripe for a national political revolution, it would have been during the period from 1929 to 1939, characterized as it was by very high levels of frustration and suffering. The New Deal programs with the ability to scrape unworkable programs and to fine tune successful ones made such radical political solutions unnecessary. Instead of a full program of nationalization of industry and complete national planning a hybrid system known as the welfare state was created. It incorporated some aspects of the European approach but left a good deal of our liberal economic traditions in place. The Great Depression and the solutions used to counter it resulted in both the massive growth of federal governmental programs and the recognition that many modern problems that faced society were beyond the fiscal means of governments the size of state and local institutions in the US. The state and local governments began to actively call upon the federal government to take over their responsibilities in areas such as public sewage systems, public water systems, bridge construction, highway construction, and the construction of schools, hospitals, and mental institutions.

Second, as an experiment in developing the concept of the modern welfare state the New Deal Programs offered a unique solution. The demands created by the depression forced the federal government to proactively respond to chronic unemployment, the failure of the private health insurance system in relation to disabilities and old age, the massive displacement of farm workers, and financial irresponsibility at all levels of government, as well as, throughout the private sector. The weakness of a reliance on the private sector for those in need of aid even when coupled with the efforts of charitable organizations became quickly and painfully apparent. All of the New Deal Programs can claim their place as national planning programs intended to handle the specific problems that arose in specific areas of the society. Problems arising in agriculture, industry, labor, banking, and investment all received direct attention under the New Deal legislation passed by the Congress. Unemployment, health insurance, disability compensation, all received direct aid from federal legislative initiatives in particular the Social Security Act. The suffering that was already being felt prior to the institution of permanent remedies was handled by the institution of temporary programs aimed at providing income and or direct grants through the state and local governments. Even the less immediately evident problems such as soil erosion, flood control, and electrification of the rural areas were handled through a national planning scheme known as the TVA. The New Deal represents national planning within the US democracy at its greatest extent; and when coupled with an adapted program of national planning that fit the needs of a capitalist system the worst effects of such planning was avoided.

Third, the New Deal Programs initially attempted to delegate as much activity as possible to the state and local governments in support of the US commitment to Republicanism. Efforts were also made from time to time to involve the private sector in the remedying of their own problems but these efforts largely were ignored by the business community in particular. The reluctance of state and local governments as well as the private business community along with the Supreme Court decisions making it difficult for their participation soon brought all efforts along these lines to a close.

By 1940 it was not clear how much of the New Deal would remain on the books as a permanent part of the federal government. It also could not be reasonably expected at that time for anyone to foresee the full development of the welfare state. Over a period of eight years the public accepted government intervention into nearly every aspect of their daily lives, indeed, not only came to accept it but came to demand it. As we shall see later the attitude that the federal government not only should have the power to fix any and all problems; but that it was the duty of the government to fix them, came to be the norm. Because of the shift in public focus brought on by World War II these issues took a position on the back burner for nearly two decades.

The suffering that was created by massive unemployment (nearly twenty-five percent of the total work force); the forced migrations of over two million people; and the discrimination that met them as well as the failure of state and local government along with traditional charitable organizations to handle the suffering, cannot be overstated. It might be fair to claim that the Great Depression was the greatest test yet faced by the original experiment in social democracy as represented by the US. It might also be fair to say that the US democracy responded very admirably to the challenge presented to it. The US emerged from the depression with the appearance of a stronger nationalistic structure but essentially with its underlying principles of republican representative democracy still intact. The programs instituted by the brain trust and the Roosevelt administration tended to show that the original principles would have to be adapted to a new modern environment requiring a shift from the republicanism of the early days to a more composite nationalistic structure today. It might be argued, from the opposite point of view, that capitalism was saved by the New Deal from a Socialist or Communist political revolution, but that Republican Democracy was scraped and replaced by a hybrid form of political socialism known as the welfare state. In support of this point of view one might claim that there is little if any state and local governmental activity today that is not funded or regulated by the federal government. It can also be argued that the public was beginning to show a willingness to sacrifice personal liberties and responsibilities and replace them with federally financed entitlement programs such as those provided by the Agricultural Adjustment Act. It is just this type of reaction that constitutes the warning given by Hayek in his book, The Road to Serfdom. It is not clear which view would have won, as the debate was suspended at this time due to US participation in World War II

The EU as it exists today is facing some of the same problems faced by the New Deal. There are very high levels of unemployment, there is a high degree of national planning, and there is a high degree of welfare participation. It is also true that the EU has developed this structure from the conscious attempts of its national members to provide just such a system. While in the US the argument is over welfare and non-welfare programs, in the EU there is no question that the welfare state is expected to remain solidly in place. In the case of many developing nations this welfare is provided by the industrialized nations. The EU has taken the lead in providing "poor relief" for the countries that have been marginalized by the global economy and which make up what is called the fourth world. The EU has also taken the lead in reducing its defense spending to the lowest possible level to enable it to maintain the highest level of "poor relief" possible both on a national level and an international level.

It should also be pointed out that the world government will face the same issues. It is likely that a significant amount of pressure will be applied to the world government to take over the various national welfare programs. There is much speculation on the part of experts today that even the most highly developed nations will find it difficult to continue to fund the levels of welfare now found in their systems. It is also apparent that most nations that have extensive welfare programs are also not going to install the austerity programs necessary to insure their continued success. In many if not most nations, no welfare system exists to handle the very evident suffering that is to be found. Pressure will also be placed on the world government to assume the duty of responding to this need for "poor relief". These two actions could only be accomplished by direct involvement of the central government through taxation or by an equitable redistribution of national wealth as is taking place in the EU. Once again it is expected that the central government would set the standards necessary to enhance the welfare programs but that the implementation and operation of the programs would be carried out at the national and local levels. Included within these programs would be the programs instituted to eliminate poverty and to equalize on a relative basis the infrastructure on a worldwide basis.

It is also possible that many of the problems that resulted in the great depression could be handled by an effective world government through a more strict application of the principles of republican democracy. In other words, the plans instituted by the central government will be implemented, enforced, and monitored by the various national and local governments. These plans would include the redistribution of wealth, the equitable distribution of employment, the use and control of natural resources, and the equitable distribution of welfare. In addition the solution to the above issues will require the central government to put into place a monitoring system to insure that the national and local governments strictly regulate the activities and expenditures under these programs. The question still remains as to how these programs will be funded but it is likely that a system of concurrent taxation will cover some portion of the programs while other funds will be directed to them from the savings generated from total disarmament and other current fixed costs.

CHAPTER 11. WORLD WAR II AND THE DEVELOPMENT OF BIPOLAR POLITICS

World War II was more the continuation of World War I than a war fought over new and differing conditions. The Treaty of Paris which ended World War I had left almost the entire gamut of problems still in place, while at the same time it created several new ones. Germany and her allies were given the total blame for World War I and were presented a bill for reparations that was totally unsustainable. Japan's aggressive imperialist policy in the Pacific was not addressed. The growth of the Soviet Union and the problems that it presented to the West were also not taken into consideration. In addition, territorial adjustments created a series of new nations that were, under the circumstances, incapable of sustaining their political stability. In short, the Treaty of Paris was essentially just an official truce that lasted some twenty years.

World War II began with the major powers, i.e., Great Britain, France, Italy, and the US essentially ignoring Japanese and German aggression. Roosevelt seemed personally to understand what was coming down the pike and took steps to prepare the US military for action. With the declaration of war the administration instituted the lend lease program which allowed the US to side step the public desire not to enter the war. This program quickly brought the full production capacity of the US on line ending the dormancy under which production had lain for nearly a decade. The full use of US production capacity brought with it an end to unemployment and also brought an end to the depression in the US. The allies with the aid of the US were guaranteed an ample supply of financing and war materials which included the effort of the Soviet Union against the Germans. Roosevelt always the practical intellect realized that the US would not be able to avoid an active part in the war and instituted the first peace time military draft in US history.

World War II also brought about some important changes in the public's attitude towards foreign policy. The war immediately solidified the principles that underlay the Monroe Doctrine. The guarantees mutually confirmed by both the US and Latin America under the doctrine allowed a level of cooperation in the region not seen prior to 1940. The war also brought to a final end any public belief in the effectiveness of the concept of isolation from world affairs. The public was now fully aware, if not totally compliant, with the fact that the US was a major world player. The war also brought some not so welcome effects into the US society. First, with the aid of defecting German scientists the US became the first nation to develop an atomic bomb. At the close of the war as everyone knows two of these devices were used against Japan causing unbelievable devastation. The US to date is still the only nation to have used a nuclear weapon of mass destruction militarily. The development of nuclear weapons followed after the war and brought about one of the most negative effects of World War II, that is, the arms race involved in the cold war. Second, the US during the war showed one of its most persistent negative traits. That is to say, the US set up internment camps and forced the internment of thousands of Japanese-Americans. In addition, the military remained segregated in support of the society's persistent discriminatory values. Lastly, the US generally, and the federal government in particular, paid little attention to the policy of genocide that was being practiced in Germany in relation to its Jewish population. All of these actions, or non-actions, indicate that racial and ethnic discrimination remains just beneath the surface in the US society and is capable of breaking into the open upon rather minor motivations. The same might be said of those countries in Western Europe that were resisting the German and Italian thrust. Third, the war allowed the revitalization of the fundamentalist religious movement in the US that had lain dormant for nearly fifty years. This revival took the form of evangelism and quickly reestablished a firm commitment from the public in general for a less frantic life style than that exhibited both in the roaring twenties and the depression thirties. Lastly, the war by its end had produced circumstances where the Soviet Union would be transformed from an ally to a perceived enemy of the United States. The quick take over by the Soviet Union of Western Central Asia and all of Eastern Europe, including the eastern half of Germany, automatically put the Soviet Union at odds with the other allies. It did not add anything favorable to the mix that the Soviet propaganda promised a quick end to capitalism and the world domination of the Soviet Communist system. The US and the other Allies including West Germany after the war took the opposite position and remained determine to defeat Soviet ambitions.

The number of people killed or wounded during the war is truly beyond calculation. The military losses of the participants alone are staggering. It is believed, for example, that the Soviet Union lost nearly twenty million people. The Germans, not including up to six million Jewish people exterminated throughout Europe, are likely to have lost a number close to eight million. In total the other Allied nations of Europe probably lost another several millions of people in the war. It is therefore possible that the number of people killed or wounded on the European continent neared sixty million. In the Pacific the number of people killed and wounded during the war is completely unknown. The number of Chinese, Southeast Asians, Pacific Island Asians, even Japanese, cannot now be counted in any degree of accuracy. It is unlikely that the numbers can even be realistically estimated although it can be guessed that tens of thousands were killed instantly in both Hiroshima and Nagasaki. Even more died or were forced to face serious maladies from the radiation poisoning distributed by the two bombs. In all likelihood the number of killed and wounded directly related to the devastation of World War II would be close to 120 million. There can be no wonder that the citizens of Western Europe and Asia lived in fear of World War III during the next four decades. The same paranoia was evident in the frantic response of both the US and USSR during the so-called cold war.

The material destruction brought about by World War II was largely isolated to the European Continent and to Asia. The whole of the European continent was brought to the point of total material exhaustion. The infrastructure of Western and Eastern Europe including that of the European portions of the Soviet Union were almost completely destroyed. The Soviet Union by grabbing the Eastern European nations after the war was able to recoup a significant portion of its losses. The French, Germans, Italians, and

English all lost their pre-war status as major powers. Western Europe as we will see was able to remain an important player in the cold war due to the effects of the Marshall Plan and NATO that the US instituted after peace was concluded. In relation to Great Britain the most important loss was that of their control of the world's Oceans which at the end of the war migrated to the United States. This in turn made it impossible for Great Britain, France, the Netherlands and others to maintain their colonial empires.

The colonial world rapidly began to decompose with the end of World War II. Wars of liberation were being fought in Viet Nam, Laos, Thailand, Burma, and India. India obtained independence from Great Britain in 1948, China became a nation in 1949, and the rest of Southeast Asia became independent after three decades of struggle in 1975. In Africa, Libya, Algeria, Tunisia, and Morocco all obtained their independence from France by 1964. The rest of Africa would continue to develop new nations throughout the remainder of the 20th century. It is of interest to note that in both Asia and Africa the struggles for independence were not so much a struggle against colonial power as a struggle between internal factions for control of the new nations as they emerged. In Viet Nam, due to US involvement, the natural process was warped but generally speaking the colonial powers were only too happy to withdraw. The people who were left with independence were incapable of establishing a viable government of any type in many cases and as a result chaos ruled. The machinations of the cold war added to the inability of the new nations to create a stable governmental system through what is known as "strings attached" foreign aid. A more detailed look at this factor will be taken later. The end of World War II also ended the British mandate in the Middle East creating as we will see the most dangerous political situation that exists in today's world.

Roosevelt was elected to a fourth term by the US public mainly due to the perception that it would be dangerous to change presidents in the middle of a war. Roosevelt, however, died shortly after he was elected, leaving Vice-President Harry S. Truman as president at the end of the war. Truman was therefore the person who made the decision to drop the two atomic bombs on Japan and who presided for the US over the peace process. Truman's presidency will be analyzed in some detail later. It must be noted that the US public quickly repented of its decision to elect one man four times to the presidency. In 1951, the 22nd amendment was ratified limiting the president and vice-president to two terms in office. This was to include the serving of another's term in case of death, disability, or impeachment. Truman, of course, served the remainder of the fourth term for which Roosevelt had been elected and was reelected in 1948. Truman could have run for another term in 1952, had he cared to, as the serving president was excluded from the 22nd amendment. Truman, however, decided to comply with the intent of the amendment and threw his support to Adlai Stevenson in the election of 1952.

The most important aspects of World War II in relation to the establishment of an effective world government revolve around several major themes. First, and probably the most difficult to solve, is the disbandment and destruction of weapons of mass destruction. The nuclear club includes a growing number of nations, with others having access to biological and chemical weapons. The largest known stockpiles of such weapons are those of the United States and the Russian Federation. The obvious distrust that still exists between these two nations presents a major obstacle to the success of any serious call for total disarmament. A very similar situation of complete distrust exists between China and the Russian Federation as well as between Pakistan and India. This distrust is, if anything, even stronger in the Middle East, even if none of the Muslim nations has anything resembling parity with Israel in terms of weapons of mass destruction.

Some steps have been taken through the offices of the United Nations and other international efforts but nothing of any substance has yet been accomplished; especially in relation to the spread of such weapons to nations that are considered to be irresponsible such as Iran, North Korea, and the former nations of the Soviet Union. The question, in essence, is not the responsibility of these nations, but rather the fact that those who possess them do not want others to have them also. There is no chance whatsoever that total disarmament will take place while the current situation of independent nationalism remains intact and the nuclear club is reluctant to dismantle its weapons. Not until there is a global power capable of inspecting, verifying, and enforcing disarmament, as well as accomplishing the destruction of these weapons and their safe disposal will total disarmament be a serious reality. Second, the collapse of Colonialism has resulted in the creation of a host of new nations. Initially these nations were collectively known as the "third world'. As such they were used by the two other worlds, that is, the "west" and the "Soviet Union" as pones in the so-called "Cold War." With the implosion of the Soviet Union the US was left as the sole remaining super power and the world was left with a single structure of independent nations. Even though there is no longer a third world there remains a vast discrepancy between those older fully industrialized nations and the new nations who are struggling sometimes without success to merely maintain their sovereignty and who have become known as the fourth world. It is only with the effective establishment of a world union that both large and small nations will be able to exist without the necessity of maintaining their independence through competitiveness, both militarily and economically, with the already existing military and economic powers. As occurred over time within the US union so with the world union, that is, the world's wealth will have to be gradually redistributed with the goal of bringing all nations, regardless of size, to a relative equality in standard of living and the understanding of the modern environment. Lastly, the question of sovereignty so important to the principles underlying nationalism will need to be seriously overhauled. Currently each nation state in existence is as jealous of its independent sovereign powers as were the thirteen original states of the US Union. The obtaining of truly sovereign status especially for those nations coming into existence since the end of World War II, and the demise of the Soviet Empire, has been reached only with the cost of large sacrifices of both people and material wealth over rather long periods of time. Maintaining sovereignty has also been the result of much suffering and sacrifice in many of the newer nations as they struggled to find a suitable government and to answer many problems involving ethnicity, economic disparity, and others. For all of these reasons a part of recent memory among the peoples involved will involve resistance against any call for them to give up a portion of this hard won sovereignty — especially to a government that requires them to institute a national government based on liberal democracy.

The European Union, however, offers a counterargument of great power in showing that peoples in both cases listed above can and will allow a diminution of sovereign power if the giving up of such power is beneficial to them in the long run. The EU has firmly grasped the importance of demilitarization and its replacement with concern for social welfare programs. This concern has not only been realized in relation to the member nations but also in relation to the marginalized nations affected by the global market. Currently the EU may be the only existing institution that is dedicated to the betterment of all people being the leader in developmental aid; a

strong advocate of international action in the area of environmental pollution and cleanup; a strong advocate of peacekeeping rather than traditional
military action; and lastly, a strong advocate for the rational regulation of
human actions in all fields of endeavor.

The US has been facing these problems within its own political system
for the last two hundred years and the reaction can be studied. The actions
taken by the US to solve the issues of sovereign power between the individual states, and between the states and the federal government, will provide clues as to how such problems should or should not be approached on
a worldwide scale. The Great Depression in the US made it clear that the
concept of "rugged individualism" could not be counted on to solve society's
modern problems; but rather, that individualism should be replaced with
some form of national planning. World War II and its aftermath has shown
that nationalism (national individualism) cannot cope with global problems and that joint action will be necessary at this level also to create viable
solutions to the problems. Such joint action can most easily be imagined in
today's world as directed by an effective world government based on a true
federalism, or an intergovernmental system such as that found in the EU.

The first eight years after the conclusion of World War II established
the political and social realities that would dominate the next seventy years
of history. The Truman administration began by making the same mistake
that had been made by the Wilson administration after World War I. Truman succumbed to public pressure and authorized the immediate demobilization of the US armed forces. The result of releasing so many people
into the labor market caused a serious dislocation of the economy. At this
time the dislocation was an inflationary spiral that was beyond the government's control. The rapidly rising prices coupled with a more slowly rising
increase in wages caused the labor unions to enter into several emotionally
charged strikes. Truman used military force to break up the strikes further
eroding the confidence of the workers in the federal government. The crisis
was short lived as the economy quickly absorbed the new work force and
rebounded due to the fact that the US was forced by the pressure of world
demand to increase its industrial capacity beyond even the limits established by the war. As a reaction to the administration's handling of the labor
unrest the midterm elections of 1946 brought a majority of seats in Congress
to the Republican Party. At the same time Truman attempted to revive the
New Deal policies under the new name of "Fair Deal."

In relation to the "Fair Deal" Truman's greatest success came in the exportation of the New Deal concepts overseas under the Marshall Program and the US support of the concept of a United States of Europe. This program aimed specifically at the rebuilding of Western Europe although in general it was offered to any nation that wished to become a part of the program. It was most effective, however, in Western Europe due to the Soviet refusal to allow the Central and Eastern European nations to participate. In connection with the Marshall Plan, the administration was able to pass through Congress several regional military and development treaties including the formation of NATO (North Atlantic Treaty Organization), a direct attempt to control the power situation created by the Soviet Union and to insure the incorporation of West Germany into the European system. The Soviet reaction was to tighten its control over the nations of Central and Eastern Europe, and thus the so called cold war was initiated.

The Soviet Union decided to test the resolve of the NATO organization by establishing a total blockade of West Berlin. Berlin had at the end of the war been partitioned into four sections of influence and was totally surrounded by Soviet-controlled East Germany. Truman was able to get Congress to authorize a forceful response to the blockade. This response consisted of a massive airlift to deliver needed supplies to allied positions in Berlin. This operation proved successful and the Soviet Union lifted the blockade after a few months.

The Allies during the peace process had no choice but to accept the Soviet Union's takeover of the Eastern European nations — unless they wished to continue the hot war. Only the US was in a position to engage in further military action, and there was little, if any, support for such action at home. The only resistance to this takeover came in the form of including Turkey in NATO to block any attempt by the Soviet Union to enter the Middle East.

When the realities of the immediate post-war conditions are taken into consideration, the policies initiated by the Truman administration appear to be practical and realistic. There has been a persistent belief that prior to the end of the war Roosevelt, Stalin, and Churchill had established an agenda that created the bi-polar environment of the cold war. According to this supposed plan, the policies of the Truman administration merely implemented an already formulated program. It does not appear that there is much, if any, truth to be found in this proposal. The geographical position of the Soviet army at the end of the war had nothing to do with any concrete plan but rather was the result of the fact that the Soviet army met less resistance than expected from the remaining German forces on the eastern front. The soldiers removed from the eastern front were used to slow down the progress of the Allies on the western front. These two conditions resulted in the geographical division of the European continent at the end of the war. Indeed, it was clearly a post-war decision on the part of the Soviet Union to remain in occupation of Eastern Europe to bolster the position it felt it had achieved. It is likely that Stalin considered these nations a just compensation for the losses suffered during the war.

The popularity of the Marshall Plan, the US support of the United Nations plan, and the signing of the military treaties, especially NATO, offset the unpopularity of Truman's domestic policies. Truman was thereby able to regain the presidency in the 1948 election and the Democrats also recaptured a majority in both houses of Congress in 1948. Truman accepted the party's victory as a mandate to continue his Fair Deal policies both domestically and overseas. Truman's Fair Deal proposals, however, were consistently defeated in Congress by a coalition of conservatives from both parties. The conservative alliances blocked all new Fair Deal proposals on the domestic front but were unable to block the final consolidation of the already existing New Deal programs. Truman was able to expand the coverage granted under the Social Security Program at the time it was adopted by expanding coverage for unemployment insurance; expanding the coverage of the rural electrification programs; and by expanding the coverage of the second agricultural act. The lesson was now being learned that skillful manipulation of these existing programs could be very effective in consolidating large voting blocs behind party platforms. As far as extensions represented by new programs, Truman was successful only in regard to the implementation of the Marshall Plan.

One set of Fair Deal proposals was aimed at the resolution of civil rights issues. The Fair Deal called for the implementation of a national health system, a restriction on the provisions of the Taft-Hartley Act (an act providing for a high level of tariff), and a new series of federal regulatory programs. All of these proposals were defeated by Congress but are still an integral part of the Democratic Party platform today.

The new conservative minority in Congress was clearly setting forth their concept of the limit to which federal intervention would be allowed in regulating the economy in the solution of social and civil rights issues, the health insurance industry, and in the labor market. The Republican Party had for some time included these limitations on federal intervention in their platform but were for the first time now joined by a strong minority position in the Democratic Party. By 1950 both parties had largely finished their readjustment to the social conditions that had been brought about by the Great Depression and World War II. Both parties had accepted the reality of the welfare state concept in the US and they had both accepted a heightened level of federal intervention in nearly every aspect of daily life, as well as accepting the leadership role of the US in the so-called "free world." By 1950 it had already become evident that the vast superiority of the US, both economically and militarily, would create what has become known as the US hegemony.

During this period several international events of great importance caught the attention of the US public. First was the knowledge that the Soviet Union had successfully completed its program of developing atomic weapons. There was no question in the US that the Soviet Union intended to develop a complete atomic arsenal. The public fear generated by this event caused the federal government to overreact and to create nuclear weapons and an arsenal that could not be surpassed. This of course gave birth to the insane arms race that made up such a large part of the cold war. One part of the arms race was the creation of an industrial/military complex that seemed to have an independent position within the US society. The arms race also allowed the public acceptance of the US role as the world's policeman.

Second, the public was shocked by the victory of the Chinese Communists under Mao Zedong. The Chinese nationalists had received massive support financially, and in the provision of military supplies, from the United States. The same had been provided the Communists by the Soviet Union although in much smaller amounts. This was seen as a victory for the Soviet Union in the cold war and a serious defeat for the US. The official US response was to continue to recognize the Nationalist government, now confined to the island of Taiwan, as the official Chinese government; while the rest of the world accepted the Communist Peoples Republic as the real government of China and allowed them to take their position on the Security Council of the United Nations. Both of these events occurred during 1949 and clearly represent a blind spot in the US vision of international affairs.

Third, the victory of the Communist Party in China, coupled with the perceived strength of the Soviet Union, led to a direct support of the Communist Party movements in North Korea and Viet Nam by both of these nations. In Viet Nam, Chinese and Soviet support of the Communist Party insurgency led to the defeat of the French in 1954. This result led to two events: the general liberation of Southeast Asia from colonial control and the ill-fated support of the US for the continued existence of South Viet Nam from unification with the Communist North. The civil war in both Viet Nam and Korea led to the unofficial adoption by the US of a policy of containment of Communist gains to the Soviet Union and China. This doctrine would operate much in the manner of the Monroe Doctrine but would apply to the whole world. Anywhere that Communist insurrection appeared, the US was committed to support the retention of whatever form of government opposed the communist takeover — whether it be a democracy, a monarchy, or a military dictatorship. It did not matter whether the people of the country involved wished to be ruled by a communist party or not. As we shall see this had very deep and profound effects upon the US public's view of international relations.

The first real crisis arose with the North Korean invasion of South Korea. Under pressure from the US and its Western European allies, the United Nations issued a mandate authorizing the use of force to remove North Korea. The Soviet Union and China did not make use of their veto power on the UN Security Council as they felt they could not defend it in light of world opinion. Western Europe was still too exhausted both financially and militarily to contribute much. The enforcement of the UN mandate therefore fell mainly to the US in terms of men, equipment, and money. The North Koreans unofficially received aid from both the Soviet Union and China. The latter, when it became clear that the US was going to drive the North Koreans beyond the line of earlier partition, entered the war with over one million troops. At this point the Soviet Union called for the UN to offer an armistice and called for putting the boundaries where they had been at the time of the initial invasion. The UN, and ultimately the US, accepted this proposal and the Korean police action ended. The Korean War can arguably be seen as the first success of the unofficial US policy of containment. As such it represents a failure of communist political systems to spread by force beyond the limits that existed in 1952 and gave false hope to the "free world" of no further communist led aggression.

In the US, the conduct of the war by the Truman administration, es-pecially the decision to prevent General MacArthur from taking the war to the Chinese, coupled with the administration's inability to control in-flation, brought Dwight David Eisenhower, one of the military heroes of World War II, into office as president in 1952. It was Eisenhower who was in office when the proposal for the armistice was brought before the United Nations. The Eisenhower administration took the opportunity to tout the result as a clear victory for the US and its unofficial policy of containment. The election of Eisenhower seemed to indicate a subtle shift in public atti-tudes brought about by the depression, World War II, the Korean Conflict, and the new problem of inflation.

In many ways by 1950 the United States had reached the point in its evolution that it occupies to this day. The most important events during the next three decades whether they were recognized or not involve nations outside the US. In two areas of the world a clear drive was beginning to form that would attempt to undo the obvious hegemony that had evolved concerning the US control of international trade and commerce. These two areas are exemplified by the rapid growth of the Japanese modernization program including the later development of the Asian Rim countries and the somewhat later evolution of the EU. In the case of the Soviet Union the effects of the prolonged arms race, the space race, and the race for client states had to wait its conclusion until 1989. Even so the lessons that can be culled from the Soviet experience, especially as it relates to our belated knowledge of what actually occurred in the Soviet Union between 1949 and 1989, is of great importance to the establishment of a world government. This will be explained in greater detail later.

In relation to the so-called third world history has tended in the past to concentrate on the struggle for release from colonial status. The collapse of the several colonial empires is less important in today's world than the results of actual release from colonial bondage. Some of the most important problems that will be faced by an effective world government will be found in these areas of the world, that is, social and civil rights issues, intractable poverty, and large scale governmental incompetence and corruption. It is likely that even with the establishment of an effective world government that many decades will be needed to solve these issues in the areas of the world where they are most prevalent.

In addition problems faced by nations such as China and India with their large land mass, huge populations and vast diversity have yet to be even addressed. Even so both of these nations have made vast strides in solving these issues on their own terms. Both are trying to smoothly enter into the world community as expressed in the concept of the global market and working within the existing international organizations.

CHAPTER 12. THE EMERGENCE OF THE EUROPEAN UNION, AND THE
COLD WAR

There is the persistent myth that developed at a later date which de-
notes the period of the 1950s as a sort of golden age in the US. On the other
hand, there is the reality represented by several major trends that occurred
largely without recognition of their long term consequences. The most easily recognized trend is found in the election, and reelection, of Dwight David
Eisenhower as president and the return of the US public to conservative
values. The election of Eisenhower clearly reflected the public's lack of desire for any further radical legislation as represented by the New Deal and
the Fair Deal.

The depression, the world war, and the post-war inflationary spiral had
shocked the US public out of its love affair with the roaring twenties. Two
trends indicate the direction of the new conservatism more than most. First
was the widely successful revival of the evangelical movement in religion.
This movement was bringing the public's focus back to a concern for personal responsibility and for moral behavior both in regard to themselves and
to others. It also focused on a more traditional attitude towards family, marriage, divorce, friendship, and other social ethics. Second was the successful
effort of the corporate community to instill a strict discipline on its employees, known generally as the "corporate life." The new standard included the
inculcation of an unrestricted loyalty to the corporation, a strict dress code,
and a strict hierarchy that ran from the ceiling to the floor of the corpora-

tion. The success of the new program led to a willingness of employees to transfer to whatever location that was demanded by the corporation even though it might mean a sacrifice of family, friends, and intermediate social institutions, such as professional organizations, churches, etc. This loyalty was also expected to be extended to the functions of government (authority generally), leading to the rather naïve belief that the government was something akin to sacred. The willingness of the employees to uproot and move with the corporation allowed the corporations to move their operations out of the expensive environment of the inner city to the more open and economical atmosphere of the surrounding rural areas. As the urban employees moved from the inner city into the small town atmosphere of the rural areas they began to take on the traditional conservative attitudes of the rural areas. In addition, those retiring from the industrial complex tended also to move to the more rural areas of the country and adopt the conservatism they found there.

These two general movements also had two rather unintended consequences. First, the employees who tended to adopt the new corporate ethic were those that were both socially and economically capable of uprooting and moving to the rural environment. This did not include those who were considered manual laborers, that is, those who manned the assembly lines and other repetitive jobs. While the white workers in this category, through the use of more extensive support networks, were in large part able to make the move, the African-American workers in this category were unable to make the move and remained in the inner city. A rapid development of discriminatory practices in the new suburbs pertaining to housing and jobs was aimed at keeping African-Americans and some other ethnic groups locked in the inner city. This trend led to a large population block that was locked into almost perpetual unemployment, lack of educational and other social services, and a dependence on crime to make ends meet. In short, this trend began the development of what we today call the marginalization of labor. By the 1950s this trend had brought about today's true middle class which represented a full sixty percent of the total population. The middle class at this time was known for its growing drive to obtain material wealth, home ownership in the suburbs, a stay at home mom, and a large family (four or more children). The middle class also professed an attachment to religion whether religion was a part of daily life or not. This class also came to be known for their ambition to create and live the "good life" (essentially a host of activities organized for both children and parents usually involving a rather extensive network of casual acquaintances). The demands of the good life, and middle class life in general, tended to cause a focus to be maintained on personal affairs and a lack of attention to state and national affairs, let alone international affairs. The 1950s have been characterized by some writers of the time as 'comfortable, but lonely'.

The persistent myth that developed, however, presents a somewhat different picture. The 1950s, according to this myth, represents a life that is wrapped in a comprehensive security. Crime, for example, was depicted as being so non-existent that one could safely leave the home unlocked while unoccupied. This would, of course, not result in any type of intrusion or crime being committed against the property. One could also leave the children unattended while at play without the least worry about them being accosted or molested. Social injustice (discrimination, racism, ethnic hatred, etc.) had been reduced to the extent that it was also almost non-existent. There were no known problems involving drugs, gun ownership, racial segregation, ethnic discrimination, or discriminatory policies towards those who were disabled, insane, or criminal inmates. The family was set forth as the most sacred of institutions followed closely by the church, fraternal and business organizations, "the company," friendships, and even government, including local, state and federal governments. While this myth may have had some basis in truth, at least, in the secluded environment of the suburbs for a short time, nothing like it could be found upon close inspection. Within the inner city, and within the environment of middle sized cities, the reality of life was much different, as it was also in the Deep South.

The realities that faced the poorer classes, particularly the African-Americans, Hispanics, and other ethnic groups, were evident to those who took the time to look. Racial and ethnic discrimination in the job and housing markets, abuse of the rights of the handicapped, disabled, and old, and the growing separation of government from the people were all plainly in sight if one cared to look. It may not, however, have been so evident concerning the negative effect the new corporate life, or the myth itself, would have on the family, the church, and the intermediate fraternal and professional organizations. All of these negatives were brought about by a gradual alteration of the traditional respect for authority. The problems that were developing in the urban centers, for example, had several interconnected causes. The major factor was due to the irresponsible recruitment practices exercised by the corporations to replace those that were called away to war beginning in 1917. The recruitment practices were irresponsible in the sense that those recruited were enticed to uproot from their homes, family, and other support institutions that normally sustained them in hard times. These recruits were also not informed, in the case of World War II that those that they replaced had been guaranteed their jobs back when they returned from the service. The success of this recruitment program is confirmed by the demographic changes that occurred between 1917 and 1960. The recruits were settled in the inner city and then abandoned when they lost their jobs with the returning servicemen, or the corporation moved out of the city into the suburbs. The origin of the ghettoes can be traced directly to the effects of this policy. It was at this time that the states of California, Michigan, Oregon, Washington, Utah, Colorado, Wisconsin, Illinois, and New York saw their greatest influx of African-Americans, largely from the Deep South. With the transfer of corporations from the inner city to the suburbs, mainly after 1945, came the development of the urban ghettoes, most evident in Detroit, Pittsburgh, Baltimore, Los Angeles, and other highly industrialized areas. When the corporations, and the service businesses that attended them, along with the majority of the workers, left the inner city so did the tax base. As a result those left in the inner city began to notice a decay in the infrastructure that served them, such as, the schools, sanitation systems, water systems, roads, bridges, etc., as well as a decline in neighborhood businesses and entertainment facilities. All these factors contributed to the formation of a population essentially left to fend for themselves. The lack of ability to gain employment and to provide for a reasonable standard of living forced a shift from independence to a dependence upon welfare. Soon even the hope that things would soon get better deserted those who lived in the inner city. All who could by any means migrate out of the inner city and into the suburbs did so during the decades of the 40s and 50s.

In addition, another mass migration was taking place. The inability of the traditional family farm to maintain itself was now becoming all too apparent to those who remained on the farm. The younger members of the farm families began to leave the farms in masse looking for gainful employment in the urban suburbs. Many of these young people were successful in finding jobs in the new industrial plants opening in the suburbs. Most of these jobs were available due to those who could not afford to move from the inner city when the factories moved out. The new interstate highways, constructed originally as a military concern, soon became the main arteries supporting the vast migration of people from the rural countryside into the urban environment. The small towns and villages that had existed to service the farm families now began to die out if they were not located geographically close to the new expressways. Those near enough to the interstate became "bedroom" communities for those who worked in the suburbs but could not afford to live there. This result was in a large degree promoted by the subsidies provided by the government and their control by large corporate farms. Therefore, the complexion of the US began to change during the 1950s and early 1960s. The great cities tended to become a two tier structure, that is, an inner city that was largely run down and composed of those who had turned to welfare and crime to make ends meet, and the suburbs that surrounded them. The suburbs were packed with malls, entertainment facilities, well maintained infrastructures, and middle and lower upper class people. A large number of well serviced intermediate sized cities grew up from their traditional small town status and became bedroom communities for those who were willing to drive an hour or more back and forth from work. These cities also had a full list of amenities and largely well to do people. The rural areas began to become towns and villages that were essentially backwaters if located any real distance from the interstate; or tourist dependent if close to the interstate. The farmland was largely taken over by large farming corporations and operated as a business, that is, very few small family farms remained in operation unless they specialized in a cash crop of some type. During this period life in the small cities, small towns, and villages could aptly be described as "provincial." This same movement passed over the Deep South during this period but eventually also overtook them during the 1970s and 1980s. The artists and writers of the period tended to accurately portray the dichotomy that separated the urban and provincial areas of the country. The most popular writers and artists, such as, Norman Vincent Peale, Norman Rockwell, Benjamin Spock, and a host of quasi-religious writers expressed the conservative ideology underlying the myth of security and white picket fences. The less popular, but more highly acclaimed writers and artists portrayed the aloneness, the superficiality, and the barrenness of life. They tended to portray the alienation and prejudice they found wherever they went, but especially in the big cities and corporate working environments. "The Naked Lunch" by Edgar Burroughs and "Death of a Salesman" by Henry Miller stand as excellent examples of what writers saw in the urban centers. While those two writers and others like them had little impact at the time, they would become the vanguard of the later reaction to the complacency of this period.

All these events and movements represent a massive adjustment required of the US public to deal with the catastrophic events that had occurred between 1912 and 1950. Included within these momentous events was the further increase in corporate size and the increase in the size of urban, state, and federal governmental structures. They all tended to decrease the population's commitment to political liberalism and to increase their support of conservative values. These adjustments were, of course, reflected in the platforms of the two political parties. The Democrats continued to be, generally speaking, the home of the liberal political platform, while the Republicans held stoutly to the conservative platform. The Democrats, because of their connection in the minds of the people with the New Deal programs, continued to garner a large share of their support from the inner city, ethnic communities, industrial workers (mainly through the effort of labor unions) and various reform movements. The Republicans, on the other hand, found their support in the suburbs, the retirement communities, and the rural areas generally. The Republican support base, therefore, tended to much more widely dispersed than that of the Democrats. The unpopularity of the Fair Deal programs after World War II led to the breakdown of the dominance of the Democrats that had existed almost unbroken since 1930. The first evidence of this breakdown came with the election of Eisenhower, which definitely represented a return to conservative values. As we have seen the Republicans had been able during the Democratic ascendency to maintain a strong minority position in Congress that was capable of blocking a large share of the liberal agenda, although they were not capable of undoing the programs instituted during the depression. Between 1952 and 1960 the Democrats were able to maintain the majority status in both houses of Congress and in the state legislatures. During this whole period of time the conservative philosophy was greatly aided by the position assumed by the Supreme Court which ruled many of the New Deal programs unconstitutional. As we will see both parties soon came to understand the power of manipulating the remaining welfare programs to benefit them at least in terms of voting blocs. The need of the Democrats to maintain their liberal stance was also the reason, in large part, for their continued focus on the area of civil rights. The Republicans, on the other hand, found themselves locked into a conservative stance that reflected the desires of the suburbs, medium and small size cities and villages, and the rural sections of the country generally. This in turn, led to their focus on the more ultra-conservative portions of the party platform.

The complacency that fell over the US public during this period also caused the drift away from interest in politics in general as stated above. This allowed the leaders of the Federal government to institute the Marshall Plan, construct the North Atlantic Treaty Organization (NATO), and support the development of a united Western Europe without much notice by the public. Most of the US public is to this day uninformed about the European Union and how it operates, even to the degree that they do not understand how the EU affects their daily lives. The European Public although now becoming much more aware of the EU was almost as uninformed during the period from 1952 to 1970 as the American public. The EU began with the hopes of some of the leading European politicians that Western Europe could evolve into the United States of Europe. These hopes were held by Winston Churchill, Conrad Adenauer, and the Italian prime minister of the time, and were supported by such men as Jacques Delors, Robert Schuman, and Jean Monnet. The Marshall Plan pumped billions of dollars into the European economies allowing the rapid recovery of almost all of the Western European nations. This money was intended to support the US desire for a more united Europe to help in the cold war against the Soviet Union and to keep West Germany tied to Western Europe. NATO was created to provide Western Europe with the military security it needed to recover from war and provide time for them to build up their own defense system. As stated earlier all of this took place without much notice on the part of the American public.

At the same time the US business community was taking advantage of the war recovery both in Europe and in Asia by providing a large share of the manufactured goods needed in these areas during the recovery period. Several international organizations were created and controlled by the US to aid in this process. These agencies included the General Treaty on Tariffs and Trade (GATT), the International Monetary Fund (IMF), the World Bank, the World Trade Organization (WTO) and others. The US during this period was able to evolve a rather solid monopoly of global economic power. The US provided nearly half of all the manufactured goods on the world market and controlled an even larger share of the trade and financial arenas on the global stage. This hegemony in the economic and monetary arenas was protected by the equally large military capacity of the US. Once again this process of global economic growth and military organization escaped the notice of a large share of the US public.

Chapter 13. The US Public Becomes Aware of the Rest of the World

The year 1950 marks the point at which the US took the position in relation to the global market that it holds today. The US essentially held this position during the first three decades after the close of World War II. At the peak of its power US manufacturing interests held control of nearly fifty percent of the world's trade in consumer goods. Taking the lead of J.P. Morgan, the US would during this period maintain a near monopoly over the international financial market as represented by the Bretton Woods system. In addition, the US expanded its shipping role during the war into another near monopoly in international shipping. The dollar, during this period, largely because of the spending occasioned by the Marshall Plan and the financial monopoly, became the international reserve currency. The US would also continue to develop its premier military position during these three decades, subject only to the ability of the Soviet Union to maintain parity with the US in nuclear weapons and missile technology.

The establishment of the US military umbrella in Western Europe coupled with the effects of the Marshall Plan resulted in a refocusing of European politics. The same military umbrella was established over the Asian nations, especially Japan which had been forced to give up all military activities under the World War II peace treaty. In both areas there was a relatively rapid recovery from the ravages of the war and a focusing of effort on political and economic stability. The initial economic recovery and modernization that took place in Western Europe was followed by the recognition that the US dominance in the global market could not be challenged by any one European Nation. This recognition was coupled to an equally clear recognition of the importance of the US military umbrella for further economic development. The result was a refocusing away from the former concern with military development, with the exception of Great Britain and France, who still held hope of regaining their world power status. The new focus both in Western Europe and Japan revolved around the desire to become competitive with the US in the global economy.

The idea received its first attention after World War II as a call for replacing the European system of nationalism with a form of federalism. Even Winston Churchill felt that this was part of Europe's destiny after the war. The federation envisioned was from the beginning based on the concept of integrating the European national economies and removing the barriers to the free movement of people, money, goods, and services. Also from the beginning it was made clear that such integration would require that Europe remain at peace with itself. Only with the building of a single European market could the Europeans compete with the US on a global scale.

The first step came in 1951 with the Treaty of Paris which created the European Coal and Steel Community (ECSC). The original six members included France, West Germany, Italy, Belgium, The Netherlands, and Luxembourg. The success of the ECSC in bringing the six members into a truly competitive stance with the US in its designated concern with coal and steel led to the signing of two additional treaties. One of these created the European Economic Community (EEC) and the other created the European Atomic Energy Community (EURATOM). The goal of the EURATOM was to allow the pooling of assets to allow the more rapid and efficient development of both nuclear weapons capability and nuclear power for domestic peaceful uses. The goal of the EEC was to establish an integrated multinational economy, a unified customs union, and to promote the standardization of laws between the members concerning trade, commercial standards, and cost and price stability among others. This effort led very quickly to a substantial increase in productivity and allowed greater investment to be made in agriculture and industry. The success attained by the original six members was duly noted by the other European Nations especially the fact that they had become competitive in the global market. In short, all the

Western European nations became aware that the six members through the EEC had become capable of breaking into the US monopoly.

By 1960 the EEC had acquired all the trappings of a fully fledged government although at this time it was not classified as such. It had its own executive branch complete with an established bureaucracy known as the European Commission; it also had a quasi legislative body known as the European Parliament; and in addition it had its own judiciary system known as the Court of Justice. The latter was accompanied by a legal system effective within all six member nations and which was essentially an economic regulatory system. The success of the EEC brought with it gains in membership. Great Britain, Denmark, and Ireland joined in 1973 and these nine members represented the EEC until the 1980s. The growth in membership however continued after the period we are now considering. In 1987 the Single European Act (SEA) eliminated most of the remaining barriers to the movement of people, money, goods, and services between the then existing twelve members. In 1993 the Maastricht Treaty changed the name of the organization to the European Union (EU) and committed the member states to the establishment of a uniform currency, a common citizenship, a common foreign and security policy, as well as enlarging the legal and policy powers of central organizations of the EU. In 1998 and 2003 the Treaties of Amsterdam and Nice respectfully altered the legal system and the powers of the existing EU institutions to prepare them for the membership of twelve additional members; all located in what before 1989 was found in the area tightly controlled by the Soviet Union.

Between 2002 and 2004 an attempt was made to replace the various treaties that stood as the legal basis of the EU with a written Constitution. In the end this attempt failed and the EU satisfied itself with the updating of the existing treaties to bring the institutional rules up to date. This is essentially where the EU stands today in relation to the legal basis for its federalist structure. The EU is governed by the following institutions: 1. The European Commission which is based in Brussels. This institution is generally considered to be the executive and administrative branch of the EU. It is responsible for developing new EU laws and policies and also for the general oversight of their implementation after passage. 2. The Council of Ministers also located in Brussels. This institution consists of members that are directly appointed by the member nations and allows for the direct participation of the various nations. Exercising this participation involves the Council in the activities of both the Commission and European Parliament. Essentially the process consists of the Commission initially proposing new laws and policies which it cannot pass into law. The Council of Ministers then takes the proposals and reviews them either approving or rejecting them. If they approve the proposals they then help the Commission draft the proposal in suitable form to be made law. The European Parliament with the help of the Council then drafts the actual statute involved and passes it into law. The European Parliament is located in Strasbourg, Luxembourg, and Brussels and consists of members that are directly elected to five year terms by the citizens of the member nations. 3. The European Court of Justice located in Luxembourg. The Court is responsible for interpreting the laws of the EU with the intent of making them compatible and operative within the legal systems of the various member nations. 4. The European Council which is composed of representatives, usually the executive leader of the member nations, is more a sub-cabinet of the Commission than an independent institution. Its main purpose is to establish the broadest of decisions on policy matters that relate to the duties of the EU institutions. This latter organization was not formally a part of the EU but has been officially recognized by treaty and operates through four annual meetings.

This brief survey of the evolution of the EU and the delineation of its institutions should clearly show the real importance of the EU as a guide for the initiation of an effective world government. It is essentially a republican federation of twenty seven independent nations that have accepted significant reductions in their sovereign rights for the benefit of all. The development of the EU during the period under consideration, as well as its importance to the world today, clearly indicate that it is one of the most important movements leading to the call for a world government. Both the US and the Soviet Union played important roles in this development, even though to a significant degree this part was a negative one.

Today some believe that the EU has become the big brother that supports the economic viability of the US. Even so, the military hegemony of the US remains unchallenged by the EU. However this view is countered by the growing belief that military power has less impact on world opinion than economic power. This growing belief includes acknowledgement of the growing dichotomy between the political policies of the US and the EU. Recently the EU has become increasingly verbal about US foreign policy, especially concerning the use of military force (both in Afghanistan and Iraq), environmental issues (global warming and the pollution of the oceans), and the proliferation of weapons of mass destruction (mainly policies affecting Israel, North Korea and Iran). It is too early yet to attempt to determine where this growing dichotomy may lead in connection with the relations between the two economic giants, that is, the US and the EU; but what is certain is that a reshuffling of priorities will be necessary to establish an effective world government.

In a second area of the world a similar result was obtained by the modernization and development of Japan. It is somewhat ironic that both of the nations that were the major military competitors of the US during World War II became the leading economic competitors during the first three decades following the war. It is even more significant that the decisions made by the US immediately after the conclusion of the war were of the highest importance in determining the success of the two movements. In the case of Japan the private industrial sector in the US initially took advantage of the cheap labor to be found in Japan. The Japanese were quickly converted to the task of assembling and producing cheap industrial products for sale in the US market. This soon led to the perception that the label "Made in Japan" was the same as the English word "junk." The inflow of US investment into Japan however allowed the Japanese government the ability to convert the feudal system that existed prior to the war to a viable modernized economy. The security afforded by the US military umbrella allowed the funneling of funds that would have normally been spent to construct a military into modernization of the Japanese industrial structure. Included within the construction of modern management and production technology was the manufacturing of products that exceeded the quality of competing American products at an equal or lesser cost. It was not long before the label "Made in Japan" was equated with quality and innovation. The Japanese broke the American monopoly of the global market and entered the US market itself.

The growing share of the global market taken by both the EU and Japan was supported by a rather unique use of the premises of republican democracy. In Western Europe as we have seen above this is represented by the EU. In Japan the movement towards federalism was more attuned to economic matters. As part of their modernization the Japanese were able to establish large conglomerates consisting of manufacturing, financial, and supply institutions that crossed national boundaries. This gave the Japanese, and somewhat later other Asian nations, a competitive edge in terms of cost and quality control over their US competitors. The US corporations although aware of the techniques being developed by the Japanese were either unable or unwilling to change their methods of doing business. Today the result has been the rather sharp decline in the position of the US in terms of the global market.

In addition to the growing challenge represented by the economic power of both Western Europe and Japan, the US was faced with the problem presented by the Soviet Union. After the war, the Soviet Union saw that the United States had expanded its power around the world and decided to challenge the "West" in an arms race, a race into outer space, a race to develop superior technology, and a race to obtain "client" nations as support in the United Nations and world opinion. This only strengthened the US determination to hold its position. Overall, the policy decisions made by the Soviet Union in response to the unofficial actions of the US policy of containment resulted in the US adopting positions that were absolutely adverse to its real interests. The space race, the arms race, the race for superior technology and the race to obtain dominance in world opinion were all unnecessary. These competitions not only caused both nations to waste huge amounts of resources but also cost them credibility on the world stage and allowed the Western Europeans and Japanese the opportunity to freely develop their current positions in relation to the global market and international affairs generally. Then, with the demise of the Soviet Union as such, the US found itself in a position that generated a great deal of policy confusion — as we will see later.

In the case of India, the first three decades after the war were taken up in the effort to establish a stable and viable government more than to become a major player in the global market. In India the drive for modernization was financed by US and European money obtained by supplying cheap labor, especially in the service sector. In India this process began early and it now appears to be bearing fruit. Although many problems still face the Indian society, a form of parliamentary democracy has been developed around the circumstances that exist within that society. India appears to be heading into a position that will either allow it to develop a stable government or that will create a scenario of political chaos that could lead to dismemberment of the current Indian nation. The jury is still out on this development, although the trend seems to favor a stable parliamentary democratic system.

China presents a rather more complex case. First, since 1949 and the Communist Party takeover China has been a relatively impenetrable nation. During the first few decades after independence China remained essentially isolated from the world except for its participation in the United Nations. During this same period, under the direction of Zhao Ziyang and other re-formers, the Chinese began to quickly convert their system of state planned economics into a mixed system of national planning and capitalism. They clearly rejected the Soviet political system and were attempting to create what they believed to be a socialist democracy. In the economic arena, in particular, the Chinese recognized that they would not be able to compete in the global market without introducing a large dose of private enterprise (capitalism). They maintained centralized control over agriculture and in-dustry generally, but within that planned economy they allowed the growth of small scale farming and industry under a relatively free market system. Over time this has led the Chinese to take advantage of the two systems. They still have the advantage of using the centralized system to tightly con-trol costs and wages, while at the same time using their private enterprise reforms to foster cooperation with foreign nations in the establishment of joint industrial and commercial projects. Although today Chinese products are very cheap and some have inherited the reputation of the early post-war products from Japan, they have also made great strides in technology and manufacturing, and probably more important, they have evolved into the major holder of the US debt structure.

The result is that China today is in an economic and political position equal to that of the US, the EU, and Japan and the other Asian Rim eco-nomic powers (South Korea, Thailand, among others) vis-à-vis the notion of any world government being imposed. In short, the refusal of any of these nations, singly or jointly, to join the world government would likely mean it could not be successfully implemented.

In relationship to the general history of the world all of these events may hold a relatively equal position of importance. In relation to the estab-lishment of an effective world government, however, the evolution of the EU seems to hold the most importance. The dream of the EU began with the hope that it would develop into a sort of United States of Europe. It actually developed into something greater than an international organization but less than a supranational government. In certain areas of law and policy, the EU actually does exercise power that is equal to any existing national government; but overall it lacks the consistent power to make and enforce its will on the citizens of the various nations that are its members. It is probably accurate to describe the EU as a modified federal institution. There are currently twelve or so federal institutions in existence. The EU is not like any of them, for example, unlike the federal systems consisting of the United States and Canada it cannot levy taxes nor can it enforce a common security and defense policy. Unlike all other federal systems the EU does not have a common military force and it cannot demand the loyalty of its citizens. It does, however, have several things in common with all other federal systems, such as laws that stand above the laws of the members nations; a democratically elected parliament; a common budget; a common currency which is in effect in twenty of the twenty seven member nations; a common executive authority authorized to negotiate and sign trade treaties and other international documents; and the fact that the member nations are increasingly known not by their national designations but rather by their membership in the EU. The major exceptions to this latter statement appear to be Germany, France, and Great Britain who are somewhat more proactive in maintaining their national identity.

To underscore an essential point, it is of the utmost importance that the world union should make every effort possible to keep the member nations and any lesser political subdivisions that are found within the member nations as active as possible in the operation of the union. The actual historical evolution of the EU is an example of how that goal can be obtained. The federal like structure of the current EU should be carefully studied for any benefit it can render to the establishment of a world union. In particular it should be clear that the various treaties used by the EU could be used as a model for the drafting of treaties covering the initial stages of disarmament, pollution control and many other issues. In the view of some scholars such as John McCormick the EU should technically be considered a confederate organization, i.e., an organization where the members retain all of the power and delegate only limited powers to the central authority. This description closely matches the description of the US under the Articles of Confederation. As we have seen this could also be seen as the major weakness of the current EU organization.

Regardless of whether or not the EU can stand as a model or guide to the establishment of an effective world government it must be respected for its position as the largest single economic market in the global market place; as one of the major influences in the development of world opinion; and as the most modern bastion of the effort to establish large scale peaceful solutions to economic, racial, ethnic, and social problems. In connection with the other eleven federal systems in existence it is likely that a world government can be created that will meet the demands of the current world situation by their cooperation in the endeavor.

It is now possible to return to a look at the position occupied by the US in relation to the developments outlined above. We have already looked at the US participation in the Korean Conflict and also have taken a short look at the social milieu surrounding the administration of Eisenhower. Little will be said about the administration of John Kennedy as it did not last long enough to establish its mark on history. We will relocate ourselves in US history by looking at the administration of Lyndon Johnson. Johnson was able to use the myths that surrounded the death of Kennedy to create a new public attitude towards the federal government under the program known as "The Great Society".

The great society programs represented the largest expansion of public expenditures in US history up to that time and possibly in the world at large. The same programs also led to the most intrusive intervention by the federal government into the daily lives of its citizens yet experienced. The consequences of the programs instituted are still evolving within the current environment of the US, especially in relation to their cost, their effectiveness, and their sustainability. There is no doubt that these programs finished the evolution of the US towards a rather unique version of State Socialism, normally within the US designated as State Capitalism.

It is ironic that the Great Society programs (which were targeted especially at the inner cities) failed to satisfy the real needs of those who resided in these areas. The discontent in the inner cities and urban centers generally continued to spawn violent reactions led by such men as Malcolm X and groups such as the Black Panthers. The violent riots that erupted in Detroit, Los Angeles, and other cities in response to worsening living conditions soon caught the attention of the public and the mainstream civil rights movement. Martin Luther King Jr., for example, turned his attention almost immediately to the problems faced in the inner cities. The public was appalled by the arson, the looting, and the general lawlessness of the urban population, which was given wide media coverage.

At the time about seventy percent of the African-American population lived in the inner cities. They had endured decades of inadequate government services, schools, hospitals, police and fire protection, and slowly deteriorating living conditions. The businesses that remained in the inner city were not generally owned by African-Americans but rather by the newly arrived Asian populations from Korea and Indochina. Lastly, they still faced consistent discrimination in the labor market.

The consequences included a long term dependence on welfare and the use of crime, especially in the form of drug trafficking, to make ends meet. The Great Society programs did not solve these real problems but did bring them into greater focus for those who were leading the civil rights movements. It was obvious that the throwing of more money at the problems would not solve anything; and the communities involved began to demand that a real effort be made to address the problems listed above. Specifically they called for quality schools, police and fire protection, infrastructure repairs, the establishment of programs to encourage black business ownership, and other quality amenities that make up the good life in US terms. Many in the inner city felt that the great society programs, especially low-income housing projects, only aggravated the problems by further isolating the community. Once again the outbreak of war like conditions put the debate on hold between the civil rights movements and the federal government.

Regardless, an effective world government must heed the lessons of the Great Society programs. Poverty, crime, welfare dependency, poor levels of education, police and fire protection, health care, and the failure to sustain infrastructure cannot be eliminated by the institution of more generous entitlement programs. These problems require on site evaluation, local implementation and inspection, and real physical changes in the manner in which life is lived. In short, care must be taken to insure that the dignity of those involved remains intact while the programs are being implemented. It is only when the people themselves are truly invested in their own future that they will become willing to put forth the effort, and to make the sacrifices necessary, to create that future. It is also clear that the future of people cannot be created by large scale planning but must be created by real human acts. This is the real import of the tenets of 19th-century liberalism.

Returning to our story, it turned out that international affairs would be the Achilles heel of the Johnson administration. Johnson had taken on the earlier commitment by Eisenhower and Kennedy to support South Viet Nam against the communist regime in North Viet Nam. The goal supposedly was not to defeat North Viet Nam militarily but rather to secure recognition and stabilization of the tentative boundary that had been established between the two countries. This solution was rejected not only by the North but also by the majority of the population in the South. Most of the people wanted, and were willing to fight for, a united Viet Nam. By 1969 the 16,000 advisors approved by Kennedy had grown to over 542,000 US combat troops committed to Viet Nam without any official purpose other than to support the Diem regime in South Viet Nam. The cost of US involvement both in terms of military causalities and in material wealth was beginning to place a strain upon the US economy and public. The actual military turning point in the conflict came with the 1968 Tet offensive (Vietnamese New Year) by the North Vietnamese and the South Vietnamese Viet Cong, when it became clear that the Vietnamese were willing to sacrifice whatever it took in lives and wealth to accomplish the goal of a united Viet Nam. It was also at about this same time that the US public began to get vocal about its dissatisfaction with the war, its loss of life, and its cost in material wealth. Some people began to ask what was our mission there and what vital US interests were at stake. Dissatisfaction was fed by the public knowledge that a significant portion of the funds earmarked for the Great Society programs had been siphoned off to pay for the war. The public reaction, especially the growing number of war marches and anti-war demonstrations, convinced Johnson that he could not win the presidency in 1968 and he announced his intention not to enter the election race. Ironically the most successful domestic president had now been forced to give up the office through his failure to control international policy. This military adventure was also the point at which the EU stopped blindly accepting US foreign policy and began to privately voice their concerns.

Two assassinations marked 1968: that of Robert Kennedy and that of Martin Luther King Jr. Robert Kennedy at the time of his death had thrown himself into the Presidential race to replace Lyndon Johnson on the Democratic ticket. Martin Luther King Jr. was the most rational and articulate spokesman in the mainstream of the civil rights movement. The loss of Dr. King threw the civil rights movement into disarray for a period of time as the community attempted to adjust to his loss. The public was also distracted from civil rights issues by the growing concern over the war in Viet Nam. The assassinations, coupled with the relatively recent assassinations of John F. Kennedy and Malcolm X, brought a level of violence into the US society that was unique in its history.

With the loss of Robert Kennedy, the Democratic Party lost its momentum in the 1968 election. The public was totally repulsed by the violence of the assassinations, as well as the violence of the civil rights protests and the anti-war protests. As a result the Republican candidate Richard Nixon was elected president.

The Johnson administration represents the end of a rather sustained return of political liberalism to dominance in US politics. This dominance had begun in the late 19th century and had continued with short breaks in 1918 and 1952 until 1968. This represented a period of time nearly equal to what turned out to be the life span of the Soviet Union. We have seen the vast changes that this seventy year domination of politics had brought. The US had in reality turned from its original commitment to laissez-faire federal government, which included a commitment to individualism, personal responsibility, free market economics, republicanism, and isolation from international affairs; and replaced these commitments the US had taken to a position favoring legalism (a lack of personal responsibility evidenced in welfare dependency, legal entitlement, and governmental establishment of formal equality by law) in regard to its citizens, group responsibility, a fully regulated economy, nationalism (that is a democracy with sovereignty only in the general government), and total involvement in international affairs. A second consequence was the failure of belief on the part of the public in the effectiveness of state and local governments, as well as private charitable institutions to cope with the personal problems facing citizens. This earlier reliance was replaced with a belief that only the federal government (the state in its corporate status) could effectively deal with these problems. This included the belief that individual citizens had little or no responsibility in the solution of social problems. These shifts were to become very evident during the next two decades as were their consequences.

The 1970s are marked by the general ineptitude of the Nixon and Ford administrations. The growing discontent evidenced by civil rights unrest coupled with the violence of the anti-war protests led directly to the withdrawal of the US from Viet Nam in 1975. The same lack of respect for authority was evidenced in the illegal behavior of Nixon in relation to the Water Gate scandal and his resignation of the office of president. Gerald Ford finished his term in office, and along with the administration of Jimmy Carter, brought the US federal government to a low point in credibility.

Be that as it may, there were several trends that began to develop during the late 1970s and early 1980s that promised an end to this type of irresponsible behavior. The breakdown of the Southern Bloc under Lyndon Johnson brought about conditions that made it possible to end the long stalemate in Congress. The Southern wing of the Democratic Party was replaced with a faction that was more liberal in its outlook and more capable of strict discipline in the control of party positions. This more liberal Democratic Party used its influence to block the attempts of Nixon and Ford to institute a more conservative approach to social problems. In addition, this shift in Democratic Party philosophy gave the civil rights movement the opportunity to reopen the issues that were of most importance to them. As evidence of the ability of the civil rights movement to work within the system is the fact that violent protest almost ceased to exist as a tactic in the movement. This shift away from violent protest took almost ten years to accomplish but was effective not only in regard to the African-American community but also in regard to the push for women's rights, gay rights, and others. All of these grassroots movements over the decade of the 70s and the early portion of the 1980s converted themselves to the position of well organized, well financed, and well staffed interest groups. As such they took their place in the US political system alongside the corporate, small business, religious, and other interest groupings. This in turn led to the dismantling of the traditional party politics of the US, i.e., the manipulation of welfare programs to gain voting blocs gave way to the courting of interest groups for the same purpose. These shifts in the political ideology of the US party system also seem to have had some unintended consequences. First, only a small number of the total citizenry was involved in the various interest groups especially in their decision making processes. As a result the vast majority of the citizens remained outside the decision making process in politics and became known as the "silent majority." The major aspects of the formation of a silent majority were, first, that the political parties spent much less time courting their views than they did those of the various interest groups. Second, the silent majority was essentially leaderless and therefore powerless in influencing the platforms of the two major political parties. As a result the silent majority was denoted by its rather consistent apathy towards politics. It is among this segment of the population that the distrust of authority had its greatest consequences.

By the end of the 1970s a startling dichotomy became evident in US politics. On the one hand a very large segment of the population took little, if any, interest in the political arena, even extending to the willingness not to vote. On the other hand, a significant minority of citizens were very active and very powerful and combined into well organized interest groups. These latter proved very effective at focusing governmental action. The result appears to be that the political parties no longer controlled the selection of candidates and issues but rather they were chosen by the effective pressure that is applied by interest groups. In short, the public at large was left to choose from the varying demands of interest groups if they decided to vote at all. As we shall see this was to change slowly during the late 1980s and 1990s with the development of such large scale interest organizations, such as the AARP and the religious right.

By 1980 it would be fair to say that the US public had accepted that the programs of the New Deal and the Great Society had largely failed to address the real problems that faced the United States. It would also be fair to accept the perception that the US public had also recognized the fact that the moderate liberal stance of the Nixon/Ford and Carter administrations had also failed to address the problems most important to the US public. This seems to point to the fact that the original political ideology of the US had failed to describe the political realities as they developed over historical time. This was particularly true in the public's perception of the accomplishments of the liberal philosophy over the preceding seventy or so years. In the public's view it was time to return to the traditional values that had made the US so important a part of the modern world. This was expressed especially by the silent majorities return to the traditional conservative values represented by the religious right. This return to traditional values was sparked in a large degree by the psychological shocks of the preceding three decades, that is, the Soviet explosion of an atomic device in 1949, the victory of "communism" in China in 1949, the war in Viet Nam, the violence of the civil rights movement and anti-war protests, the scandals that arose in both the business and political communities, and the assassinations of the late sixty's.

On the international front the US began experimenting with programs aimed at sustaining the position it had obtained in the world market at the end of World War II. As will be remembered at that time the US was directly responsible for about fifty percent of all the products found on the global market. By 1980 Japan and Germany (Western Europe generally under the EEC) had proven themselves competitive in this market system. They were on the brink of breaking the long US domination of the world market. The realization that others were about to take a significant portion of the US economic position on the world market brought with it the realization that unrestrained foreign aid, support for unpopular governments, and the use of covert operations were the main cause of this erosion of economic power. The response brought about an almost total collapse of US foreign policy. In the area of international relations the US public again began to call for a reinstatement of more traditional approaches, such as a relative isolationism.

By 1980 the public was thoroughly convinced that the New Deal and Great Society programs had failed to address the underlying problems. The conditions in the inner city had become worse, the denial of civil rights across the board had become more persistent, and the lack of authority was evident everywhere. The economy had entered into what was perceived to be a permanent stagflation. In short, political liberalism whether overt or moderate, had failed in the eyes of the public to address the most important social issues. The public understood with clarity that public education was still failing to meet the needs of a modern society, the infrastructure was failing to meet the needs of a rapidly increasing social mobility, and that government policies had receded into a type of antiquated past. The public was about to express its desire to return to the more traditional reliance on democratic republicanism, the free market, and individual responsibility for social problems. The failure to address the underlying causes of social instability may in fact be a product of the failure to recognize what they were at the time; but the bankruptcy of New York City, and the failure of the Savings and Loan Institutions should have been a clear warning as to the failures of the system of regulations that was then in place.

It is clear that the establishment of an effective world government will need to take cognizance of the fact that welfare capitalism (state capitalism) coupled with a system of internal dollar diplomacy (the throwing of money at problems in hope that the problems will disappear) does not work within the traditional ideology of republican representative democracy based upon the US model. It is therefore incumbent upon those who would establish an effective world government to devise a plan that would address the existing social problems that face the world without any intention of throwing money at them to quiet the social unrest contained within them. A world government will have the opportunity to offer and institute substantive programs for the elimination of poverty, infrastructure inadequacies, economic marginalization, and many others.

The US reaction to the perceived failure of the liberal platform was to elect Ronald Reagan as president of the US.

CHAPTER 14. THE BEGINNING OF A NEW ERA IN US POLITICS

Ronald Reagan was in many ways the most unlikely of men to lead the resurgence of an ultra-conservative revolution in US politics. In other ways, however, a better candidate could not have been selected by the US public. His early political career included a beginning that put him solidly in the tradition of the New Deal. He became even more involved with the liberal philosophy when he became the president of the Actors Guild in Holly-wood. After some experience with the liberal tradition, especially with the infiltration of the Actors Guild by suspected communists, Reagan turned to conservatism. He had experienced a wild swing from ultra-liberalism, as represented by the actors' union, to the ultra-conservatism of the religious right expressed as resistance to the suspected communist penetration of American society. By the late 1950s he was solidly behind the Eisenhower campaign for the presidency. At last in 1962 Reagan switched his party loy-alties to the Republican Party.

Reagan first came to public attention with his passionate support of the campaign of Barry Goldwater. Goldwater was totally unsuccessful in his campaign even to the point of nearly discrediting the ultra-conservative wing of the Republican Party. Reagan, however, in some manner was able to escape the debacle of the Goldwater campaign and became the acknowl-edged leader of the ultra-conservative wing of the Party. With the support of the wealthy members of the ultra-conservative wing Reagan was able to win the governorship of California in 1966. This in regard to the normal liberal bias of California politics was something of a surprise. Reagan entered the governorship on the promise that he would reduce state spending. California at that time had one of the largest if not the largest state budget deficit in the nation. The deficit had resulted in large part from the state expenditures in relation to welfare payments to individuals under various federal entitlement programs. Reagan was not able to push his legislation through the California legislature and in the end saw the California welfare payments nearly double. It was true, however, that he had succeeded in reducing the total number of people covered by the welfare programs. The public impression as a result was that Reagan had reduced the tax burden of the citizens of California; and had effectively reduced the size of state government in California. In fact, Reagan had accomplished neither of these goals as both the state government and the welfare budget increased as did deficit spending. This mistaken perception throughout the country made Reagan the "star" of the ultra-conservative faction.

From the date of his election as California Governor Reagan had set his goal to become a president of the US. The 1970s were not very conducive to the rhetoric of the ultra-conservative wing of the Party and Reagan was forced with them to take a back seat in national politics. A shift in demographics was occurring during the same time period that would change the political mood in the US. The changes were based on the gradually increasing age of the US population coupled with a massive migration of retirees to both the Southwest and the Southeast portions of the US. Both of these regions had for most of the later history of the US been the main bastion of conservatism. Conservatism in these areas was affected in a very significant manner by the views of the so-called religious right, a brand of ultra-conservatism. As a general rule, as a person gets older they also tend to become more conservative in their views, in particular their political views, that is to say, they become less comfortable with change. One of the most surprising reactions to the violence and chaos of the seventies was the reawakening of a new evangelical movement. This awakening differed from those that had occurred in the 19th and early 20th centuries. The latter had been largely local, or at most regional, in extent and were not particularly commercialized. The new movement was not only nationwide but worldwide in extent and was very highly commercialized. Some of the most prominent evangelists of this awakening owned their own television and radio networks as well as publishing companies that put out weekly and monthly magazines and papers. They would at times rent out entire stadiums in which to hold revivals as was the practice of Billy Graham one of the more widely known evangelists. Oral Roberts was able to establish and operate his own university solely from the donations of his faithful followers. The movement was able and did over a short time span reach millions of individuals in many cases changing their lives. In 1977, for example, a survey revealed that 70 million people claimed that they were "born again" Christians. The main goal of most of these evangelists was the bringing back to a belief in Christ and Christianity those who had slipped away earlier. The movement was successful through the decisions of the Supreme Court in obtaining a relaxation of the rules banning prayers from public schools, abortion on demand, banning the teaching of the creation story in public schools, and the enforcement of a stricter definition of pornography. The political arm (expressed in the formation of a well organized interest group) became known as the religious right and held forth a philosophy that included a return to an unregulated economy (a free market system), a reversal of Roe v. Wade (they sought a total ban on abortion — except when needed to save the mother — that became known as the "right to life" movement), a return to the concept of a limited federal government, and an open resistance to the Soviet Union (a battle against paganism). A curious fact regarding the political arm of the religious right was its failure to support the campaign of Jimmy Carter for president. Carter professed openly to be a born again Christian but the religious right did not throw him their support. It is probably true that his overall political views were so liberal that they could not in earnest accept him as one of their own. Ronald Reagan when he ran for his first term as president was very careful not to commit himself concerning his religious views. He was on the other hand openly in favor of the whole platform outlined by the religious right. As one would expect, this only shows that the secular arm of the religious right was more concerned with political views than religious ones.

At any rate, Reagan won the election of 1980 in large part because of his promise to oversee and promote the programs sought by the religious right. This election was the first time in US history that it was noticed that less than fifty-three percent of those registered to vote actually voted in the election. This figure does not include an estimate of the number of people who were eligible to register to vote but did not do so. It is likely that the fifty-three percent who did vote were composed of older voters and in a large degree were representative of the religious right. The forty-seven percent who did not vote, according to experts at the time, consisted largely of people under the age of thirty, urban dwellers, and union workers. This supports the contention that a definite shift had taken place in voting demographics. The shift was one from the dominance of union workers and urban dwellers to one expressing the dominance of the middle and upper class suburban dwellers. At the time this shift, if permanent, was expected to lead to a shift to a long term commitment to a conservative philosophy.

Reagan's first administration was highlighted by the proposals submit-ted with the intention of bringing stagflation under control. His program consisted of a concept known as supply side economics which was quickly dubbed "Reaganomics." The intention behind supply side economics was based on the theory that federal intervention in the market system coupled with high taxes was responsible for the nearly stagnant growth of the econ-omy, a high rate of inflation, and high rates of unemployment. The first two proposals offered by the administration were intended to remove federal intervention in the market by eliminating price controls on oil and by re-moving the embargo on wheat sold to the Soviet Union. Although Congress passed them neither of these measures appear to have been particularly effective in the short term. During the campaign Reagan had promised a "new beginning" consisting of large tax reductions to stimulate the growth of investment and thereby the economy. The new beginning also included a promise to reduce the size of the federal deficit to free up more funds for private sector investment. In lieu of these promises proposals were sent to Congress requesting significant tax reductions coupled with equally large reductions in government spending although an increase in the military budget was included. The latter increase in spending was connected to Rea-gan's promise to end the cold war in his generation through the introduction of a program named "star wars." The intent was to force the Soviet Union into a military spending race that would in the end bankrupt them. Most experts at the time predicted that Reagan's programs would fail mainly be-cause they relied on additional revenue that was expected to be realized from the growth in the economy. Under normal conditions it is likely that Congress would not have passed the legislation proposed by the adminis-tration. Conditions were altered by the assassination attempt made on Rea-gan's life and his rather flippant response to the attempt. Under these con-ditions Reagan's popularity with the public reached an all time high in US history. As a result, at least partially because of public pressure, Congress passed the proposals before them in 1981. The overwhelmingly positive vote in Congress lends creditability to the counter argument that it was less due to Reagan's popularity and had more to do with the shift in congressional seats due to the religious right. Both parties during the 1970s had seen a shift in their political philosophy towards the moderate conservative side of the ledger as well as the growing strength of the ultra-conservative wing in the Republican Party. This alone could explain the ease with which the package passed through Congress.

The Act itself was known as the Economic Recovery Act and set forth a twenty-five percent reduction in income taxes across the board (the reduction was spread over a three year period); it called for the maximum tax rate to be cut to fifty percent in 1982; it cut capital gains taxes to a maximum of twenty percent; and added a variety of tax concessions (loop holes). This package was essentially the whole supply side economics offered by the administration. The theory itself was clearly set forth back in 1789 by Alexander Hamilton in its simplest form, that is, 'that the more cash that was put into the hands of the public, especially the wealthy and business interests, the better it was for the economy.' At the same time the Congress passed the Recovery Act they also approved the requests for an increase in military spending. The combined short term effects of Reaganomics were a large increase in the federal deficit that exceeded the total of all his predecessors combined. The largest share of the federal budget was still for payments to individuals, i.e., Social Security, Medicare and Medicaid reimbursements, pension checks, veteran's benefits, and entitlement payments. About forty-eight cents of every dollar of revenue was spent on the above payments; another twenty-five cents was spent on the military; ten cents was spent to pay the interest on the national debt; and the remaining seventeen cents was split between encapsulated programs such as the FBI, CIA, National Parks, The National Weather Service, highway programs, and services to the handicapped, etc. Even with this, however, the first Reagan administration was able to reduce the federal budget deficit by 35.2 billion dollars largely through cuts in social services programs such as education, urban housing, food stamps, school meals, and health services. The reductions in federal spending in these areas were forced upon the state and local governments to keep the services intact. It is of interest to note that the cuts included a complete abandonment of the alternative fuels research program.

By the end of 1982 the public began to believe that the efforts by the administration had failed to improve the quality of their lives. This in turn forced the administration to reverse much of its former tax reduction policies even though a real reduction in taxes and deficit spending had occurred. The fact that the economy overall had not yet responded to these changes brought about the perception that they had failed, i.e., the National debt had grown significantly due to the failure of the expected new revenue from economic growth.

The administration of Ronald Reagan then shifted its focus to a second area incorporating an attempt to deregulate the economy. Reagan took the approach of appointing directors to the various regulating agencies that were committed to not enforcing the regulations that were on the books. In the field of labor relations the administration consistently fought against increases in both benefits and wages. The most prominent event in this field was the firing of all federal air traffic controllers after their refusal to compromise on working conditions. This treatment of the traffic controllers had been empowered in the president during the New Deal, i.e., the power to reduce, reorganize, or create new agencies by executive order. During his service as President Reagan was able to break the political power of the giant AFL-CIO setting the labor union movement back thirty years.

The administration also consistently resisted any of the issues involved in women's rights, or the civil rights movement generally when they touched on welfare issues such as abortion on demand, single parent issues, even at one point resisting the call for equal pay for equal work. The administration also took steps to eliminate existing affirmative action programs and to deny any further expansion in this area. The effect of the latter policy is evident in the reduction of appointments given to women and ethnic minorities during the Reagan presidency.

The proposals submitted by the administration to reduce the size of the federal government (bureaucracy) and the federal spending programs were largely still-born in Congress. Although conservatives were capable of garnering the votes to pass such legislation the desire to take such a risk did not exist. The failure of this legislation to pass, coupled with the revenue failure, made it evident that executive orders alone would not solve the problems facing the federal government particularly in the area of the economy.

Foreign affairs during the Reagan administration still captured the majority of the coverage offered by the mass media. As a result foreign affairs were also the most prominent part of the public's interest in the federal government. During his first term foreign affairs were a mixed blessing for Reagan. On the positive side Reagan began by blaming all of the world's problems on the policies of the "evil empire" (the Soviet Union). His solution was to create a military spending program that would make it impossible for the Soviet Union to maintain parity. Reagan was successful as we have seen in increasing military spending on a program intended to provide the US with an outer space missile defense system (star wars). The spending was also intended to revitalize the conventional weapons capability of the US military. It is likely, at least from the perspective of hindsight, that the Soviet Union was already incapable of maintaining industrial parity with the US. The consumer demands for domestic products although hidden from Western view were continuing to grow and were causing serious political problems for the Soviet elite. At any rate, the Soviet Union did not display any intentions of initiating a similar program of their own although very little time was left before the Soviet system broke apart. The US public gave its full support to the star wars program and the buildup of our conventional forces. On the negative side two events erupted that caused the US serious embarrassment in the area of foreign policy. First, the nation of Iran was taken over by the branch of Islam known as the Shia. This had happened even though the US had provided massive financial and military support to the Shah of Iran, a virtual dictator, and a member of the Sunni branch of Islam. This was correctly seen as a failure of US foreign policy. Second, the US had sent a peace-keeping force under the auspices of the United Nations into Lebanon. The militant arm of the Shia branch borrowed the insurrectionist tactics of both the Irish Revolutionary Army and the Palestinian Liberation Front, and attacked the US barracks in Beirut in 1983. The explosions from the truck bombs killed 241 US Marines. The US did not retaliate in this case but did quickly remove the remainder of its troops from the peacekeeping mission in Lebanon. The overall foreign policy mission in the Middle East remained the same, i.e., the continued support of Israel and moderate Arab leaders but the policy was now limited to doing only what was minimally required to support the policy. The Arab world and the Arab insurrectionist organizations in particular immediately interpreted the US pull out as a sign of weakness or lack of will power. The success of the insurrectionist actions in Lebanon made such tactics a standard weapon in the arsenal of Mid-Eastern insurrectionist organizations. The US, on the other hand, was faced with the lessons learned by both Great Britain and Israel that there is no such thing as a compromise when dealing with insurrection. The first term ended with the occurrence of a strange event centered in the Caribbean. The US, the perceived giant of giants, invaded a tiny island known as Granada, ostensibly to protect the lives of US citizens there as tourists or on business. Granada was a member of the British Commonwealth at the time. The mass media was on hand live as the invasion took place, providing film to millions of television onlookers. The results of the invasion were happy for the US and bolstered the public's spirit and Reagan's popularity; but for others it was only a sort of theatrical performance. Little notice was publicly taken by the EU but it was known that they disapproved of the invasion privately.

The second Reagan term in office began with the submission of another tax proposal to Congress. This proposal called for a reduction of the maximum tax on the lowest income brackets to fifteen percent; and the maximum rate of tax on the highest brackets to twenty-eight percent. At the same time the number of income tax brackets was to be reduced from fourteen to two. This tax legislation represented a retreat from the traditional reliance on a progressive income tax and was largely only beneficial to the wealthy. The proposal also was intended to close some of the most abusive tax loopholes offered in the former tax package. The package was passed rather easily by Congress and represents the high point in domestic policy during the second term in office.

The second term (as has been the case with most administrations since the end of World War II) was dominated by international affairs. The two major events that plagued the administration were the establishment of a détente with the Soviet Union and the revelation of the Iran-Contra scandal. First, the detente with the Soviet Union was mainly a symbolic term used to express the hope that the summit meetings being planned would led to a substantive change in the relations between the two nations. In reality the talks resulted in little more than progress in the ability to keep talking. What it did produce was a perception on the part of the public that the administration had made some real substantive advances in the talks. Second, the Iran-Contra scandal began with the revelation of a covert sale of armament to Iran for Iran's help in getting prisoners still held in Lebanon freed. Investigation soon revealed that the profits from the sale of arms to Iran were being covertly used to support the Contra faction in the civil war in Nicaragua. This type of aid had been specifically denied to the executive branch by congressional action. The resulting investigation conducted by Congress in public revealed a high level of financial and military incompetence. This included orders from the executive branch to execute a cover up consisting of false testimony and the shredding of pertinent documents. The public was left with a picture of military profiteering and misguided patriotism.

The embarrassment on the international front was matched by an equally embarrassing scandal on the domestic front. The financial mismanagement that had occurred within the Savings and Loan industry due to the failure to maintain strict regulation finally came to a head during the second administration. It is noted in passing that both the Iran-Contra scandal and the Savings and Loan debacle came to the public's attention by leaks to the mass media on the part of executive branch employees. The Savings and Loan institutions had been created as a conservative banking measure to aid in the financing of home ownership in the lower and middle classes. The system however became involved in what was known as the practice of leveraged buyout (LBO). Under this procedure a group of investors would buy the controlling interest (the majority of the stock) in a profitable business. The investors would then liquidate the company's real assets leaving the creditors with a bankrupt company. The Savings and Loan institutions due to the lax regulation instituted by Reagan became the major source of the loans used by the investors to make the initial purchase of the business. They also held most of the worthless assets. In the same connection the Savings and Loan associations also became the primary lending institutions involved in the purchase of "junk" bonds. In this case investors would buy large blocks of bonds on margin (a small percentage of their projected value) using loans obtained from the Savings and Loan institutions. The investors would again manipulate a profit from the bonds while at the same time leaving them as worthless collateral for the loans made on them. This was merely a new twist on the old game of profiteering. It was not long before the Savings and Loan associations were technically bankrupt. Their bankruptcy would have cost the savings of millions of ordinary investors (in the form of a loss of their savings deposits). The federal government under the conditions that existed could do little else than provide for the largest private bailout yet known to US history. In short, the taxpayers paid for the financial irresponsibility of the Savings and Loan industry and the illegal, or at the very least immoral and unethical tactics, of the individual investors. The combined effect of these two scandals was to destroy the credibility of the administration in the eyes of the public.

The eight years of the Reagan administration exceed all other periods in US history in regard to the public's willingness to accept both private and public debt. The relaxation of the conservative attitudes towards debt affected individuals (a massive increase in per capita credit card debt among other debt), corporations (the use of debt to maintain antiquated facilities and to finance profiteering), and governments (deficit financing at all levels of government). The national debt, for example, grew from 908 billion dollars in 1980 to 2.9 trillion dollars in 1989. The average US citizen saved about ten percent of their income in the 1960s and only 4.6 percent by the end of the 1980s. In Oct. of 1987 the creditors began to put calls for the redemption of this huge debt. The stock market crash that triggered this call on the debt structure of the US was short lived but did focus attention on the fact that conditions could arise that would in fact force the immediate repayment of large segments of debt. Attention was turned to the control of public debt and the rising imbalance of trade between the US and rest of the world.

These policies still in large part govern US policy. The US is the largest debtor nation on Earth by a sizable margin. It also is carrying a very substantial balance of trade deficit with the EU, Japan, and as of late with China. The US has been able to carry this huge internal and external debt structure largely due to the dollar's position as the main reserve currency. So far the wealthy countries of the world have been willing to lend the US money to cover its deficits in the form of purchasing US bonds and then turning around and reinvesting the dollars in the US economy. This is, however, beginning to change as the Euro challenges the dollar as the main international reserve currency. As this happens the EU is also enforcing through its economic power a stricter regulation of the global market in spite of the US demand that the global market be unregulated. As a result it may not be many years before the US will be forced to take the steps necessary to reduce its budget deficits, its trade deficits, and the US citizen's love affair with private debt. The adjustment when and if it comes will be painful to say the least. The fact that military power now seems to be taking something of a back seat to economic power may be a bright spot for the US. A huge reduction in military spending of all kinds would free up enough money to reduce the budget deficits to near zero. The US may not be able to reduce its trade deficits unless it accepts a non-hegemonic position in the global market and the need to continue to heed EU regulations in regard to the global market. It can be argued that the severe recession that has struck both the US and global economy is the first round of the adjustment needed to realign debt spending. The approach to date is to throw good money after bad in the form of massive bailouts of private corporations, private financial institutions, governments, and massive stimulation programs. They have all seemed to fail, at least in the short run. Many experts expect the economy will not recover in the foreseeable future. The funds generated by a full disarmament could go a long way in relieving this debt.

In relation to the establishment of a world government the return to the fundamentalist tradition of conservatism may be the major factor. There has been a sharp growth in the tendency for the US to act in a unilateral manner, for example, as it did in the case of the invasion of Iraq. This seems to stem from the negative side of the conservative movement, that is, the call for a return to isolation from world affairs, a return to the free market system, and an obsession with internal policies. In this case a call for a world government would probably evoke a considerable reaction in the US public against relinquishing even a minimal amount of national sovereignty. The same problem was faced in Great Britain as it made its decision to enter, or not to enter, the EU. In all cases, however, the opportunity to join, or not join, the world union should be debated much in the same manner as the US Constitution was debated in the Federalist Papers. Most nations appear to react favorably to any proposal that they perceive to be in their national interest. Under the system proposed the various nations would be capable of retaining a large share of their sovereignty while at the same time reaping the economic benefits of a world union.

In total the Reagan administration closely followed the platform laid out by the ultra-conservative wing of the Republican Party, in particular, the wishes of the religious right. The platform included the reduction of federal taxes, a generalized deregulation of the economy, a return of civil rights issues to the state and local governments for solution, a dismantling of the federal welfare programs, a return to the moral and ethical tenets of Protestantism, a balanced budget, and a reduction of the federal debt. The Reagan administration was able to obtain, although not totally maintain, major tax reductions, a major deregulation of the economy, a reduction of certain federal welfare programs such as food stamps and housing subsidies, a return of civil rights issues to the state and local level especially individual entitlement programs. Attempts were made but unsuccessfully to dismantle major portions of the existing welfare legislation, to establish protestant ethics, to balance the budget, and to reduce the federal debt. As was stated earlier there is as yet no means to make a conclusive determination of the effectiveness of these measures as they are still in the process of development. The administration especially after 1986 was unable to get its programs passed into law. The public perception, whether fair or not, or whether pre-mature or not, was that the programs of the ultra-conservatives had failed to touch the underlying economic and social problems. The public also perceived that the ultra-conservative policies had created a serious embarrassment in US foreign policy. These negative perceptions were more than offset by the positive response of the public to both the reduction of inflation and the reduction of unemployment. These were both signs of the slowly improving economy that still remained largely hidden to the public. As a result of this latter public satisfaction Reagan was able to handpick his successor George H. W. Bush.

In relation to the EU it became increasing apparent that differing policy issues were beginning to arise. The EU and its leading citizens were beginning to become public about the US debt structure, the growing US tariff increases in reaction to its imbalance in trade, as well as to other trade barriers. Although these reactions were beginning to surface they were largely hidden from public view for two main reasons; first, the EU and US were each others' largest trading partners and two, the EU still was in reliance on the US commitment to provide military security if needed. As we have seen the EU continued to expand both in terms of its share of the global market and in terms of its total number of member nations. The growing concern of the EU with US policies would become even more defined during the next two decades.

Chapter 15. The Policies of George H.W. Bush and Their Effects on US Foreign Policy

The election of George H.W. Bush in 1988 as the handpicked successor to Ronald Reagan can be interpreted as the willingness of the US public to continue the experimentation with ultra-conservative programs. The non-voting trend continued in the 1988 election with a drop from fifty-three percent of eligible voters voting to fifty percent. This trend at the time was believed to have been the result of the breakdown of the political power exercised by the large labor unions; and the inability of interest groups, especially the civil rights groups, to pull out the vote. It appeared evident that the working class, the urban dwellers, and those under the age of thirty were not motivated by the growing use of conservative party politics. Party politics are under normal conditions controlled by those members in the upper middle and upper classes especially those with large business interests. As party politics came to more tightly control the candidates and the issues the voting demographics shifted in favor of those classes within the society. The voting system in all democratic systems tends to be complicated but all voting blocs need to be coaxed a little to motivate them to vote. It is also fair to say that without this special coaxing the concern with self-absorption and apathy in politics decreases the public interest in voting. If the trend continues in the US and voter participation reaches a point at which less than forty percent of those registered to vote actually vote then a point has been reached where elections can more easily be manipulated.

This would mean that one very large interest group, the religious right for example, or a combination of two or more large interest groups, the corporate and industrial interest groups for example, will be able to control both the candidates and the issues. This in turn would create conditions under which a minority of the citizens could exercise tyranny over the majority.

Therefore, one of the most important early functions of the new world government will be to create a voting system that is easy, convenient, and capable of maintaining a maximum level of interest in voting. In the US, at least theoretically, it appears that a majority of the voters have the perception that their vote does not count for much or represents anything that is important to their personal freedom. This made the difficulty and inconvenience in voting greater than the motivation to vote. In other democracies the vote can and is easily manipulated by special interest factions based on religion, ethnic considerations, gender, tribal concerns, among many others. What needs to be accomplished by whatever election system is used within the world union is the control of manipulation of any kind in the operation of the elections. It is proposed under our scheme to return to the original voting system used at the beginning of US constitutional history. It is clear from the Federalist Papers, as shown in Volume One, that this system is most likely to result in the election of the most able representatives with the least opportunity for manipulation.

The four year term of George H.W. Bush was focused on the reduction of federal deficit spending and the reduction of the national debt on the domestic front; and the fighting of an unwanted war on the international front. The implosion of the Soviet Union occurred at this time, and the establishment of twenty or so new nations from the allies of the former Soviet Union caused some international tension, but these were overshadowed by a new turn in events. One of the most remarkable results of the demise of the Soviet Union was the reunification of the two Germanys. This was the first experiment in the combining of nations, one of which was a fully industrialized modern democratic state and the other a much weaker planned economy. The effort and cost of reuniting the two Germanys put a real strain on the West German system; but the reunification was accomplished with a minimum of individual suffering.

One of the most confusing results was the fact that the US was forced to consider a readjustment of its foreign policy on the basis that it was the sole remaining superpower. Both Central Asia and Central Europe are still undergoing rapid changes and little can be predicted for the future in these areas.

In relation to world government the most important aspect of the Reagan and Bush administrations is the continuing readjustment that is occurring within the US, and to some degree world-wide. There has been a distinct increase in US attempts to control and manipulate national insurrections wherever they occur. This is how the US has responded to its position as the sole military superpower. The US forced deregulation upon the global economy and this has resulted in two further economic failures: first, the financial irresponsibility of the banking system worldwide, and second, the increase of national debt in almost every nation of the world.

It will be the duty of the world government to provide a peaceful forum for the discussion and solution of all existing insurrections. The violence associated with these insurrections, if any, should and will be controlled by true peacekeeping forces provided by the world government. The solutions to the underlying causes of these insurrections will be found in a more creative manner, by allowing more flexible responses such as nation creation, the option of migration, etc. The financial problems will be handled under the world government by enforcement of laws against the type of financial transactions that led to the housing crisis and the general financial crisis now facing the US and the EU. A system of rational regulation will be instituted and enforced by law rather than through bailout and the suffering of individuals bilked of their homes and savings.

CHAPTER 16. THE "LIBERAL BIAS" OF THE CLINTON ADMINISTRATION IN
COMPARISON TO THE EUROPEAN UNION

In 1993, William Clinton took office and bought a temporary end to the
conservative domination of the federal executive office. Clinton represented
himself and his party's platform as centrist or moderately liberal in political
philosophy. He promised to cut the defense budget, which made sense in
relation to the demise of the Soviet Union; to provide tax relief to the middle
class as opposed to the Republican tax relief to the wealthy; and to provide
a massive aid program based on the Marshall Plan used at the end of World
War II to the Russian Federation in support of democracy in that nation.

However, he tended to be inconsistent in the positions that he took even
during the campaign and appeared to be willing to compromise his principles to obtain votes. He used the various media polls almost to an obsessive
amount in determining the stands that he would take on various issues. It
also appeared at times as if he was abjectly catering to the demands of various interest groups to obtain votes. This, however, may have just been his
recognition that elections were now dependent upon the ability of interest
groups to get out the vote.

The first Clinton proposal that passed into law was the Family Leave
Act. The proposal was quickly passed even though it had been vetoed twice
in different forms by the Bush administration. The act allowed government
employees and the employees of companies with more than fifty employees
the right to take up to twelve weeks of unpaid leave to deal with family mat-

ters and for family sickness. The second proposal submitted was a combination of tax increases and spending cuts that were intended to reduce the expected federal budget deficit spending by $493 billion. The tax increases were mainly aimed at the wealthy and corporations while the spending reductions were aimed at the military. In addition, the package offered sixteen billion in an attempt to stimulate the economy with public works projects. This money was to be spent mainly on urban transportation, urban utilities, and social entitlements such as general education, technical training, and health and welfare subsidies. This proposal was the first causality of the administration. The opposition to this bill in Congress adopted the old tactic of the filibuster to defeat its being brought to a vote. The Clinton forces were unable to garner the necessary votes to end the filibuster (a two-thirds vote) and the proposal was eventually withdrawn. The same package put together in another format finally passed with Vice-President Gore casting the tie-breaking vote in the Senate. The third and major battle for the administration during its first year in office was the debate over the NAFTA Treaty (North American Free Trade Agreement). The treaty had been negotiated by the Bush administration between the US, Canada, and Mexico. The debate finally settled in on the argument as to whether the tariff rate should be higher or lower. In this case the business community, which was now fully integrated into the global market, favored a low tariff and ratification of the treaty. The South (the textile industry) and the labor unions, on the other hand, favored a high tariff (to protect the textile industry and the jobs it represented) and a non-ratification of the treaty (for fear of the loss of jobs to Canada and Mexico). The treaty was finally ratified and went into law in November 1993. The last proposal submitted by the administration during the first year was a package intended to establish a national health program. This issue had been one of the major platform planks for the progressives, the New Deal, and the Great Society program before Clinton democrats took up the cause, and still it would prove impossible to gather the support to pass it into law.

The first year in office was clearly a mixed blessing for the administration. Two bills had passed that were in fact not brought to Congress by the administration, that is, the Family Leave Act and the NAFTA Treaty. The administration had lost on the two most important proposals that it had submitted to Congress, that is, the economic package and the health insurance bill. The former was finally passed but only in a form that was acceptable to the Republicans.

Lastly, the administration had put together an economic aid package for the Russian Federation consisting mainly of technical advisors, industrial equipment, and trade arrangements. There were also several proposals still waiting in line for congressional approval. Another attempt was being made, this time through formal congressional action, to reform the military recruitment practices to include homosexuals; the Goals 2000 proposal had been submitted with the intention of greatly increasing the amount of federal aid available for higher education; the Clinton proposals to be submitted at the next session of GATT (General Agreement on Trade and Tariffs) intended to improve the trade position of the US with the European Union and the Pacific Rim countries were all pending debate in Congress. The military recruitment bill was passed but the other measures were put on hold as a result of external events — the revelation of a scandal involving the personal actions of the Clintons in a transaction known as White Water and the attempted cover-up. As a result of these events the 1994 mid-term elections continued a Republican majority in both houses of Congress and a substantial republican majority in the state legislative and executive branches. It was the most widespread defeat the Democrats had suffered since prior to the Great Depression and the greatest Republican victory since 1952.

Events occurring internationally then come to the fore. The administration was quickly challenged by the UN mandate to send a military peacekeeping force in the Balkans to end the civil war there. Clinton agreed to provide the normal financial and military aid to the effort but in addition appointed his Secretary of State Madeleine Albright to open a diplomatic effort in the region and persuaded NATO to contribute the needed military forces. The peacekeepers (mostly West Europeans) were faced with the consequences of the attempted genocide in regard to the dissolving of the former Soviet of Yugoslavia into its constituent parts. The West Europeans proved incapable of handling the military activity (to the great embarrassment of the EU) and Clinton sent the US Air Force in to bomb the Serbs into submission. Albright was able to arrange for Western European peacekeepers and an armistice. It was not long before the Balkan military crisis had been brought to an end through this use of global resources. It must be noted, however, that many of the underlying causes of the Balkan crisis remain in place today.

Clinton concluded that the US could not successfully sustain either financially or militarily two or more engagements at one time. The US foreign policy position shifted to a policy of waiting to see what happened, reacting only in the case of a perceived crisis. This was a retreat from the proactive approach taken by prior administrations and Clinton's foreign policy actions were seen as being inconsistent and confused. It was in fact a creative new approach to the problem of how to use America's military dominance in a constructive way. Hindsight would indicate that this approach would have been more fruitful and less costly if America had stayed with it.

The Clinton administration had obtained a financial and technical aid package for the Russian Federation geared to influencing public perception of the US and encouraging a stronger commitment to liberal democracy within the Federation. However events conspired to make the program unpopular in the US and Congress limited it in every way possible.

The Clinton administration also continued the US policy of supporting negotiations between Israel and the Palestinians. The administration was able to get Israel to agree to allow the PLO a seat in a conference to be held in Jordan. In connection with this Middle East peace initiative the administration confirmed a peacekeeping mission in Somalia that had been undertaken by the Bush administration covertly through the CIA. This peacekeeping mission did bring some semblance of order to the area but was quickly defeated by an increase in insurrectionist activity. The arrangement between Israel and the Palestinians also later broke down. Lastly, again through a skilful use of diplomacy the administration was able to avoid a dangerous situation in the island of Haiti. All of these foreign policy initiatives had obtained a degree of success but due to reasons outside the control of the US they did not bear much fruit.

In relation to world government, the most important aspects of the first term of Clinton is the use of treaties to increase the ease by which the flow of goods, people, services and finances could travel in inter-nation trade (NAFTA), the use of a small, rapid, and well equipped military to respond to multi-level insurrections (the Balkan Response) and the use of diplomacy for the settlement of difficult political issues (the Mid-Eastern Peace Initiative), and the desire to cut budget deficits and the national debt. All of these solutions will need to operate within the response of the world government to global problems. That is to say, negotiation (whether by treaty or through the courts) will be the only form of response available to the world government, the ease of flow of goods, services, finances and people are the foundation of a single world market, a small, well armed rapid deployment force is all that will be expected for peacekeeping and disaster control purposes, and balanced budgets and the maintenance of zero national debt will be mandatory.

By Clinton's second term he faced a hostile Congress, a hostile Supreme Court, and a hostile public motivated by the media and talk shows. He further damaged his image with two more scandals.

US voters, who tend to be conservative in their philosophy in general and ultra-conservative in their most vocal wing, perceived Clinton personally as an ultra liberal. From this point the US public accepted the conservative viewpoint that Clinton was personally immoral and politically inept. On the other hand, in terms of political philosophy Clinton would in fact be a moderate liberal by European standards, if not downright conservative. Many of his actions were very popular in Europe and fit well with the policies favored by the Europeans. They clearly approved of his domestic policies, especially favoring a more disciplined budget, a stronger emphasis on civil rights, and the tendency to use negotiation rather than military means in international relations. Europe was both in favor of Clinton's acceptance of their military role in Eastern Europe and appreciative when the US finally agreed to come in and settle the issue when they had failed. They were also in favor of the US approach in the Middle East as it almost duplicated their own. In short, the foreign relations policies of the Clinton administration matched well with those promulgated by the EU. His domestic policies also fit well with that being practiced in most of the national members of the EU as directed by the supranational institutions. This latter approach to evaluating the Clinton administration is the one that holds the most promise in relation to the establishment of a world union. The liberal position taken by the Clinton administration would be the one necessary to find agreement between the US and the EU to support the establishment of a world government or at least a quasi world government.

The US public, however, rejected this line of thinking and returned to the ultra-conservative position by electing George W. Bush as president in 2000.

CHAPTER 17. THE GROWING UNILATERALISM OF US FOREIGN POLICY

George W. Bush has been out of office less than two years at the time of this writing, so that any analysis is difficult. What can be said, for certain, is that using the attacks of September 11, 2001, as a stepping-off point, his administration "declared war" on "terrorism" in general and then invaded and attacked specific countries.

The first target chosen by the administration was Iraq and the regime led by Saddam Hussein. This target, of course, immediately brought charges that the administration was just attempting to finish the job started by George H.W. Bush. The world quickly took the position that it would resist the use of force in Iraq, and the UN rejected the US demand for a mandate but did allow that force might be approved if definitive proof were found that Iraq had stockpiles of, or was producing, weapons of mass destruction. Weapons inspections failed to turn up any evidence of such weapons or any capability of producing them in Iraq.

The US and British intelligence agencies however produced evidence that Iraq had both stockpiles of chemical weapons and the capability to produce nuclear weapons. In connection with the release of this information the US, Great Britain, and a small coalition of nations unilaterally invaded Iraq. It was soon revealed that the intelligence information presented was faulty and that there were no weapons of mass destruction in Iraq and that the Iraqis had no capability to produce them. However, by this time the regime of Saddam Hussein had been overthrown, Saddam had been captured, and a provisional government composed of Iraqi refugees had been installed. At this point the world was forced to accept the fait accompli.

The US and coalition forces after nine years have been unable to generate any political progress in Iraq especially in relation to the rights of the Kurdish, Sunni, and Shia factions and the distribution of oil revenue. The replacement of the Iraqi infrastructure destroyed in the short war has been painfully slow and the level of insurrection activities has threatened consistently to break out into a civil war. The US has also failed to bring the UN into an active attempt to resolve the stalemate it has created.

Dissatisfaction at home has recently resulted in a persistent call for the US to withdraw its troops from Iraq. The Obama administration, as one of its first acts, has agreed to withdraw all US troops by mid 2011. The public, at least at this point, seems to accept that going into Iraq was a fatal mistake that needs to be quickly repaired. The capture, trial, and execution of Saddam Hussein did not bring about any softening in the world opinion concerning its position on the War in Iraq.

On the domestic front the "war on terrorism" has had some serious collateral effects. Essentially the administration established secret prisons throughout the world for the detention of persons they claim are suspected of terrorism and for information gathering. Detainees there and in Iraq have been tortured. US conduct during the war on terrorism has broken international law and stands in stark contradiction to the values America has prided itself on.

Second, a strong reaction to the Patriot Act (a measure passed shortly after the attack of 9/11) has taken place especially in private legal circles. The Act was passed to give the government rather wide powers of investigation including wire tapping and access to private banking records without a court order or warrant. This has been interpreted as a direct violation of the constitutional guarantee against illegal search and seizures and the due process of law.

Third, the establishment of a new Department of Homeland Security seems to be only the first step in the militarization of the police and of US society more broadly. Nominally this department was to take responsibility for the creation, implementation, and enforcement of measures for the protection of US citizens against any further terrorist attacks. So far this has included increasingly intrusive and restrictive inspections at airports and ports, national monuments, public offices, and among other places, in ways that are hard to correlate to any imaginable threat of terrorism but that surely abrogate any sense of liberty, and significantly limiting access to information on military operations and the military/industrial complex, reining in what used to be hailed as freedom of the press. It has also been used to establish stronger security at the US borders with Canada and Mexico.

Fourth, public support for the war on Iraq as a separate issue from the war on terrorism has largely dissipated. President Barack Obama has promised to wind down the action in Iraq but according to the *Washington Post* (January 13, 2009) the US Army is still building $4 billion worth of bases and other installations in Afghanistan — signaling a long-term military commitment. It is still open to question what goal the US is actually attempting to achieve in Afghanistan or Iraq, as well as in its war on terrorism. It may be time for the US to drop its use of the term "terrorism" and to concentrate on the solutions to the problems that create a desire of people involved in insurrections around the world to attack the US.

It became clear under George W. Bush that the goals of ultra-conservatism, that is, deregulation, shifting taxes away from the wealthy and the business communities, and greater independent use of US military power, is out of step with the demands of the US public and with world opinion. It is clear that it is also out of step with the policies of most of the world's leading economic powers, especially the EU. Before Bush, there were many disagreements between the US and the EU but they were mainly withheld from public airing. Since Bush, however, the EU has become much more vocal and very public about its displeasure with US policy, especially the unilateral use of US military power. With the election of Barack Obama, there were hopes that policy would at least be switched back to the more liberal approach found in the Clinton era, i.e., the use of diplomacy rather than military force, international cooperation on trade and commerce, and a concern for human rights. These are definitely more in tune with the policies of the EU, but already Obama has lost momentum and the results of the mid-term elections of 2010 would seem to indicate that the strongest interest groups want a strong return to conservative values.

In the last ten years the US has increasingly been at odds with world opinion, even as it is increasingly subject to economic pressure applied by the EU and other developed nations such as Russia, China, India, Japan, and others. This type of pressure will, of course, be a major political tool in the hands of a world government for the peaceful resolution of today's more violent problems.

Conclusion

A beginning can be made towards concluding this work by noting how the worldwide recession that is in progress affects the attitudes of the US public. In the case of the US economy, the public perception is that a large share of the blame for the recession can be placed on the deliberate fraud and excesses found in the financial industry. Yet the Obama administration's response has centered on corporate bailouts, the bailout of large financial institutions, and measures to prop up the failing housing industry. Meanwhile average Americans are losing their homes in record numbers, and a large segment of the population is suffering from long term unemployment.

In the international arena the same malfeasance of corporations, financial institutions and the housing market are also to be found. In addition, governments at all levels need to be bailed out as they are virtually bankrupt.

Economic problems on a worldwide scale could also arise from uncontrolled pollution of the environment; the abusive depletion of the world's natural resources; the monopolistic control of world markets by a few huge multinational conglomerates or national consortia; the irresponsible use of weapons of mass destruction; and the increasingly unequal distribution of the world's wealth. The use of outer space and militarization, security, and privacy concerns regarding communications technology and cyberspace could also lead to economic problems in the absence of coordinated international policy and regulation.

Whether or not regulation is necessary to control honest commercial and social behavior, it is needed to control those who would take advantage of others. Such problems as those set forth above can only be solved by resolute international action overseen by a worldwide organization. It is the conclusion of this work that this can only be obtained by instituting an effective federalized world government. The founding documents and institutions of the United States and those of the European Union provide the best working models so far that can guide us in shaping a world that works to the benefit of a majority of people.

There is substantial agreement that in the long term liberal democracy (in whatever form) is the best for everyone. However, in the short term it may be necessary to use non-democratic systems to produce the environment in which liberal democracy can thrive. The history of "poor relief," "colonialism," and "imperialism" has proven inadequate to the task. The immediate establishment of liberal democracy where it has not emerged locally has also failed. It would seem reasonable, then, that an effective world government will be needed to institute programs to eliminate poverty, ignorance, subsistence agrarianism, and the lack of infrastructure to allow the growth of a stable middle class and an economy that will result in the possibility of stable democracy.

This book was based on the assumption that a republican representative democracy would be used in the creation of the world government and that all nations would become members, either initially, or shortly after its formation. It was also assumed that all nations would over a period of time be required to adopt some type of democratic government.

The growing unilateralism of the US has also made more urgent the need to consider worldwide disarmament. A continued dependence on military force by the US to protect what it sees as its national interests can only lead to a failure of the underlying trend towards liberal democracy throughout the world. At this point in time the only real control over the unreasonable use of military force on the part of the US is world opinion coupled with sustained economic pressure. It can be hoped that the US will see the benefits that it would reap from a commitment to global cooperation, but only the future will tell.